Rhetorical Argumentation

Rhetorical Argumentation

Principles of Theory and Practice

CHRISTOPHER W. TINDALE

Trent University

SAGE Publications
International Educational and Professional Publisher
Thousand Oaks ▪ London ▪ New Delhi

For information:

Sage Publications, Inc.
2455 Teller Road
Thousand Oaks, California 91320
E-mail: order@sagepub.com

Sage Publications Ltd.
1 Oliver's Yard
55 City Road
London EC1Y 1SP
United Kingdom

Sage Publications India Pvt. Ltd.
B-42, Panchsheel Enclave
Post Box 4109
New Delhi 110 017   India

Printed in the United States of America

Library of Congress Cataloging-in-Publication Data

Tindale, Christopher W. (Christopher William)
Rhetorical argumentation: principles of theory and practice / by Christopher W. Tindale.
    p. cm.
Includes bibliographical references and index.
ISBN 1-4129-0399-8 (alk. paper) — ISBN 1-4129-0400-5 (pbk.: alk. paper)
    1. Persuasion (Rhetoric) I. Title.
PN207.T56 2004
808—dc22   2004004419

This book is printed on acid-free paper.

04   05   06   07   08   10   9   8   7   6   5   4   3   2   1

Acquisitions Editor:	Todd Armstrong
Editorial Assistant:	Deya Saoud
Production Editor:	Julia Parnell/Tracy Alpern
Copy Editor:	Diana Breti
Typesetter:	C&M Digitals (P) Ltd.
Cover Designer:	Janet Foulger

for Cait, at the start of a great (ad)venture

Contents

About the Author

Christopher W. Tindale (PhD and MA, University of Waterloo; BA, Wilfrid Laurier University) teaches and conducts research in the areas of argumentation theory, ethics, and ancient philosophy. Since 2000, he's been an editor of the journal *Informal Logic: Reasoning and Argumentation in Theory and Practice,* and he presently sits on the editorial board of *Controversia.* He is the author of *Acts of Arguing: A Rhetorical Model of Argument* (SUNY Press, 1999), coauthor of *Good Reasoning Matters* (3rd edition, Oxford University Press, 2004), and coeditor of *Argumentation and Its Applications* (forthcoming CD-ROM) and two other CD-ROMs, *Argumentation at the Century's Turn* and *Argumentation and Rhetoric.* Recent work of his has appeared in the following journals: *Argumentation, Informal Logic, ProtoSociology,* and *Social Theory and Practice.* In addition to teaching at Trent University in Peterborough, Ontario, Canada, in 2001–2002 he was a research fellow at the Centre for Interdisciplinary Research in Bielefeld, Germany.

Preface

To be a part of the social world is to experience it as an audience, to be "in audience," and a fundamental way in which that world addresses us is argumentatively. These are the basic premises from which the current account of argumentation and communication proceeds. The book is the culmination of over six years' reflection on the relations between rhetoric, argumentation, and communication, and on how best to present these relationships to an audience of senior students and scholars. Approaches to argumentation vary from those that lay emphasis on the logical product, the "argument," that results; to those that investigate the procedures involved in argumentative exchanges, exploring and devising rules to facilitate this; to those that stress the processes involved in the argumentative exchanges between arguers and audiences. While all three must play some role in a complete model of argumentation, it is the last of these that is being stressed in this book. For a number of reasons, we tend most to associate the practice of argumentation with the production of arguments according to the first approach mentioned. Yet this is the approach least able to capture and express the dynamics of argumentation as a communicative process. If we want to explore and understand the latter, we must begin with the underlying rhetorical features and view argumentation as an essentially rhetorical activity.

Initially, the task was to make the model of rhetorical argument attractive to philosophers, since this is the discipline in which I was trained. It is one of the ironies associated with philosophy departments, so steeped in traditions of careful argument and logical procedure, that little attention may be paid to engaged argument, to the ways argumentation is experienced by audiences. In particular, there seems little interest in teaching such matters in courses that seriously address the complex problems involved. While some people regard this as a scandal, others believe it is just a matter of time before the merits and promise of studying argumentation make themselves felt there. Still, I decided during the writing that this was not the project with which to directly engage that audience, although there is much here that I hope they will appreciate and find provocative. What dissuaded me most from this course, though, was the recognition that there is a far more receptive audience for these ideas and for whom a book of this nature would be most useful. Communication departments are seriously interested in the study of argumentation and its developments, and in teaching these things. This was brought home to me by the range and nature of interest shown in my work as I was preparing this manuscript. Thus I decided to strengthen a foothold that exists, teach to receptive minds as it were, and leave for later the audience that still must be challenged and persuaded. On some level, I hope that accomplishing the first task will set me on my way to the second.

Reinforcing through teaching the principles and developments of a perspective is, I believe, one of the most effective ways to increase its profile and emphasize its value. Thus I present the book with the firm hope that readers will come away from it with a better sense of what constitutes a rhetorical approach to argumentation, and also persuaded that it is through its rhetorical features that argumentation as a communicative practice can best be understood and adopted. This involves both the construction and evaluation of good argumentation. Of course, what counts as "good" in this case remains to be explored in the pages ahead. However, crucial to good argumentation, I believe, is an understanding of the ways arguments are experienced, and of how audiences collaborate with arguers in an argumentative situation so as to invite reflection and self-persuasion rather than impose a view on passive minds.

A number of the details of rhetorical argumentation presented in the book are the result of discussions with colleagues or responses to concerns raised by some of them in written work. For criticism and encouragement of this nature, I would particularly like to thank Tony Blair, David Godden, Hans V. Hansen, Hans Hohmann, Ralph Johnson, Fred Kauffeld, Mike Leff, Arno Lodder, and Charlie Willard. Deserving of quite separate mention is Jean Goodwin, who read the entire manuscript and suggested many improvements. Others who have read parts of the book in earlier drafts and offered comments include Randy Harris, Maged el Komos, and Andreas Wenzel. I am grateful to them all for their interest in the project. Likewise, the reviewers of the initial proposal and subsequent manuscript made many useful suggestions that have found their way into the finished text, as well as directed me away from errors and confusions. This is a better book for their diligence. Many thanks to Alan Gross, Karen Rasmussen, Raymie McKerrow, Kathleen M. Farrell, and Michael Osborn.

Drafts of sections of the book were written in 2001–2002 during my time as a research fellow at the Centre for Interdisciplinary Research (ZiF) in Bielefeld, Germany. The subject of the research group was conflict resolution, and while none of the work specifically done there has found its way into the book, I trust participants will see the influence of the ideas and discussions that resonated in that rich, vibrant environment. Among the members of the group with whom I was pleased to have the opportunity to interact, I would like to thank Matthias Raith, Andreas Wenzel, Olaf Gaus, Wilfried Hinsch, Christoph Fehige, and Kirsten Schroeter. I am particularly grateful to Matthias for the invitation to join the group.

Parts of Chapter 5 were read to audiences at the University of Dundee and the Open University in April of 1999, and a shorter version of Chapter 7 was read at the "Informal Logic at 25" conference in Windsor, Ontario, May 2003. In each case, I am grateful to members of the audience for helpful comments.

During the time that I worked on this project, I was fortunate in having two excellent research assistants—Ashraf Lalani and Daniel Farr. Daniel in particular made a number of direct contributions, including formatting notes and references and preparing the index. Many others have made contributions to whatever positive features this book may have; if I tried to mention them all, I'd be sure to overlook someone, and some may even prefer to go unmentioned, happy in the knowledge that their conversations played a part in what eventually resulted. To all of these colleagues, students, and friends I owe a debt of gratitude.

Finally, I would like to thank the editorial staff at Sage who made working on the production of this book such a pleasure. Thanks to Todd Armstrong, who became excited about the project and enthusiastically pursued it, and to Julia Parnell, Tracy Alpern, and Diana Breti for the care and detail they have given to the production and editing of the book.

1

A Rhetorical Turn
for Argumentation

Alice couldn't help laughing, as she said "I don't want you to hire *me*—and I don't care for jam."

"It's very good jam," said the Queen.

"Well, I don't want any *to-day,* at any rate."

"You couldn't have it if you *did* want it," the Queen said. "The rule is, jam to-morrow and jam yesterday—but never jam to-day."

"It *must* come sometimes to 'jam to-day,'" Alice objected.

"No, it can't," said the Queen. "It's jam every *other* day: to-day isn't any *other* day, you know."

"I don't understand you," said Alice. "It's dreadfully confusing!"

(Carroll 1993, 87)

❖ ALICE'S PREDICAMENT

For many people, argument and communication would seem strange companions. When we argue, in the sense of a quarrel or bitter dispute, communication is the very thing most in jeopardy, often impeded by heightened emotions and a refusal to listen. Yet this book is about argumentation as good communication. In it, I will explore the ways in which arguers communicate with their audiences, and the positive results that emerge from the processes of anticipation, involvement, and response that are integral to argumentative interaction. We must begin by rethinking, or at least greatly expanding, the meaning we give to "argument." As suggested, many of us associate it most readily with quarrelling. We think of it as an activity that defines our dis-agreements. Sometimes it may promise ways to resolve those dis-agreements, although our performances on this front have often been less than impressive. More formally, "argument" has been understood in the western academic tradition as having a particular structure with fixed ways of understanding that structure. An argument on these terms has a conclusion and premises in support of it. It is a reason-giving use of language, and its success is determined by evaluating the strength of such reasons and the appropriateness of their connections to the claims they allegedly support, employing notions like "validity" and "soundness." If we have thought of "argumentation" at all, it may have been as an activity in which this structure is embedded: argumentation is the giving, receiving, and assessing of arguments, understood in the terms just presented.

This understanding of "argument" has been seriously challenged by scholars interested in the nature of argumentation and reasoning. In a recent posthumous work, Grice (2001, 8) points out that most actual reasoning does not conform to what he calls "canonical inference patterns." This agrees with the views of those who deem the traditional concept of argument too narrow to account for much of what should pass as argumentation, when we enter debates, negotiate agreements, investigate hypotheses, deliberate over choices, and persuade audiences. Obviously, these ideas considerably expand the notion of argumenta-tion in the previous paragraph. In general, to think of argumentation this way is to appreciate it as an activity that changes how we perceive the world by changing the way we think about things. But if we are going to expand this idea, it is natural to revise the notion of argument at its heart. To do otherwise, to stay with the notion that we have inher-ited, invites problems of confronting argumentative situations for which our idea is inadequate.

An argumentative situation, as this book will explore, is a site in which the activity of arguing takes place, where views are exchanged and changed, meanings explored, concepts developed, and understandings achieved. It may also be a site in which people are persuaded and disagreements are resolved, but these popular goals are not the only ones, and too narrow a focus on them threatens to overlook much for which argumentation is a central and important tool.

As a "site," the argumentative situation is a nongeographical space, located in and created by discourse. We inhabit such spaces with different facility, some of us with ease, others with discomfort. Yet they are crucial to our self-understanding and our understanding of others. Exploring these spaces, then, should be a priority and not an incidental by-product of an otherwise specialized education.

Potentially argumentative situations are not restricted to overt disagreements. They include situations in which ideas are reinforced, proposals are introduced and explored cooperatively, and parties struggle to achieve understanding and agreement even when the starting position of each is virtually unrecognizable to others. Communication faces its greatest challenge in these last kinds of cases, particularly where values and the meanings of terms are not held in common.

As an extreme and artificial example of this, but one that will be widely familiar, consider Alice's interactions with the White and Red queens in Lewis Carroll's fantasies. The queens do not view experience and the language that describes it in the way that Alice does, and we share her confusion because of this unfamiliarity. The queens refuse to conform to the rules that govern communication and logic as we understand them. The White Queen, for example, wants Alice to believe impossible things, suggesting she just needs to practice to do so. She wants her to admit the value of punishing people before they commit crimes, on the grounds that Alice has benefited from past punishments. And when Alice points out, reasonably we might think, that she was punished for things she *had* done, the Queen observes how much better it would have been had she not done them and prior punishment would encourage this. When Alice responds to the offer of jam every other day with the remark that she does not want any today, she is told that she could not have it even if she wanted it. Jam every other day means "jam to-morrow and jam yesterday—but never jam today." The Red Queen is no easier. She dazzles Alice with exaggerated claims about gardens like wildernesses and hills like valleys, forcing her at last to disagree: "a hill *can't* be a valley, you know. That would be nonsense." But that would be sensible compared to some of the nonsense the Red Queen has heard.

This playful recalling of a childhood favorite has a point: Alice's discourses with the queens in *Through the Looking Glass* are like interactions with intractable people. It is not that they are particularly hostile to her perspective; they simply do not recognize it as significant. Alice cannot get a level foothold in her conversations with them, cannot manage herself in those conversations (really, *have* conversations) because they insist, stubbornly, on seeing things their way, whether it be the language they use or the reality around them, and they don't admit a perspective other than their own. As a potentially argumentative situation, with terms to explore and disagreements to resolve, the tools of traditional argument ill-equip anyone to deal with it.

We may ask of situations like these: What must take place in them for real communication to occur? And what perspective on argument best serves our needs? This book answers these questions by proposing a model of argument that is characterized as rhetorical. This is to contrast it, as we'll see in the next section, with perspectives that are primarily logical or dialectical. As we will see, the rhetorical model is the best candidate for grounding a theory of argumentation that manages both everyday situations and extreme aberrations like those between Alice and the queens.

❖ MODELS OF ARGUMENT

Following scholars like Habermas (1984) and Wenzel (1979), those working with theories of argument have been attracted to the divisions suggested by Aristotle's triumvirate of logic, dialectic, and rhetoric. These are three distinct ways of conceiving argument, the first of which, the logical, has been the one to dominate the tradition to the extent that many people are accustomed to the idea that arguments are no more than logical products. In this book, I will challenge such thinking by presenting the case for a rhetorical notion of argument. But in order to better appreciate the benefits of the rhetorical model, we need first to understand what is at stake in the alternatives.

The *logical* emphasizes the product of statements collected in the relationship of premises and conclusions. As its name implies, the logical sense of argument has occupied the attention of logicians, both formal and informal. Minimally, an argument under this definition requires one premise in support of one conclusion, as in:

Premise: Most people believe that incidents of crime in large cities are on the increase.

Conclusion: More money should be put into law enforcement.

Beyond this structure there is a further component: an argument has an intention behind it, namely to convince others to accept the proposition put forward as the conclusion.

The *dialectical* sense of argument focuses attention on the argumentative exchanges within a dialogue and the moves that might be involved. There are several dialogues of interest, such as the quarrel, the negotiation, the debate, or the inquiry. Theorists who study the dialectical sense of argument uncover and devise rules governing the correct procedures by which such arguments can be conducted. Hence, the dialectical focus stresses argument-as-procedure.

The third division is the *rhetorical*, which emphasizes argument as a process. Here attention is paid to the means used in argumentative communications between arguer and audience. Questions are asked about the nature of the audience, what subgroups might comprise it, and what beliefs are involved. The character and interests of the arguer are also important, as are the background circumstances in which the argument arises. Such components contribute to a full sense of the context in which arguments are embedded.

Consider these three perspectives in light of an example that illustrates what each has to offer and the particular power of the rhetorical. Imagine the following argumentative exchange on the justification of the 2003 Iraq-US war.

Bob: The United States and its allies were justified in waging a war to free the Iraqi people from a dictator.

Susan: If such a war was necessary, it was the role of the United Nations to determine this and act accordingly. Without their endorsement the war was illegal.

Bob: That's not my point. I said they were justified in acting, not whether they had anyone's permission. The reasons were there to support the war.

Susan: That's consistent with my point. *If* the reasons were there, it was the UN's role to decide so and determine what action was necessary.

Bob: But the world couldn't wait forever for the slow wheels of diplomacy to turn while Iraq became an increasing threat to global security.

Susan: That's a different point altogether from the one you claimed justified the war. It's not that insecurity leads to war, but that war leads to insecurity.

The logical approach to argumentation would extract the separate arguments of Bob and Susan, lifting them out of the exchange and rewriting them in premise/conclusion form, and then test those arguments for validity and strength (basically internal assessments of the relationships between the propositions). A logical analysis might focus on whether Bob has committed a fallacy by bringing in another point in his last statement.

The dialectical approach to argumentation would test the exchange against procedural rules (which vary according to the dialectical account employed): Are the arguments relevant? Does each of the arguers adequately deal with the objections of the other? A dialectical analysis might focus on whether a fallacy has been committed through the violation of a rule of discussion.

The rhetorical approach to argumentation insists that far more is involved in appreciating this exchange, and that the other two approaches miss what is really happening as communication by failing to attend to these rhetorical features. What is said has to be considered in relation to who is saying it and why (something both other perspectives overlook). We need, for example, to look at the features of the context (insofar as this is available): How has this dispute arisen? What do the participants know of each other, and the commitments involved? What are the consequences of this exchange in the lives of those involved, and how might this affect what is being said? Moreover, how well do these two people reason together in addressing the issue? How might they improve this? That is, what collaborative features could emerge here? How effective is Bob's metaphor of diplomacy progressing like a slow-turning wheel, and how are we to evaluate Susan's refutation by reversal in the antimetabole she provides at the end? More importantly, from the rhetorical perspective, how is this exchange being *experienced* by the participants, and how does that affect their understanding? All this is to rethink what it means to be an arguer, and what it means to have an argumentative situation. Learning about and seeing these features at work provides for both better argumentation on the student's part and better evaluations of others' arguments, because one can now see much more involved in both activities.

Of course, the focus on the rhetorical does not mean that the other two perspectives can be dismissed. Product, procedure, and process are each important ideas in the understanding of and theorizing about arguments. While they can be discussed and studied in isolation, in actual argumentative contexts we might expect each to be present, and a complete theory of argument will accommodate the relationships among the three. Still, it is the rhetorical that must provide the foundations for that theory, and it will influence how we understand and deal with the logical and the dialectical in any particular case.

The remainder of this section has something to say about the logical perspective that has dominated our tradition of argument and its recognized ineffectiveness for dealing with argumentation in the kinds of situations we are envisaging here. The subsequent sections will consider some recent developments of the dialectical and rhetorical perspectives that provide considerable advances in our understanding of argumentation. Yet, they remain wanting in several significant ways.

In spite of the playfulness of some of his characters, Lewis Carroll was a traditionalist when it came to "argument." He lived in exciting logical times, if such can be imagined. His career coincides with the breakdown of Aristotelian logic and the flowering of Boolean algebraic logic (Carroll 1977, 19), as the discipline went from a period of stagnation to one of serious study and publication with many significant treatises appearing, including the works of John Neville Keynes and John Venn, and Carroll's own *Game of Logic* and *Symbolic Logic, Part 1* (dedicated to the memory of Aristotle). Carroll's work was in the algebra of logic, developing and modifying techniques of Boole and Venn.[1]

While traditional logic was undergoing change, one of its core concepts—that of "argument"—was not. This is reflected in Carroll's own treatment.[2] Simply put, Carroll adheres to the traditional way of viewing arguments merely as premise/conclusion sets. We find fairly standard "logical" appreciations of "argument" and its attendant terms: the standard for an argument is introduced as the Syllogism (1977, 107) and defended against detractors who would argue that "a Syllogism has no real validity as an argument" (128–129). And a term like "Fallacy" is defined in the standard Aristotelian way as "any argument which *deceives* us, by seeming to prove what it does not really prove" (129). Nothing here would help Alice manage her misunderstandings with the queens, because what is needed, beyond an assessment of the "validity" of the reasoning, is some appreciation of those involved in the exchange, the arguers themselves, their beliefs and backgrounds, their styles and strategies. And once we entertain these ideas, we have already turned to the underlying rhetorical features of the situations.

Resistance to such a traditional way of conceiving argument has come from scholars of varying stripes. Chief among these was the Belgian philosopher Perelman who, along with Olbrechts-Tyteca (1969), set the foundations for modern studies of rhetorical argumentation. Their work will be of considerable importance in the chapters ahead. A thinker sharing more of the logical approach is Toulmin, whose *The Uses of Argument* (1958/2003) delivered a tremendous wake-up call.

Toulmin's primary target is, in fact, formal logic, which he claims is unable to serve as a model of everyday argument. More precisely, he identifies different types of argument in a range of fields, none of which is amenable to the procedures and standards of formal argument. For his own part, he develops a model of argument that makes use of more informal ideas like "warrant" and "backing," ideas that better account for the complex relations between evidence and conclusions.[3] His general model of "data" leading to a claim, mediated by a "warrant" with any necessary "backing," has been very influential as a new standard of logical thinking, particularly among scholars of rhetoric and speech communication. He takes seriously the contexts in which arguments emerge and looks to evaluate them in ways relevant to those contexts.

While this model is not without its critics, it stands out as among the first to seriously consider the range of problems with the traditional logical idea of argument and try to ameliorate those concerns. Still, there is here a dependency on the product itself. Insofar as that approach (even in the "updated" version of 2003) lacks a sufficient attention to features of the argumentative situation, Toulmin's model suffers also.[4]

❖ BEYOND THE LOGICAL

A more recent model of argument that looks to wed the logical with the dialectical is that of Johnson (2000a). Along with his colleague Blair, Johnson is one of the originators of what is called "informal logic," developing it on both the pedagogical and theoretical levels. Informal logic, as here conceived, attempts to bring principles of logic into accord with the practice of everyday reasoning. At first this was done through an analysis of the traditional fallacies, but more recently informal logicians have been looking to develop it as a theory of argument. Johnson's book *Manifest Rationality* is a major contribution to that project. In that work, "argument" is defined as "a type of discourse or text—the distillate of the practice of argumentation—in which the arguer seeks to persuade the Other(s) of the truth of a thesis by producing the reasons that support it" (168). This "distillate" is described as the illative core of the argument. In addition to this, an argument possesses a dialectical tier in which the arguer discharges various dialectical obligations.

While he acknowledges the influence that Toulmin has had on the study of argumentation and much of the impetus behind informal logic, Johnson's concept of argument is a considerable advance on that proposed by Toulmin. Most distinctive is the inclusion of the "dialectical tier" wherein dialectical obligations are recognized and met.

This is not an incidental feature in Johnson's mind; the provocative nature of the definition enlivens one of the stronger claims associated with it: that "an argument without a dialectical tier is not an argument" (172). The way in which the dialectical combines with the logical deserves attention, and I turn to it here in part to investigate why Johnson has not taken the further step of explicitly including the rhetorical. This is explained by his more traditional and negative position on the relationship between logic and rhetoric, but in many ways Johnson's account anticipates and requires a rhetorical aspect.

To define an "argument" as, in part, "the distillate of the practice of argumentation" in the way that Johnson does serves to place primary emphasis on the *product,* in turn stressing the logical grounding for this model of argument. In fact, Johnson wants to include more than what has traditionally passed as the product. He invites us to view argument within a practice of argumentation, "which includes as components (a) the process of arguing, (b) the agents engaged in the practice (the arguer and the Other), and (c) the argument itself as a product" (2000a, 154). These are dynamic relations, including the distilled product. Yet to speak in such terms for (c), the product, is to suggest something that is finished, while to place it alongside (a), the process, suggests something that is yet to be completed. This hints at a tension between process and product. As much as Johnson encourages us to see them as interrelated, it is the nature of that interrelation that appears particularly elusive.

Another important aspect of his notion of argument is the aim he assigns to it: "the arguer seeks to persuade the Other(s) of the truth of a thesis by producing the reasons that support it" (168). In various forms throughout his work, Johnson offers two components of this aim. The following statements capture them:

(i) By the term "argument," I understand an intellectual product . . . that seeks to persuade rationally (24).

(ii) [T]he fundamental purpose, although admittedly not the only one, is to arrive at the truth about some issue (158).

As (i) suggests, *rational* persuasion is emphasized and valued over any other. This is the feature that will distinguish the better arguments (189). Hence, the *argumentum ad baculum* or appeal to force would not be considered an argument "because here the reasoning is being used to threaten someone" (145). It isn't a matter of it being a bad move in argument, Johnson suggests, it is simply a non-argument.

In this definition of argument and argumentation, rationality is a goal in itself. In terms of the dual nature of the aim identified in (i) and (ii), while (ii) is more evident in the definition, (i) is the larger purpose that Johnson promotes. The *argumentum ad baculum* fails to be simply a bad argument because its attempts at persuasion are not rational to both parties involved. The character of manifest rationality, which is not explicit in the definition of argument, turns out to completely underlie it.

At the heart of Johnson's definition is the illative core[5] of premises and conclusion. But, as we saw, added to this core is the "dialectical tier in which the arguer discharges his dialectical obligations." Because of the underlying project of manifest rationality, the illative core cannot be enough; the best practitioners "always take account of the standard objections" (166). It is this taking account that constitutes the dialectical tier. More precisely, it is the addressing of alternative positions and standard objections.

There seem to be two things to address here: (i) the relationship between the illative and dialectical tiers with respect to the product itself, and (ii) the relationship between the arguer and Other(s) implied by the dialectical tier.

That we should take account of and anticipate objections seems noncontroversial, even if it has not been a feature of the tradition. But that this should be such an essential component of *what an argument is*, such that its absence excludes a discourse or text from being an argument, is controversial. It must be asked whether this dialectical tier is a part of the product or, rather, is something that arises afterwards, as participants reflect on the initial argument or an evaluator begins to work on it.[6] On the whole, insisting that an arguer complete the argument by showing how he or she intends to handle certain objections is a positive development in theory. It forces the acknowledgment that arguing is a complex activity and that many textbook treatments are inadequate. On the other hand, it appears to have some unfortunate consequences. Chief among these, since one of the things that separates rhetoric from Johnson's approach to argumentation is the requirement of manifest rationality (163), is the slim prospects the proposal projects for the advance of rhetorical argumentation.

Critics object that an argument should not be considered incomplete simply because it fails to address all objections and alternatives (Govier 1998, 7). Johnson agrees, but insists that what is important is that an arguer has dialectical obligations (1998, 2). Thus, we might surmise, to be an "arguer" (and so to produce an argument) the fulfilling of one's dialectical obligations must be part of one's practice. Thus, again, an arguer must address *some* obligations for an argument to be complete. Apparently, different understandings of "complete" are in tension here: one sees it objectively in terms of covering all possible objections, the other views it contextually in terms of the arguer's recognition of obligations.

This helps. But we could take things further by observing that the context restricts the possible objections and alternatives to those relevant for the audience in question and so likely to be raised by that audience. That is, insofar as the dialectical relationship between arguer and audience is integral to a specific argument, then the relevant objections should be those internal to that relationship. Possible objections that could be brought against the argument-product dislocated from its dialectical context are not at issue here.

This call for a dialectical tier deserves further support because, if we view it now from a rhetorical perspective, we should see it as part of the essential argument, although not exactly on terms that Johnson proposes. There is a profound way in which the anticipation of the Other's objections informs and *forms* the arguer's own utterances, and in this sense the dialectical tier cannot be divorced from the structure. Understood this way, the line between the two tiers really begins to dissolve.

Johnson accommodates this up to a point. He acknowledges that the arguer is only half the story and that the process is incomplete without the Other, and he gives us a dynamic relationship of back and forth responses between the two (2000a, 157). This, however, still implies a temporally extended process. To better capture and reflect the activity of arguing some compression is required, and Johnson later suggests just this:

> Genuine dialogue requires not merely the presence of the Other, or speech between the two, but the real possibility that the logos of the Other will influence one's own logos. An exchange is dialectical when, as a result of the intervention of the Other, one's own logos (discourse, reasoning, or thinking) has the potential of being affected in some way. Specifically, the arguer agrees to let the feedback from the Other affect the product. The arguer consents to take criticism and to take it seriously. (161)

In Chapter 4, I will return to this idea and examine a proposal drawn from the work of Bakhtin. On the terms developed there, an argument is always addressed to someone and that is its most telling feature. The argument is co-authored by the arguer and addressee. This is more than the accommodation of a reply and the anticipation of objections. This is to suggest that a more accurate description of what is involved in arguing sees the anticipated components as influencing the structure of the argument. The dialectical is not something that takes place after the illative is fixed; it precedes the development of that "core" (which ceases to be so core since such terminology is no longer warranted if the dialectical infuses it rather than surrounds it).

In the passage given above, Johnson moves toward this position in the remarks made about the logos of the Other influencing the arguer. But he draws back from it in the final two sentences where the references to feedback and criticism suggest a more traditional separation of opposing discourses.

In the previous few pages, several features of rhetorical argument have been drawn upon in both addressing problems with Johnson's model and offering support for it. The attention to audience and the dynamic relationship between arguer and addressee with its rich sense of context are points more characteristic of a rhetorical approach. Johnson, however, resists too strong a rapprochement with the rhetorical. While his model of argument is notably nontraditional in its melding of the logical and dialectical, his attitude toward rhetoric is anything but.

Johnson does recognize a working alliance between the new logic he advocates and the new rhetoric that has been ushered in by Perelman and Olbrechts-Tyteca (1969), but he is still at pains to stress the differences between the two. Both logic and rhetoric, for example, see argumentation as governed by rationality. But while rhetoric sees considerations of character (*ethos*) and emotion (*pathos*) as important as *logos*, the new logic assigns these only a secondary role.

Of greater concern is the difference in purpose. Rhetoric aims at effectiveness rather than truth and completeness. That is, if there is an objection to the argument of which the arguer is aware, from the point of view of rhetoric he or she has no obligation to deal with it; the argument is effective without it. In other words, rhetoric has no dialectical tier. But from the point of view of logic, the arguer is obligated to deal with it,

> [b]ecause even though the audience does not know of the objection, and so the arguer could get by without dealing with it, the argument will be more rational in substance and appearance if it can meet the test of this objection. (Johnson 2000a, 270)

This requires a much stronger interpretation of Johnson's concept of argument because this implies that rational persuasion works by degrees and the *more rational*, the better the argument. However, as suggested above, rather than having no necessary dialectical tier, rhetoric, conceived now in terms of rhetorical argument, subsumes such dialectical features into its very core. This is partly because, unlike the purpose of rhetoric that informs Johnson's discussion, rhetorical argumentation does not aim at effectiveness alone. Chapter 2 will introduce other aims of rhetorical argumentation. As a venture that seeks and requires the cooperation of the parties involved, rhetorical argumentation cannot ignore the dialectical dimension understood in ways that Johnson has presented it. But it subsumes them in a way that addresses any gap between the illative and dialectical.

As we have seen, while there is much to welcome in Johnson's manifest rationality project, in the positive ways that it takes us beyond the traditional logical approaches to argument, there is also a serious question of whether the underlying concept hangs together. Earlier, I noted the tension between the process and the product in the practice of argumentation. Does the relationship between the illative and dialectical tiers suggest something that is finished or in process? This is never completely answered. Johnson resists a firm reading of "complete," yet at the same time claims that rhetoric aims at effectiveness while logic aims at truth and completeness. What sense of "complete" is at work here? Especially since the better arguments are the more complete ones. The problem is this: while the dialectical tier captures the dynamic process between those involved, the illative retains much of the fixedness of earlier models. For Johnson, premises are true or false in and of themselves and not in relation to an audience. But this understanding would seem to conflict with the positive reading I gave to the dialectical tier. Rhetorical features like audience and context are indeed at work in this model, but to a degree and at a depth beyond what its author acknowledges. Where Johnson does challenge rhetoric, he addresses it in its traditional guises. While this is useful for bringing out the problems that are inherent in how many people may still understand rhetoric, it fails to appreciate how truly "new" rhetoric can be conceived, particularly in its relation to argumentation.

❖ BEYOND THE DIALECTICAL

A recent model of argumentation that combines the dialectical approach to argument with a refreshing acceptance of rhetorical features is the pragma-dialectical model developed in a series of papers by van Eemeren and Houtlosser.

As its name implies, pragma-dialectics is a dialectical perspective that melds an approach to language use drawn from pragmatics with the study of critical dialogue. Advanced by Dutch theorists van Eemeren and Grootendorst, it has developed into a comprehensive theory of argumentation, alert to the exigencies of everyday argument and accommodating a full range of features, including a theory of fallacies as violations of rules that govern critical discussions. Within certain limits, it is a powerful model of argumentation that promises to become stronger still as more people turn their attention to the eclectic program of its research agenda.[7]

Pragma-dialecticians conceive all argumentation as part of a critical discussion aimed at resolving differences of opinion. They approach this through the identification and clarification of certain procedural rules, hence conforming to the dialectical perspective's interest in argument as procedure. For example, one rule requires someone who has advanced a standpoint to defend it if requested; another forbids regarding a standpoint as conclusively defended if it has not involved the correct application of an argumentation scheme (van Eemeren and Grootendorst 1992, 208–209). These rules govern four stages of dispute resolution: a confrontation stage, an opening stage, an argumentation stage, and a concluding stage.

In recent years, van Eemeren, now working with Houtlosser, has tried to strengthen pragma-dialectical analysis by drawing on the insights of rhetoric. This "rhetorical turn" seems born of a recognition that the model itself was incomplete without such an accommodation. As they write,

> Until recently, pragma-dialectical analysis tended to concentrate on reconstructing primarily the dialectical aspects of argumentative discourse. It is clear, however, that the analysis and its justification can be considerably strengthened by a better understanding of the strategic rationale behind the moves that are made in the discourse. For this purpose, it is indispensable to incorporate a rhetorical dimension into the reconstruction of the discourse. (van Eemeren and Houtlosser 1999a, 164)

There is no question, however, about the appropriate relationship here—rhetoric is the handmaid of dialectic, and rhetorical moves operate *within* a dialectical framework (van Eemeren and Houtlosser 1999c, 493). This contrasts markedly, as they note, with rhetorical theorists Perelman and Olbrechts-Tyteca, who bring elements of dialectic into rhetoric (van Eemeren and Houtlosser 1999a, 165). The preference should be unsurprising since it seems a natural extension of the commitments already made in the parent project. There are also explicit reasons for this position. Dialectic, they indicate, deals with general and abstract questions, while rhetoric concerns itself with specific cases (van Eemeren and Houtlosser 2000a) and with the contextual adjustments required to convince specific people (van Eemeren and Houtlosser 2002, 15). It seems natural, then, that the specific should be embedded in the general. Furthermore, theoreticians have characterized rhetoric's norm as that of effectiveness, while dialectic embraces the idea of reasonableness. Although van Eemeren and Houtlosser insist there is no incompatibility between these norms (2002, 15), they do not resist this traditional characterization of rhetoric and so, again, it seems natural to ground effectiveness in reasonableness. As they remark, "effective persuasion must be disciplined by dialectical rationality" (2000b, 297).[8]

For van Eemeren and Houtlosser, the main way in which the rhetorical affects argumentation is the way people's own interests direct and influence the resolution of a dispute. Here, rhetorical strategies are used to achieve the outcome people desire, while still fulfilling their dialectical obligations. "[T]hey attempt to exploit the opportunities afforded by the dialectical situation for steering the discourse rhetorically in the direction that best serves their interests" (2000b, 295). Thus the real rhetorical aspect of argumentation for van Eemeren and Houtlosser comes through in the strategic attempts to personally influence the resolution process. This can take place at each of the four stages as the arguer exploits opportunities made available to advance her or his own interests.[9] At each stage, strategic maneuvering may involve three distinct aspects or dimensions, and these are important for the combined role they play in deciding the completeness of rhetorical strategies.

The first dimension involves the selection of topics from those available. Van Eemeren and Houtlosser call this the *topical potential* of each discussion stage. That is, arguers will select materials from those available according to what they believe best advances their interests. At the confrontation stage, the speaker or writer will select or exclude in an attempt to dictate how the confrontation is defined. In a dispute over foxhunting in Britain, for example, the key idea might be defined in terms of maintaining rural traditions or in terms of cruelty to animals (2000a). At the opening stage, participants attempt to create the most advantageous starting point. This may be done by establishing agreements and winning concessions. At the argumentation stage, the best "status topes" will be selected from those appropriate for the type of standpoint at issue. And at the concluding stage, attention will be directed to achieving the best outcome for a party by, for example, pointing to consequences (1999a, 166).

The second dimension involves adapting to *audience* (auditorial) *demands*. In general, this will amount to creating "empathy or 'communion' between the arguer and his audience" (van Eemeren and Houtlosser 2000b, 298). But this adaptation works in specific ways at each stage, depending on the issue and the nature of the audience involved. For example, in their analysis of an advertorial defending Shell's actions in Nigeria, they show the adaptation to audience at the argumentation stage by the employment of two types of maneuvering that address the audience's expectation (2001, 21).

The third dimension involves exploiting the *presentational devices* appropriate at each stage. Here, rhetorical figures are used to impress moves upon the mind, thus compounding their effect. In their case study of William the Silent's discourse, for example, van Eemeren and Houtlosser see *praeteritio* being used as the confrontation stage, effectively making a point while claiming to pass over it (1999b, 169).

The key criterion for assessing whether a rhetorical strategy is "being followed" (1999a, 166; 1999b, 170) in any stage is that of *convergence:* the selection of materials, the adaptation to audience, and the use of rhetorical devices must all converge.

But "being followed" is inherently vague. It is not clear whether this is merely an identification criterion to determine that a rhetorical strategy is fully present, or a measure of quality by providing a criterion of success. Van Eemeren and Houtlosser suggest the latter of these. With respect to the foxhunting case, they observe: "Strategic maneuvering *works best* when the rhetorical influences brought to bear at each of the three levels are made to converge" [italics added] (2000a). The pro-hunting lobby, they argue, has fused the three dimensions of topic selection, audience adaptation, and device presentation in the tradition of a treasured past. In doing so, the lobby has more than just strategically maneuvered, it has "displayed a genuine rhetorical strategy" (2000a). In the same paper, the authors speak of a rhetorical strategy being "optimally successful" when such a fusion of influences occurs.

We might ponder the nature of this success. In rhetoric, it is usually tied in some way to effectiveness of persuasion, according to van Eemeren and Houtlosser's own understanding. But success in terms that they have now set out may mean no more than being able to match one's own rhetorical interests with one's dialectical obligations through strategies that exploit (in a neutral sense) the opportunities in an argumentative situation.

More clearly identified is a negative requirement governing appropriate strategies. Being persuasive would not be sufficient to count rhetorical strategies acceptable if they are not also reasonable (2000b, 297). And the key way in which they must meet this condition, as with pragma-dialectical assessments generally, is by avoiding fallaciousness (1999c, 485). Fallacies in pragma-dialectics involve violations of one or more rules that govern critical discussions. In the view of van Eemeren and Houtlosser, it is "possible to identify specific 'types' or 'categories' of strategic maneuvering that can be pinned down as fallacious for their correspondence with a particular type of rule violation in a specific discussion stage" (2001, 24). The requirement of reasonableness represented by the rules for discussion serves as a check on the arguer simply having her or his own way. Such would occur should the arguer's commitment to proceeding reasonably be overruled by the aim of persuasion (in other words, when the correct relationship between the dialectical and the rhetorical is inverted). When this happens, van Eemeren and Houtlosser say that the strategic maneuvering has been "derailed," and hence a fallacy committed. Clearly, this is a point they wish to fix in the minds of their readers, because they adopt the figure of antimetabole (reversal of pairs) to present it: "All derailments of strategic maneuvering are fallacious, and all fallacies can be regarded as derailments of strategic maneuvering" (2001, 23).

The success of pragma-dialectics as a model derives to a large extent from the way it conceives of argumentation in terms of a critical discussion. As its proponents present it, pragma-dialectical theory gives us just the right model for testing the acceptability of a standpoint by dealing with all the doubts and criticisms that might be brought against it. Thus whether argumentation is private or public, whether it has the form of a dialogue or a monologue, and regardless of its subject matter, it can be described as if it were aimed at resolving a difference of opinion (2000b, 294). But doubt has been cast on whether all argumentation can be fruitfully addressed this way (Crosswhite 1995; Woods 1988, 1994), and we may question whether our evaluations strive to do no more than test the acceptability of standpoints. Once we see argumentation as representing more than a critical discussion, whether its goal is consensus, persuasion, or understanding, we find more to say about rhetoric's role. Beyond this, some of van Eemeren and Houtlosser's own case studies used as vehicles to demonstrate rhetorical maneuvering seem hard to cast as critical discussions involving conflicts of opinion. In the cases of the fox hunt and Shell in Nigeria the conflicts of opinions are evident. But other cases, like that of the R. J. Reynolds tobacco advertorial (2000b), are less convincingly expressed in such terms. The tobacco company advertorial aims to give advice to children on the issue of smoking. The discourse is rhetorical in force and aims to be persuasive. But the "opposing opinion" is by no means clear. In fact, we might expend considerable energy debating what actual conflict exists in this case, if there is one at all.

This is not to suggest a problem with the account per se, and the task set for this book of identifying and elaborating the *fundamental* importance of rhetorical features to argumentation can benefit from several components of van Eemeren and Houtlosser's work. For example, the choices speakers and writers make in selecting the terms and structures of their statements are aimed at giving their ideas *presence*. That is, statements are designed to capture the attention of the audience so that specific ideas stand out in their minds. Even the first dimension of selecting issues has this intent (1999b, 168). But it is with the use of rhetorical figures as presentational devices that this becomes most apparent, as they "make things present to the mind" (1999a, 166; 1999c, 485). This is an important echo and acknowledgment of Perelman and Olbrechts-Tyteca's stress on the way rhetorical figures attract attention (1969, 168).

The second point of interest is the argumentative role suggested for figures of speech. These figures have their own distinct structures and effects such that they can appear and act very much like types of argument. In fact, Chapter 3 will explore the proposal that we should go further and understand some of them as actual arguments when they are employed in specific ways.

❖ RHETORIC AND RHETORICAL ARGUMENTATION

Perelman (1963, 195) conceived of rhetoric constructively as "the study of the methods of argument" and saw in it the potential to clarify diverse areas of human thought. This contrasts noticeably with some of the more popular, but negative, uses of the term. We are exhorted to get beyond the rhetoric to what is real, to what is serious. And the reference is often to a rise in incendiary language, where emotion and reason have lost their natural relationship of balance and special interests have given vent to provocative invective. The chapters ahead echo Perelman's constructive understanding of rhetoric insofar as approaching argumentation in this way encourages us to view it as fundamentally a communicative practice. But as a *practice*, as a central human activity, argumentation is essentially rhetorical in ways that far exceed methodology alone. Bitzer (1968, 4), in a seminal essay on the rhetorical situation, comes closest to the way I am conceiving of rhetoric here when he describes it as "a mode of altering reality . . . by the creation of discourse which changes reality through the mediation of thought and action." Whether we see the aims of rhetorical argumentation as leaning towards persuasion, deliberation, or inquiry, the ways in which it helps us change our point of view and directs our actions reflect this understanding.

Rhetorical argumentation draws features from the rhetorical tradition and mixes them with newer innovations. For the core of what the tradition provides, another Aristotelian triad is useful: that organization of the rhetorical that distinguishes *ethos, pathos,* and *logos.* The processes of rhetorical argumentation meld together these three bringing into relief, and inextricably wedding to one another in the argumentative situation, the arguer, audience, and "argument." To understand argumentation is to understand the interactions of these components; to evaluate argumentation is to do the same.

Rhetorical ethos, or the consideration of character, has been given serious consideration by several argumentation theorists (Brinton 1986; Walton 1996a). In the *Rhetoric,* Aristotle introduces a basic sense of *ethos* with respect to the speaker who wants to establish credibility and demonstrate positive character traits (1.2.1356a; 2.1.1377b). Of particular value to Aristotle were the qualities of practical wisdom (*phronesis*), virtue (*areté*), and goodwill (*eunoia*), character traits essential to the virtue ethics he develops elsewhere. Ethotic argument, as it has developed, is not necessarily restricted to the character of the speaker or writer (the arguer, in our terms), but can involve any argumentation that deals with matters of character generally. Leff (2003) stresses the importance of *ethos* by relating it to three special dimensions: embodiment, enactment, and evocation. Embodiment involves the arguer embodying the correct values for a relevant audience. The rhetorical problem for Martin Luther King, Jr., in the *Letter from Birmingham Jail,* was not to embody the civil rights movement, since this was already clear in the public mind, "but to establish a persona that embodied the values and interests of his target audience" (Leff 2003, 261). King accomplished this by associating himself with core American values of freedom and independence, and situating himself within the Christian faith. There are echoes here of van Eemeren and Houtlosser's dimension of adapting to audience demands to create "communion" between arguer and audience. In Chapter 3, we will also meet an earlier instantiation of this in the rhetorical effect that Perelman and Olbrechts-Tyteca (1969, 172) refer to as "communion."

Leff's second dimension, enactment, arises from what a text *does,* rather than what it says. A text is not something that is inert, but it constructs representations and relationships as it develops. We will explore such a dynamic view of argumentative texts in Chapter 4. In the case of enactment, the text constructs the persona of the author (Leff allows that enactment and embodiment overlap in well-designed texts). Again, King's text illustrates this. To have the appropriate effect on his audience, King must escape the view that he is a radical whose ideas contrast with American society. The text works to accomplish this.

Finally, evocation involves the representation and apprehension of a situation as a whole in which everything else makes sense. Evocation makes evident "suppressed or undetected inconsistencies that block genuine argumentative engagement" (Leff 2003, 257). Thus, in King's text, the audience is brought to recognize a gap between their beliefs and the discriminatory practices of their society. Evocation here expresses rhetorical *ethos* in the way the text presents King as a prophetic voice, operating from among his audience rather than beyond them. Evocation also presupposes embodiment and enactment.

What Leff demonstrates is that an arguer is not a simple predetermined author of argumentative texts in which he or she is uninvolved. The arguer is implicated in, and in ways constructed by, the text. Thus attention to *ethos* is important for appreciating the full nature of argumentative situations and for recognizing the importance of rhetorical argumentation over and against its logical and dialectical cousins. More will be said about rhetorical *ethos* in later chapters.

The role of *pathos*, or the psychology of the emotions, in argumentation, will be seen in this book through the attention paid to the rhetorical audience. Aristotle defines *pathos* as "disposing the listener in some way" (*Rhetoric*, 1.2.1356a). While this directs us to attend to emotional appeals, it more importantly brings the audience into the picture and leads us to ask about the nature of audiences and their role in the argumentative situation.

The rhetorical audience is a complex and fluid idea. Audiences change, even in the course of argumentation. In fact, the very conception of audiences may "always be modified" (Perelman and Olbrechts-Tyteca 1989, 44). This refers to more than the composition of the audience—it includes its attitudes and adherence to positions: "We must not forget that the audience, to the degree that speech is effective, changes with its unfolding development" (Perelman 1982, 149). The emphasis on change indicates a further important feature of the rhetorical audience: it is not a passive consumer of arguments but plays an *active* role in the argumentation. The nature of the audience sets the terms of the premises, which are formulated in light of theses accepted by those to be addressed. The audience also contributes assumptions to the reasoning. And the audience can interact with the argumentation in the mind of the arguer or in dialogue with the arguer and become a co-arguer. Here "audiences can . . . take these arguments and their relation to the speaker as the object of a new argumentation" (49).

An interest in the assumptions and beliefs of audiences leads us to consider the environments in which audiences assess arguments and make their judgments. The crucial idea of interest to us here is that of a "cognitive environment," drawn from the work on relevance by Sperber and Wilson (1986). Suspicious of such catchphrases as "mutual knowledge" and "shared information," Sperber and Wilson observe that although we may share a physical environment, our differences seem to preclude any further generalizations about us: we represent the world differently and our perceptual and inferential abilities vary; we possess different belief structures through which we understand the world, and quite different sets of memories. So our *cognitive environment* would be different for each of us (38). Several things about this idea need to be understood for the discussions in this book.

A cognitive environment is a set of facts manifest to us. This idea involves an analogy with our visual environment. That environment comprises all the phenomena in our visual field at a particular time, even though we may not notice them. Likewise, we can imagine a cognitive field composed of all the facts manifest to each of us, which we could potentially perceive or infer. However, while our visual abilities may be fairly common, our cognitive abilities will differ, and hence so will our cognitive environments. One consequence of this is that we will differ in our ability to infer other facts from those we directly perceive. Memory will also come into play here, since knowledge previously acquired affects our ability to work with new information.

Where our cognitive environments overlap, they will give rise to a shared cognitive environment. This idea replaces that of "mutual knowledge" or "shared information." The same facts and assumptions can be manifest in the cognitive environments of two people. Insofar as their cognitive environments intersect, then that intersection is itself a cognitive environment. Where it is clear, manifest, which people share a cognitive environment, then this is a *mutual cognitive environment*. Texans, for example, share a mutual cognitive environment. As individuals they are essentially different, but there is an overlap in that certain facts and assumptions, within a shared physical environment, are manifest to them. They may not make the same assumptions, but it is possible for them to do so. Mutual manifestness, then, is weak in the right sense, since a claim that an assumption is mutually manifest will not be a claim about actual states or processes but about cognitive environments.

The last of the three core ideas important to rhetorical argumentation is *logos*, or the "argument." This introduction will have less to say about this concept because, even though it has a rich history, as we saw in the opening sections of the chapter it is one of the key ideas that will be developed throughout the book. The next chapter begins exploring the kinds of discourse that will qualify as rhetorical "argument." While the succeeding chapters will show that it is not a case of "anything goes" when it comes to what qualifies as argument, it is the case that we cannot anticipate the range of things that may be deemed to count. Our focus on the argumentative situation, with its necessary components of arguer, audience, and argument, creates a structure in which the last of these three terms is determined by the other two even more than they are each determined by the other components.[10] In a very general sense, an argument is the discourse of interest that centers, and develops in, the argumentative situation. The detailed discussion of "context" in Chapter 4 will further our understanding of the relationships between these three components.

Woven throughout contemporary discussions of traditional rhetorical ideas like *ethos, pathos,* and *logos* in the book are contemporary features of rhetorical argumentation, or notions that arise from it, that serve to fill out the account.

Of principal interest here is the idea of an "argumentative situation" that has already been mentioned a number of times. This is the dynamic "space" in which arguer and audience interact, but interact in a way that makes them coauthors. To understand this we will need to explore concepts like "addressivity": the way that a speaker addresses an audience already anticipating a reply in the very words that are used. Again, we will understand this further in a later chapter by exploring how we are always "in audience" to some degree, and hence able to appreciate what it means to be addressed by argumentative speech. Connected to this idea is the way that rhetorical argumentation is singularly concerned with how argumentation is experienced and how it invites collaboration. This means that the argumentation of interest to us is an invitational one. Rather than persuasive discourses that impose views on an audience, rhetorical argumentation, through the situation it enacts, invites an audience to come to conclusions through its own experiencing of the evidence. This idea, too, will be developed in the pages ahead.

The ideas of the last paragraph are presented with only the merest sense of what they involve, unlike the more detailed features of rhetorical argumentation elaborated in the previous pages. But this is because these are the innovations being brought to the study and developed here. Their details and justifications await us. As we proceed, fleshing out the ideas involved and showing how fundamental rhetoric is to actual argumentation, we will address arguments in all their diversity, from the traditional sets of premises and conclusions to the frustrating interactions demonstrated by Alice's encounters with the White and Red queens. In the process, ways will be suggested for both understanding and dealing with the full range of contemporary argumentative situations.

❖ THE PATH AHEAD

This chapter has already indicated a number of the discussions that are to come and the chapters in which they take place. Generally, the treatment of rhetorical argumentation proceeds from an investigation of its roots in the ancient Greek world, through several chapters that explore some of its central features and detail the core of the account, to chapters that take up questions of assessment and appropriate criteria for the evaluation of arguments from a rhetorical point of view.

The study begins in Chapter 2 by addressing the basic questions of how argument can be rhetorical and how exactly we are to understand "rhetoric." For answers to both questions we explore the emergence of rhetoric and argument in the ancient Greek world, not principally as these ideas came to be employed by Aristotle or even Plato, but prior to them in the writings and practices of the Sophists. This move necessitates a rehabilitation of Sophistic argument, demonstrating its variety and multiple goals, and thus challenging the traditional view that sees it trading only in eristics and aimed only at persuasion. The constructive model of argument drawn from these early practitioners sets the standard for what is to come.

Chapter 3 reverses the question of the previous chapter and asks rather how rhetoric can serve as argument. The particular devices of interest here are rhetorical figures like the antimetabole and prolepsis. Drawing on Fahnestock's provocative study of figures in scientific argumentation, we can see not only how figures facilitate argumentation, but actually serve as arguments in some contexts. Important here is the way in which such regular patterns of discourse are experienced by audiences, as arguers make certain things "present" to them to encourage the movement from the evidence of the premises to the conclusions.

The discussions of arguers and audiences in Chapters 2 and 3 raise the question of how such parties can best communicate argumentatively. Chapter 4 provides the heart of the current account in the way it addresses this question by drawing from the work of Bakhtin. A Bakhtinian model of argumentation, as developed from the suggestive discussions scattered throughout his works, is dialogical in the surest sense. The argumentative situation, as it is revealed here, encompasses a dialogue characterized by anticipation, involvement, and response, in which the arguer and audience become defined by the presence of the other party and co-construct the "argument." This model is illustrated through a traditional and a contemporary text.

With Chapter 5, attention shifts to how argumentation ought to be evaluated and judged. Such questions arise from the account of audiences developed in the preceding chapters. If the success of rhetorical argumentation is accounted in some way by the appropriate audience response, then what makes the choices of a specific audience reasonable? More importantly, from where do we get any standards for making such evaluations ourselves? Chapter 5 begins to discuss what is at stake in such questions by exploring some of the ways in which allegedly "objective" standards of reasonableness have been employed. In particular, we look at the so-called Martian standard, which represents a perspective quite foreign to our own point of view. In seeing why this standard fails, we begin to appreciate what is at stake in pursuing standards of reasonableness and the direction in which we should go in such a pursuit.

That direction takes us in Chapter 6 to a staple of rhetorical argumentation—the universal audience, as this notion was put forward by Perelman and Olbrechts-Tyteca. In visiting again this idea and reconsidering some of the problems that have been associated with it, we see how it can be developed to address the problem of the previous chapter. The universal audience is the source for our standard of what is reasonable. Rooted in real audiences, this idea represents the moving face of reason over time and human communities. Latter parts of the chapter show how a universal audience can be used both in constructing argumentation and, importantly, in evaluating it.

The evaluation of arguments leads to the final substantive investigation of the book: from a rhetorical perspective, what criterion best serves us, truth or acceptability? The challenge comes from a logical perspective on argumentation that specifically rejects rhetoric because of its abandonment of a truth criterion. In showing instead how acceptability not only avoids the problems associated with truth, but better meets the requirements of argument evaluation and communication, the chapter offers once again a defence of rhetorical argumentation as the one best suited to form the foundation of any comprehensive model of argument.

Chapter 8, in summary, recalls the principal features of the account that has been developed, and shows how they address the questions left unanswered by logical and dialectical accounts of argument. While there is much we can conclude about the rhetorical, in bringing form and substance to this sometimes inchoate force, ultimately it escapes firm conclusions. Like the argumentative situations it reflects, its boundaries are unclear and its components always undergoing change. What we can say about it is only part of an ongoing discussion that will enrich as much as it challenges.

❖ NOTES

1. For an assessment of Carroll's logic and its place in history, see William Warren Bartley III's *Introduction to Lewis Carroll's Symbolic Logic*, 1977.

2. The difference between the two "logics" is reflected in the types of exercises offered in the textbooks. In the traditional textbooks the problem is to test syllogisms for validity, or, where the example is not in syllogistic form, to reduce it to that form. This kind of exercise is missing from post-Boolean logic, including Carroll's text. There, the problem is to determine what information propositions provide for any given term or combination of terms.

3. For a more detailed assessment of Toulmin's model see Tindale 1999a, 24–25; 28–30.

4. For detailed appreciations of the problems involved see, for example, van Eemeren et al. (1996) and Johnson (1981).

5. The term is taken from Blair (1995).

6. Trudy Govier suggests as much when she writes that "an argument is one thing; objections to it, another; responses to those objections yet another" (1998, 7).

7. For details on the model, see van Eemeren and Grootendorst 1984, 1992; and van Eemeren 2002.

8. They note more than this, however: there is an intersubjective reasonableness prevalent in rhetoric and this is "one of the pillars of the critical reasonableness conception characteristic of dialectic" (van Eemeren and Houtlosser 2000a).

9. Available strategies abound. At the confrontation stage, for example, an arguer may employ evasion; at the opening stage, perhaps "smokescreen"; at the argumentation stage, "knocking down" an opponent could be used; and at the concluding stage, one may force an opponent to "bite the bullet" (van Eemeren and Houtlosser 1999a, 166).

10. Of interest here is one of Feyerabend's (1967) occasional remarks on argument. In discussing how arguments are observed in theatre, he noted that "an argument is more than an abstractly presented train of reasoning, for it involves the behavior, strategies, and appearances of the disputants and onlookers" (Preston 1999, 10).

2

Argument as Rhetorical . . .

❖ INTRODUCTION: RHETORIC'S ORIGIN

Argument, like rhetoric, comes out of the ancient Greek world. Also, like rhetoric, its emergence is to some degree indistinct and carries with it elements of controversy.

In Plato's *Gorgias,* the Sophist claims to have gone with his brother to the bedside of a sick man who had refused medical assistance, and persuaded the man "by means of no other art than rhetoric (*rhētorikē*)" (456b). This fits squarely with the traditional understanding of the Sophists as practitioners of the art of rhetoric. In fact, the "traditional" conflict between philosophy and rhetoric is often identified in the conflict between Plato and the Sophists (Mailloux 1995, 20). As Kerferd (1981) notes, various concerns have been deemed the distinguishing mark of a Sophist, and one of these was clearly "the educational ideal of rhetoric" (35). But just as it is difficult to assign any common interest to the Sophists, so, far more surprisingly, it may be difficult to attribute to them the teaching of rhetoric as it was understood by Plato and Aristotle.

Schiappa (1991, 1999) offers a persuasive argument for locating the origins of *rhētorikē* in the works of Plato and no earlier.[1] The standard account of the origins of rhetorical theory, as expressed in Kennedy (1980), ascribes the "invention" of rhetorical theory to Corax and Tisias, with this attributed to the authority of Aristotle (Schiappa 1991, 50). By the end of the fifth century BC, handbooks of rhetoric were available to students and the Sophists earned large sums of money teaching rhetorical techniques. It was their limiting of the uses of rhetoric to personal gain and success that prompted Plato and Aristotle to develop more philosophical accounts. Thus, as Schiappa summarizes the matter, "three traditions of rhetorical theory are identifiable in the fifth and fourth centuries: technical, sophistic, and philosophical" (40).

It is with this standard account that Schiappa takes issue. Simply put, he argues that *rhētorikē* is a product of the fourth century, first introduced in the *Gorgias* by Plato, who essentially "invents" rhetoric (1991, 40).[2] "Prior to the fourth century the key conceptual term associated with Sophists was usually logos and sometimes legein—terms broader in meaning than any ancient conception of rhētorikē" (71). Elsewhere, Schiappa (1995, 42) identifies in Isocrates' fourth-century *Against the Sophists* the earliest surviving use of *rhetoreia* for "oratory." The claim is not that evidence of interests in what we would take to be rhetorical matters is missing from accounts prior to Plato. As Johnstone notes, "[c]lassical rhetoric may have been an invention of the fourth century, but it was invented using tools and materials that had been crafted during the preceding two hundred and fifty years" (1996, 16). Nor is Schiappa denying that the Sophists belong to the development of rhetorical theory (Schiappa 1999, 28). His challenge is to the standard belief that they composed a systematic and deliberate set of procedures and practices under the rubric of "rhetoric." What they provide for such a history of rhetoric would, he argues, be "better described as predisciplinary rather than as a consciously held theory or definition of Rhetoric" (1999, 28).

As partial evidence for his thesis, beyond the absence of any use of *rhētorikē* in fifth-century fragments, Schiappa cites Aristophanes' failure to exploit its use in his treatment of the Sophists. Had they used the word, Schiappa suggests, Aristophanes would surely have targeted it (1991, 41). Again, the anonymous text *Dissoi Logoi,* as well as extant texts of the Older Sophists like Gorgias's *Encomium of Helen,* would be expected to mention it, given their interest in persuasive speaking (1999, 16).

The instructive aspect of this thesis for our purposes lies in what Schiappa proposes the Sophists *were* doing with language. Principally, he identifies a theory of *logos* rather than a theory of rhetoric. He identifies this in Protagoras's thinking but also notes that "[t]hough Protagoras seems to have been the first Sophist to privilege *logos* over the mythic-poetic tradition, virtually all the Sophists can be so characterized" (57). Protagoras is viewed by Schiappa as a transitional figure between myth and argument, as seen in his fragment on the existence of the gods. In challenging the tradition of *mythos*, Protagoras inaugurated a more anthropological approach. "This called for *arguing* rather than merely *telling*. The substantive challenges to traditional ways of thinking brought a new humanistic rationalism of *logos*" (1991, 56). By identifying arguing with *logos* and opposing it to rhetoric, Schiappa challenges the popular distinction between success-seeking and truth-seeking (rhetoric vs. philosophy) that has influenced so many accounts. Such "rhetorical" readings serve to understate the philosophical (90) and give a one-sided portrait of Protagoras and the other Sophists. To do so downplays not only their contributions to philosophy, but also reduces their many useful insights into language and argumentation to a singular interest in persuasion, an interest deemed unworthy because of the perceived ends involved. Gagarin (2002) would appear to agree. The images of rhetoric as "the art of persuasion" and the Sophist as "the craftsman of persuasion" are both caricatures that have distorted our vision. Few of the fragments of the Sophists even mention persuasion. Rather, Sophistic *logos* had other aims, "such as exploring methods of argument" (30).[3]

As noted above, Schiappa is not making the counterintuitive claim that we don't see in the Sophists the use of rhetorical devices but, as he insists, "there is a subtle but historically significant difference between describing early sophistic efforts at theorizing about *logos* and the world, and later efforts to organize and improve discursive strategies as part of a discrete and clearly conceptualized art of rhetoric" (1991, 71). For example, the distinction between a theory of rhetoric and a theory of *logos* can be recognized in the practices advocated by Aristotle and Protagoras. Aristotle's approach involves categorizing the occasions for rhetoric in the law courts, assembly, and civic ceremonies, and delimiting the sphere of rhetoric as distinct from the roles of logic and dialectic. In contrast to this, Protagoras's view of *logos* "was undifferentiated and precategorical; that is, it was independent of context and did not distinguish between types of discourse on the basis of distinctive principles or degrees of certainty" (1991, 200). Following Schiappa's lead, any apparent theory of rhetoric in the Sophists appears only in retrospect and results primarily from reading them through Platonic and Aristotelian filters.[4]

❖ ARGUMENT'S ORIGIN

Similar things can be said for the origins of argument. Feyerabend (1987) points to the vagueness surrounding its origins when he notes that

> [a]rgument, like language, or art, or ritual, is universal; but, again like language or art or ritual, it has many forms. A simple gesture, or a grunt can decide a debate to the satisfaction of some partici-pants while others need long and colourful arias to be convinced. Thus argument was well established long before the Greek philosophers started thinking about the matter. (8)

Indeed, we could no more hold otherwise if we are to contend that argument is a primary mode of communication and a means to gain understanding. As long as language has been in use, elements of argu-mentative speech must have occurred. But with the Greeks, "argu-ment" starts to take on specific forms. Participants become reflexive about their argumentative practices, studying them for best effect and purpose. There may be some indication of this in the writings of Homer. Enos (1993, 4–8) draws some murky references, principally from the *Odyssey*, that suggest emerging heuristics (as opposed to eris-tic, which is the term he associates with argumentation). In the *Odyssey*, for example, Odysseus, trapped with his men in the Cyclops's cave, takes counsel with himself on how they might escape, weaving "all manner of wiles and counsel" (9.421–423). On balance, however, it is difficult to attribute more here than the awareness of a shift from reliance on the gods to a trust in human reason.

Feyerabend sees the Greeks standardizing a particular way of arguing that they believed "was independent of the situation in which it occurred and whose results had universal authority" (1987, 8). In this way, argument, as something abstract and objective, became a tool for finding "truths" that were independent of any tradition or perspective. Later in the same work, Feyerabend clarifies how he understands what is at stake here: "What the early Western rationalists did invent was not argument, but a special and standardized form of argumentation which not only disregarded but explicitly rejected personal elements" (87). In this Feyerabend suggests (and indeed makes explicit in the surrounding discussion) that arguments should be directed at particular people, that for an argument to be "argument" it must take into account the beliefs and attitudes of the participants.

In saying this he is only telling one side of the story of argument in its Greek emergence, or at least, in stressing the "invention" of formal argument he implies that this is the sole sense of "argument" active and valued among the Greeks. This is a dangerously selective picture. As we saw in Chapter 1, the three distinct senses of argument, as logical, dialectical, and rhetorical, can all be traced to the early Greeks, and specifically to Aristotle. Feyerabend draws attention to the emergence of the logical, and perhaps what he is decrying is its perceived prominence. But he overlooks the emergence of dialectical and rhetorical argument, the second of which does take into account the beliefs and attitudes of the participants.

To get a clearer sense of this we need to look briefly at the argumentative practices of Plato and Aristotle, and their often overlooked predecessors, the Sophists.

❖ RHETORIC AND ARGUMENT IN
    FIFTH- AND FOURTH-CENTURY GREECE

Aristotle's *Organon* is a source for far richer ideas concerning argument than Feyerabend's dramatic exposition would suggest. It is the case that his logical use of "argument," centered on the development of the syllogism, has received primary attention in the tradition. But it is this very primacy of value that is being questioned in recent work on dialectical and rhetorical argumentation. In his *Posterior Analytics,* Aristotle advanced the syllogism as a structure of necessity, whereby some things are assumed and something other than what is assumed follows from them (I.1.24b). In this way, he strove to develop a formal system of inferences that would disclose the kinds of objective, independent truths about the world that concern Feyerabend. On Feyerabend's terms, such sets of inferences are not arguments. But it is by no means clear that Aristotle intended us to think so, at least not in the sense that Feyerabend wishes to attribute to "argument." In the

Topics, for example, Aristotle discusses reasoning as it is employed in dialogues and debates. Very different premises are employed in this reasoning, ones that are probable. Such premises allow us to "reason from reputable opinions about any subject presented to us, and . . . when putting forward an argument, [to] avoid saying anything contrary to it" (*Topics* 100a21–22). The sense of "argument" being understood here is not one that would be recognizable from the discussion of the *Posterior Analytics*. Rather than logical, it is dialectical. Concerned with dialogue and debate, it has as its primary interest the types of procedures that should be used to reason well. Again, in the *Rhetoric* we find a further shift of emphasis, which inaugurates for Aristotle a third sense of "argument." As we saw in the previous chapter, while rhetoric is deemed to share features with dialectic, it also contains distinctly separate elements, like *ethos* and *pathos.* At the same time, while rhetorical arguments are concerned with proofs or convictions (I.1.1355a), the logic here is more informal than that of the *Posterior Analytics.* As Burnyeat (1994, 31) observes of Aristotle, "not all the patterns of argument he illustrates can be fitted into the syllogistic mold." At the heart of the account in the *Rhetoric* is a notion of rhetorical enthymeme that, among other characteristics, relies on its audience for understanding and even completion.[5]

Moving further back in the Greek corpus of relevant texts, the work of Plato presents more than a few challenges to those interested in the emergence of senses of argument. This is in part due to the form that his writings take, conversational dialogues in which an authoritative voice cannot always be assumed in the way that it can with authors like Aristotle. Beyond this, Plato is an inveterate imitator of other people's styles and voices. Discourses that appear to reflect the styles of Sophists like Thrasymachus and Hippias, for example, are contrasted with the question-answer discourse attributed to Socrates, and such discourses are all argumentative in different ways, with the eristics of the *Euthydemus* being the more extreme example. Again, the very attribution of a method to the Socratic figure of the early dialogues is challenging insofar as it raises questions about the discourses of the historical Socrates and the degree to which Plato captures something of his voice, if he captures it at all.[6] The so-called "Socratic Method" of the early dialogues, with its characteristic of ending in perplexity or difficulty (*aporia*) and its apparent goal of holding up an interlocutor's speech before his mind, as if it were a mirror in which he might see his own ignorance, itself contrasts with a later, "Platonic," hypothetical method that eschews *aporia* and employs a type of counterfactual argument, whereby the participants in a dialogue can pursue what might be the case if a certain statement is assumed to be true.[7]

One aspect of the treatment of argument in Plato's texts that we should consider here, since it is relevant to the concerns raised by Feyerabend, is the apparent distinction between public argument and what begins to appear as the use of private argument. Such serves as a plausible bridge from the discourses and public interests of the Sophists to what has become by the time of Aristotle an introspective tool for exploring the nature of truth.

The opposition between the public and the private is a common feature running through what I will call the "Sophistic Dialogues."[8] Plato's Sophists are exponents of public argument, as indeed they would seem to have been in real life. Hence, their interests are focused in this direction. The Socrates of the dialogues, on the other hand, prefers private argument, fostering the Platonic interest in internal reflection—a different motivation and a different end. Nowhere may this be more apparent than in the *Greater Hippias*.[9] Hippias has a desire for speech making (304b). He accuses Socrates and those with whom he speaks of producing only "flakings and clippings of speeches." They take the entirety of things, and cut them up with words, freezing things in isolation for examination. This tears them from the natural flux, making the treatments, in Hippias's view, inadequate and, it might be implied, without context.[10] Hippias, after all his failed attempts to define the "fine," insists at the end,

> here's what is fine and worth a lot: to be able to present a speech well and finely, in court or council or any other authority to whom you give the speech, to convince them and go home carrying not the smallest but the greatest of prizes, the successful defense of yourself, your property, and friends. (304b)

Clearly from this, what Hippias values is the public performance and his speech is directed toward an outer audience that he must convince.

The dialogue between Socrates and Hippias does not continue. In part, this is because a continuation is not welcome—the attack on Socrates' "small-talking" can be taken as a refusal to engage further in it or be subjected to it. But it is also because an answer has already been suggested in the dialogue. Plato employs a very strange device in the

Greater Hippias. Rather than have Socrates directly attack the points
raised by Hippias, he has him invoke a shadowy dissenter (someone
who has questioned him quite insultingly) (286c–d) and then take on
the persona of that other man, so that Hippias is to answer Socrates as
if this other is the questioner (287c). Socrates stresses how important it
is that he, Socrates, be able to convince this other man, who he eventually identifies as Sophronicus's son, that is, Socrates himself, "who
wouldn't easily let me say those things without testing them" (298c).
What is Plato's purpose in employing this device? Is it to allow
Socrates to insult Hippias without appearing to do so himself? After
all, Hippias, as a model of self-sufficiency, who makes his own clothes,
shoes, and jewelry, who writes poems and all sorts of prose (*Lesser
Hippias* 368b–d), is the antithesis of the Platonic individual who knows
one thing well and does that thing, and so is thought to be the Sophist
who Plato sees most fit for ridicule. But Socrates states often that
he agrees with the insults of this other man, so he is hardly a buffer
between the insult and the insulted. Rather, we might see in this device
Plato stressing a preference for private argumentation over the public.
Where Hippias longs for the whole speech to be addressed to a public
audience, and *defines the fine in these terms,* Socrates' speech is internal,
the one to be convinced is himself (Sophronicus's son), and the payoff
is private, not public.

This accords, to cite a further supporting reference, with the discussion of argument given in the *Phaedo,* where Plato has Socrates
attack those who are quite uneducated and engage in argument not
with any thought to the truth but only to get the better of others.
Socrates confesses,

> I differ from them only to this extent: I shall not be eager to get the
> agreement of those present that what I say is true, except inciden-
> tally, but I shall be very eager that I should myself be thoroughly
> convinced that things are so. (91a)

For him the value of argument is not as a public display, but as a
tool to achieve inner conviction (cf. also *Theaetetus* 189e–190a). These
two purposes, the Platonic and the Sophistic, are quite distinct.

The inner argumentative speech of the Platonic dialogue is, then, a
fitting precursor of Aristotle's more systematic structuring of private
argument, developing a tool that can be employed by the individual
inquirer to explore what is true. As a bridge stage in the emergence of

argument in forms recognizable to us, the Platonic dialogue would combine both the public and private senses, as indeed the dialogue method would seem to do. Clearly, the emergence of one sense of "argument" does not preclude the continuation of other senses. Plato, for instance, is developing both the dialectical argumentation of the academy, reflected in several dialogues, and the public argumentation of the Sophists. It is this latter that has been sorely neglected in historical treatments of argumentation, but in my backwards chronology of argument's emergence, it is the last stop.

By the time we reach Aristotle's *Rhetoric,* rhetorical argumentation has taken on a relatively clear focus and set of ideas. But this understanding is in turn matched with a philosophical perspective, that of Aristotle's truth-seeking epistemology. And we might wonder both whether there are useful ways to conceive of rhetorical argument outside of such an understanding, and what kinds of precedent were available from which Aristotle could structure his own ideas. Pursuing these two lines of inquiry will allow us to further explore the origins of the ideas that interest us—rhetoric and argument.

❖ SOPHISTIC ARGUMENT

If Schiappa's account for the Platonic origins of rhetoric is plausible, and the presentation of his case above would suggest that it is, it raises several questions about the nature of Sophistic discourse and even the practices of Socrates and *their* appropriate categorization. For example, when Plato takes pains to distinguish Socrates from the Sophists he is in the process understanding "Sophist" in a particular way that deviates from earlier practice. As Protagoras himself is allowed to say in the dialogue that bears his name, the extension "Sophist" covers such workers with language as Homer and Hesiod (*Protagoras* 316d). It is Plato who reworks the concept so as to focus on a particular type of practitioner, and in the process distinguishes Socrates from that group. But if we for a moment ignore Plato's categorization, are the distinctions quite so clear, particularly when it comes to the two concepts we are exploring: "rhetoric" and "argument"?

The essential feature of any notion of rhetoric is the employment of discourses in social contexts. Primarily we might think of persuasive discourses, but even here the senses of persuasion can be varied. Prior to Plato we find a rich tapestry of emerging discourses, from the narrative to the historical, the scientific and the philosophical, and even perhaps the sophistical. In each of these, *logos* is approached in some specific way, and in each the power of *logos* to effect change and influence is recognized, even if only in how to understand the descriptions of reality that it offered. Two primary uses of *logos* (as a generic term for discourses) are suggested here: to describe the world and to influence people's beliefs and behavior. These conform well to modern uses that we can appreciate. But we might raise the question of whether this distinction is so finely understood during the periods under discussion.

In the history of argumentation, Plato and Aristotle, particularly the latter, dominate the early voices. Even more significant, any other voices that might be recovered from that period come to us through the "filters" of Platonic and Aristotelian texts. In the case of the Sophists, we have very few original fragments with which to work. Any judgment about what constituted a Sophistic position or attitude, or even whether there was agreement on any point, must be made in light of a plethora of conflicting interpretations and an attempt to reconstruct the contexts in which the statements were made.

Yet the Sophists' positions on and use of argument are important, not least because of the obvious influence they had on Plato and Aristotle, both of whom went out of their way on repeated occasions to contest points they attributed to Sophists. The Sophists represented an "other" against which the pillars of Platonism, and to a lesser extent Aristotelianism, were erected. The Sophists promoted practices at odds with those advocated in the dialogues and which bear directly on the understanding and value of "argument." And they further represented, in some way, the infamous "sophistical refutation" in Aristotle, out of which a long and standard history of fallacy, or incorrect argument, has developed.

In spite of the rehabilitation that the Sophists have enjoyed in recent studies (Kerferd 1981; Guthrie 1971), the negative judgments of Plato and Aristotle have tended to be endorsed by those who study the nature of argument.[11] A major text that aims to capture the current state of affairs in the study of argument (van Eemeren, Grootendorst, and Snoeck-Henkemans 1996) conveys what is indeed a standard story. Referring to the Sophists of fifth-century Greece, the authors tell us that they "were itinerant scholars who taught lessons in argumentation and social and political skills" (30). But the argumentation that they taught was presumably bad argumentation. The authors transfer the advocacy of relativism, often attributed to the Sophists as a group, to the field of argumentation where they identify as a Sophistic standpoint the view that

> objectively speaking, there can be no such thing as good argumentation. If one person convinces another with his arguments, this is because the other person accepts what he says. The first person is, in other words, agreed to be right, but that does not necessarily mean that in objective terms he actually is right. (30)

What appears here to be a description of Sophistic practice is on closer scrutiny a prescription. Behind the account stand the assumptions that *good* argumentation must have standards outside of social agreement and that the Sophists recognized no such standards. Both assumptions may prove questionable. But what is notable here is that a particular conception of argument, and indeed *good* argument, is being projected onto the Sophists and used to find their practice inadequate. In this respect, such recent authors still follow in the steps of Plato and Aristotle.

One argumentation theorist who is cognizant in his work of the controversy surrounding Plato and Aristotle's interpretations of the Sophists is Walton. This is significant because in many respects Walton's own dialectical model of argument has much in common with the Sophists' interest in probability and plausible inference, as he himself recognizes (1995, 4; 1998a, 15–16). The problem, as Walton suggests it, is that the denouncing of the Sophists by Plato and Aristotle was so widely accepted as correct that any interest in a notion of argument based on presumption and opinion was in turn regarded as less than respectable. This, however, does not prompt Walton to go back and investigate the argumentative practices of individual Sophists (beyond a recognition of Antiphon's predilection for the argument from probability) (1998a, 15). Instead, he directs his attention to salvaging the disfavored aspects of dialectical argument.

Again, while Walton acknowledges the recent controversies surrounding Plato and Aristotle's interpretations of the Sophists, he does not himself pass judgment except to accept their condemnation of eristic argument.[12] Eristic argument is a form of argument that aims at victory at any cost.[13] The standard example of this is found not in any of the Sophists' writings but in Plato's *Euthydemus.* In fact, the *Euthydemus* examples often seem to be taken as *the* examples of

Sophistic argument, even though, or perhaps because, the *Euthydemus* constitutes Plato's most derisive treatment of "Sophistic thought." That it is countered by a greater number of respectful portraits of Sophists in other dialogues is often overlooked. Certainly, the depiction of Sophistic argument presented in the *Euthydemus* fuels the judgment that the Sophists were not serious arguers inquiring after truth, but perpetrators of fallacious reasoning and seekers of personal profit. At least, this is the view that Walton follows Aristotle in sharing. Aristotle links sophistical argumentation and fallacies (or sophistical refutations) to eristic argument. That Walton is in agreement with this move is indicated when he relates it to his own new dialectic: "Aristotle is also making an extremely important statement about the analysis of fallacies that is preserved in the new dialectic. Fallacies are associated with deceptive shifts from one type of dialogue to another in the new dialectic" (1998a, 191). The stigma of deception clings to eristic argument, and in turn to the Sophists who are deemed its exponents. Even when the controversial nature of Aristotle's interpretation is recognized, the association holds firm. Yet, as we will see, there is more to Sophistic argument than eristics, and not all Sophistic argumentation can be equated with fallacy even if we permit ourselves to view it only through Aristotelian lenses. Eristic argumentation itself may even be seen to have some merit to it (Grimaldi 1996, 29).

The foregoing treatment of the Sophists—what really amounts to a nontreatment—is the standard story to be found in studies of argument, if the Sophists are mentioned at all. But there are exceptions to this rule.

Notably, Perelman and Olbrechts-Tyteca (1969) question the received view when they observe that the value of the Sophists' enterprise depends very much on the value we place on the type of argumentation involved. Plato considered truth to be more important than gaining the adherence of an audience. But for Perelman and Olbrechts-Tyteca, "as soon as these procedures are examined from the angle of argumentation, a justification can be found for them which makes them less offensive" (319). The implication is, of course, that there is still some offense committed by the Sophists, but at least they understand a model of argumentation, and perhaps good argumentation, that can be reconciled with Sophistic practice.

A more complete positive engagement with the Sophists is provided by Poulakos (1997). He goes beyond simply noting the antipathy that Plato and Aristotle felt toward them to ask what exactly it was that

Plato and Aristotle were rejecting: "How did the Sophists reason? Why? On what grounds did philosophers of the fourth century BC reject the logic of sophistical thought?" (13). Such questions guide our thinking in useful directions. Poulakos also introduces several methodological principles in approaching these questions. Of most significance is the understanding that logic is "time- and place-specific" (13). Rather than progressing over time, Poulakos sees different logics arising in response to different cultural situations and declining when those conditions no longer pertained. Such might be reflected in a shift from the oral-based, itinerant teaching, and communal contexts of the Sophists to the emerging text-based, institutional, and private contexts of Plato's writing.

In accordance with this, Poulakos follows the principle that a logic can be derived from studying the practices and ideas of the Sophists (1997, 14). There is ample material for following this direction. Although we are limited to fragments of the Sophists, there are many corroborative accounts of their practices and positions, including those of Plato and Aristotle, "the informational aspect of the critics' comments" (14). The difficulty, as already noted, is to distinguish description from interpretation in these accounts. But while this difficulty will loom large over any such project, it ought not to deter us from employing the approach. In Poulakos's study it is the culturally derived sense of spectacle that comes to the fore (along with the Sophists' associations with the Presocratics and poets), presenting the Sophists as figures interested in competition and exhibition, with modes of reasoning (like the eristic argument) developed to those ends. Sophistic logic, he concludes, concerns itself "with situational forces, specific points of contention, and new visions of linguistic expression. In short, it must be a circumstantial, agonistic, and exhibitive logic" (16). This logic is founded around three notions that he develops in a general discussion without direct reference to any of the individual Sophists involved. The first notion is that of the opportune rhetorical moment, or *kairos*. This involves speakers responding spontaneously to fleeting situations marked by their unique features (18). The second idea is that of playfulness (*paignion*), seen in the making of the weaker argument stronger and the way in which the language was exploited in the coining of new words and arguments (20). The final notion is that of possibility (*to dynaton*), which refers to things that are not but can be. Here, Poulakos argues, the Sophists introduced a third possibility between the strict opposition of the actual and the ideal (21). The merit of Poulakos's essay is the way he culls these features from the cultural and political contexts in which the Sophists worked and further explains how each notion served as a target for Platonic and Aristotelian criticisms. Several of his points will enrich some of the discussions that follow.

❖ SOPHISTIC ARGUMENT
AND THE NOTION OF "FALLACY"

While theories of good argument have not given much space to the ideas of the Sophists, theories of fallacy certainly have. As has been noted above, it is taken as a commonplace that the paradigms of fallacious arguments are found in the reasoning of the Sophists, as exemplified in Plato's *Euthydemus* and Aristotle's *Sophistical Refutations*. Here the judgments of Plato and Aristotle have been decisive in establishing the deeply entrenched opinion of the tradition. In modern parlance, the fallacy and the sophism are deemed synonymous. There are several questions that can be raised here, but principally we might ask whether the historical assumption that equates fallaciousness with Sophistic argument is fair? And, whatever answer we give to that question, whether all Sophistic modes of argument are reflected in the types presented in the *Euthydemus* and *Sophistical Refutations*? A full exploration of these questions is beyond the scope of this text, but enough can be said here to fuel the thesis that Sophistic modes of argument far exceeded the feeble simulacra in these works.

Poulakos (1997) asks questions that seem so obvious once posed that our failure to have asked them earlier is itself instructive: "If the philosophers were right, how on earth did the Sophists' contemporaries believe them? Couldn't they see through their deceptions, inconsistencies, and contradictions?" (13). While the reaction to the Sophists seems to have been mixed, several of them at least were highly respected and enjoyed positions of responsibility. Protagoras, for example, was well regarded by Pericles and commissioned to write the laws for the Athenian colony of Thurii; and Gorgias was sent as an ambassador from Leontini, his home, to Athens. On the other hand, there is no doubt that the Sophists also could be the subjects of humor and derision. Aristophanes' *Clouds* would have contributed to this perception, even if it was not descriptive of it (that is, there is a question whether Aristophanes is reflecting a common mood toward the Sophists or creating it). This mixed portrait does nothing to clarify matters, but it does suggest that no simple equivalence between Sophistic argument and fallacy is plausible.

The problems with this way of thinking are well illustrated in Sprague's (1962) study of the use of fallacy in Plato's dialogues. Her intention is to defend Plato against the charge that he engages (unintentionally) in fallacious argumentation. Her thesis is that all his uses of fallacy are conscious. The bulk of the work is given over to a detailed analysis of the *Euthydemus*, where the nature of eristic argument is explained and illustrated. The key distinction lies in the intention behind the use of "fallacy," here equated with eristics: the Sophists, represented by Euthydemus and his brother Dionysodorus, aim for victory in argument; Plato, on the other hand, employs fallacy to advance his argument, to demonstrate the flaws in such discourses and hence their inadequacy. However, Sprague's study also examines parallel arguments in the *Theaetetus* and *Cratylus* and some similar arguments in the *Hippias Minor*. In defending Plato's use of eristic arguments here, and particularly in the *Theaetetus*, she makes an important claim: "that arguments which may, from their resemblance in form to arguments in the *Euthydemus*, be called 'eristic,' need by no means be employed in an eristic spirit" (81). This serves to emphasize several points. The commitment of a fallacy, in Sprague's eyes, lies not in the argument form itself, but in the "spirit" of its use. This allows her to salvage Plato's logical reputation; his facility is such that he can employ both good and bad arguments to positive ends. But if such a charitable judgment can be extended for Plato, one wonders why it should be withheld *carte blanche* from the Sophists, who also have a remarkable facility with argument. By Plato's own depictions, the intentions of Sophists like Protagoras and Gorgias were by no means bent on deception. Certainly, given Sprague's results, we cannot cast the mantle of deceiver over *anyone* who employs eristics.[14] Furthermore, this split between form and intention can itself direct us to the very different practices and values that separated the Sophists from Plato.

Equally interesting in Sprague's study is how she understands the central term of her investigation, "fallacy." We must wait until her concluding chapter before being offered even an indirect attempt at defining the term. Prior to that, it is simply assumed to be eristic argument. Examples of individual fallacies, like that of Equivocation (a form prevalent in the *Euthydemus*), are adopted with their Aristotelian understanding. In her concluding remarks, Sprague notes: "If fallacies are, after all, bad arguments, it might be asked whether it is fair play on the part of Plato to employ them" (80). Hence, the indirect definition: fallacies are "bad arguments," and bad arguments, in the context of the study, are eristic arguments. But this kind of categorizing will require much closer attention as we ask wherein the "badness" of such arguments is to be found.

The seminal work on fallacies in the last thirty years is that of Hamblin (1970), although we cannot ignore the wealth of treatments that his study has encouraged.[15] Hamblin takes his standard of what should count as a fallacy from Aristotle's account in the *On Sophistical Refutations*, whose list, Hamblin observes, has endured with little change for two millennia (9). Specifically, "a fallacious argument, as almost every account from Aristotle onwards tells you, is one that *seems to be valid* but *is not so*" (12).[16]

Hamblin introduces the Sophists in connection with Aristotle's treatment of contentious arguments in competitions and contests. In Athens, he notes,

> [w]e meet professional debates [sic] called 'sophists' who make a practice of taking part in contests and train students to do the same. The better-known sophists such as Gorgias and Protagoras are worthy philosophical foils for Socrates, and Plato's dialogues named after them relate encounters that are more than mere debating competitions. (1970, 55)

But, he immediately observes, Plato and Aristotle have a low opinion of the Sophists, and after quoting Aristotle's meaning for "contentious" in the *Topics* (100b23), Hamblin writes: "A contentious inference is called a *sophism* (162a17), so that it is written into the definition that the stock-in-trade of sophists is fallacy" (1970, 55). Here, Hamblin has directly taken the association of Sophists with fallacy from Aristotle. He then continues: "We have no detailed account of an actual sophistical contest. The best example, in Plato's dialogues, of the kind of argumentation he and Aristotle have in mind is the *Euthydemus*" (55). In the space of a few lines, Hamblin has gone from Gorgias and Protagoras to the *Euthydemus* as if "Sophist" has a common currency throughout.[17] Passages like this, which fail to make important distinctions, leave the Sophists as a group infected by the association with fallacy that belongs at most to a subset, and this a subset whose practices may well be born of the pen of Plato.[18] While it would be unwise to minimize the eristical side of sophistry, it is just as problematic to overemphasize this aspect.

In presenting several long passages from the *Euthydemus*, Hamblin (1970) indicates that Plato's response to eristic arguments was mixed. Aside from the lack of serious intention that seems to mark the brothers' approach, the puzzles themselves, achieved through exploiting the richness of language, seem to fascinate Plato. As such, the arguments await treatment in a relevant logical theory, and Aristotle's *On Sophistical Refutations*, Hamblin believes, is the first step in that direction (59). That work contrasts arguments (or refutations) that are real and those that are only apparent. It is the latter, in Aristotle's judgment, that characterizes the Sophists' manner of arguing. Hence, the Sophists are drawn into the arena of Aristotle's metaphysics, and their practices interpreted from that perspective. Hence, further, the *apparent* validity that is stressed in Hamblin's definition of fallacy. Insofar as we might come to question how appropriate it is for the Sophists to bear labels drawn from Aristotle's metaphysics, so we might also question whether their argumentation is suited to his designation of "fallacy." The adoption by the tradition of a model of logic and argument with a rich Aristotelian heritage includes a concept of fallacy that appears fixed and universal (as seen in the assumptions driving Sprague's study). It will pay us to consider how much that concept is a product of Aristotle's own way of looking at the world and, in particular, a product of his debate with a group of thinkers who did not share that vision and all it entailed.

So if the charge of "fallacy" is inappropriate as a general description of Sophistic argument, it is important to ask what kind of description would be accurate—how did they understand the nature and use of "argument"? To a certain degree, this topic deserves a study of its own. The Sophists introduced interesting and varied strategies or types of argument, some of which are reflected in current forms of argumentation. There is the strategy, attributed to Protagoras, of setting opposing arguments against each other, on the premise that for any position that can be put forth an opposing argument can be made that is equally compelling. There is the important and wide advocacy of probability argument (*eikos*) that strives to show which things are likely rather than certain. This is a type of argument employed famously by Antiphon in his instructive speeches (which also involve opposing arguments). And there are schemes like the *peritrope*, which involves the reversal of positions and has one of its most effective demonstrations in the first book of Plato's *Republic*.

Such strategies and schemes also serve to indicate how Sophistic argument must have aims beyond the simple persuasion of an audience. How, for example, would presenting arguments on both sides of an issue be persuasive (Gagarin 2002, 31)? It makes more sense to see this as a use of argument to achieve understanding, to open up perspectives, and to explore an issue. Nor should we miss the echoes of this in the writings of current argumentation theorists who advocate the importance and value of considering all sides to an issue, including that of one's opponent.

To gain some appreciation of the variety and flavor of Sophistic argument, I will look at two examples, both drawn from what is available in extant fragments of the Sophists. The first, from Gorgias, involves current recognizable patterns of argument. The second, from Antiphon, is less familiar, at least in the form that he uses.

Of those Sophists who *might* be seen as trading in persuasive discourse, Gorgias would seem the primary example. And yet his texts also demonstrate a clear commitment to what he calls "reasonings" and a fine logical structure. His extant speeches, *Encomium of Helen* and *A Defense on Behalf of Palamedes,* regardless of his purpose in constructing them, both reveal what Kennedy (1963, 167–68) calls the apagogic method of listing possible outcomes and dealing with each in turn. We might think of this now as counterfactual reasoning. Consider the way Gorgias phrases this argument in the *Palamedes.* Palamedes is defending himself against Odysseus's accusation that he has betrayed Greece to the barbarians. Palamedes insists he was not capable of performing such a deed, because for him to have met with the barbarian or exchanged messages would not have been possible when neither could speak the other's language. So a third person, an interpreter, would be necessary. He continues: "But assume that this too has taken place, *even though it has not.* Next it was necessary to give and receive a pledge . . ." [italics added] (frag. 11a, 8).[19] Palamedes (or Gorgias through him) uses the phrase I have italicized here to invite his audience to think counterfactually, and then proceeds to show how unlikely the hypothesis is, since no one would trust a traitor. There is an element here also of the argument from probability, of what is likely to have happened. But for our purposes, it is sufficient to emphasize the contemporary character of the argument and also the rhetorical effectiveness of proceeding on the terms of the case that has been made against one, of drawing the audience into the account and inviting them to "see" the consequences of the proposal. In light of the discussion of rhetorical ethos in Chapter 1, drawn from Leff (2003), we might consider how Gorgias constructs the text so that Palamedes embodies the appropriate values for the audience.

Such a "method of logical proof" (Kennedy 1963, 168) is used to even greater effect in the structure of the *Helen*, where Gorgias sets out four possible causes for Helen's behavior and then deals with each in turn. "For either by will of Fate and decision of the gods and vote of Necessity did she do what she did, or by force reduced or by words seduced or by love possessed" (frag. 11, 6). It is to the third of these, "by words seduced," that Gorgias gives the greatest attention. If it was *logos* that persuaded Helen, she is not to blame. For *logos* is a powerful lord, since it can invisibly "stop fear and banish grief and create joy and nurture pity" (frag. 11, 8). Of this claim he realizes "it is necessary to offer proof to the opinion of my hearers," and he proceeds to do so by showing how through the "agency of words" the soul can experience the sufferings of others as they are relayed to it (frag. 11, 9). In a similar way, sacred incantations can bring pleasure to the soul, affecting it in some magical way (frag. 11, 10). Such words that persuade, he then implies, do so "by molding a false argument" (frag. 11, 11) because it seems we must rely on opinion as a substitute for knowledge and thus are susceptible to what is "slippery and insecure." *Logos* can bewitch and drug, compelling people to act against their wills. The wrong lies with the persuader, not the (passive) persuaded, and he cites examples that demonstrate the power of persuasion, from the words of astronomers to the verbal disputes of philosophers (frag. 11, 13).

In this way the *Helen* both pays homage to the power of *logos* to create impressions and at the same time uses it to do so. In fact, one of the principal things it evokes is an understanding of the power of discourse itself.

Equally interesting in their treatments of *logos*, but less familiar to a contemporary audience in some of the forms used, are the writings of Antiphon. One set of his texts that displays a range of Sophistic argument is the *Tetralogies*, demonstrative court speeches with four parts, written as teaching tools. They are particularly noteworthy for their use of opposing arguments and the strategy of appealing to what is *eikos*.

We have three tetralogies, each one involving speeches by the prosecution that are then countered by the defense. The first case involves an assault of a man and his attendant (or slave). The man died in the attack and the attendant died shortly after being discovered. Antiphon presents two exchanges between the prosecutor and the man accused of the attack (the defendant). Each of the four speeches points to probabilities, with the prosecutor arguing in the first speech that the jury "must place great reliance on any kind of probability which [they] can infer" (Sprague 1972, 137), and the defendant concluding in his second speech that "it has been demonstrated that these probabilities are in general on my side" (147).

The first speech of the prosecution draws attention to several probabilities, including that the criminals were not professional killers, since the victims were still wearing their cloaks, and it's likely professionals would have taken them; and the killing was not the result of a dispute, because people do not become involved in disputes in the middle of the night and in a deserted spot. In fact, who is more likely to have committed the crime than a man who has already suffered injuries at the victim's hand and expected to suffer more? And this describes the defendant—an old enemy who had recently been charged by the victim with embezzlement.

To these particular charges, the defendant offers an opposing argument in his first speech: it is not improbable but probable that a man would be attacked in the night and killed for his clothes. That they still had them suggests that the killers panicked. On the other hand, maybe the man and his attendant were witnesses to a crime, the perpetrators of which silenced them. Or, isn't it more likely that others who hated the victim would have committed the crime, knowing that suspicion would have fallen on the defendant? To this particular charge of the prosecution (that the defendant was the most likely person to commit the crime), the defendant responds in terms that clearly anticipate those Aristotle will later use in an example in the *Rhetoric* (Bk. 2, Chapter 24): "Indeed, if on grounds of probability you suspect me because of the intensity of my hostility, it is still more probable that before I did the deed I should foresee the present suspicion falling upon me" (Sprague 1972, 139). Antiphon invites the reader (or listener, were this to be a real court case) to consider the case from the perspective of what their experience tells them is likely to have happened, or what might reasonably be extrapolated as probable from the details provided. The procedure seems aimed at arriving at a determination about a case where the question "what actually happened?" seems inappropriate. The structure of opposing arguments can be seen clearly in the following paraphrase of some of the exchanges involved:

Prosecutor, first speech: The attendant was still conscious when found, and before he died he named the defendant as the attacker.

Defendant, first speech: It is not probable that the attendant would recognize the killer in the heat of the moment. And, besides, a slave's testimony is untrustworthy, which is why slaves are submitted to examination [torture] to extract the truth from them.

Prosecutor, second speech: The testimony of the slave *is* trustworthy, since in giving evidence of this kind, slaves are not examined.

Defendant, second speech: We should not trust the testimony of an attendant over that of a free man (the defendant himself).

Each contribution to this exchange is designed to get the listener (or reader, in our case) to revisit the details of the case, replacing one likelihood with something deemed more probable. Each contribution changes the context relevant for the judgment. Each opposing argument constructs the details of the case to favor a specific way of experiencing it. In this way, the speeches are attempting to modify the listener's experience as it is to be applied in this particular case, to think of the world as a place where what is proposed seems most likely to have happened.[20]

This is seen even more vividly through one of the *peritropes* (reversals) demonstrated in the second tetralogy. This is a case where a young man, practicing the javelin with his classmates in the gymnasium, accidentally kills another boy who runs in front of the javelin as it is being thrown.[21] Again, the prosecution and the defense exchange two speeches. What is at issue is whether the dead boy should be avenged by the death of the boy who threw the javelin, even though it is agreed he did so unintentionally. In the second speech the defendant (the accused boy's father) argues that the dead boy is avenged if the killer is punished, and in this case such has occurred: "The boy, on the other hand, destroyed by his own mistakes [in running in front of the javelin during the class], simultaneously made the mistake and was punished by his own motion. Since the killer [i.e., the victim himself] has been punished, the death is not unavenged" (Sprague 1972, 155). Here, the tables are turned so that the victim is made to seem the killer. This may appear a clear traditional "sophism," or case of trying to make a weak case seem strong. But Antiphon's understanding of language allows that when someone speaks there is no permanent reality behind the words. Only the senses tell us what exists, and "names are conventional restrictions on nature" (213). This is to suggest that the meanings of "victim" and "killer" need to be worked out by exploring the context of a particular case. The same will hold for what is understood as "justice." These ideas come from the fragments of Antiphon's *On Truth,* where the position is held that rather than there being a truth underlying things, truth is something to be made known through experience. It is on such a fundamental point that the distinction from Platonic and Aristotelian views become most apparent.

❖   RHETORIC AS INVITATIONAL

One compelling feature of the arguments of Gorgias and Antiphon illustrated in the previous section is the way they invite the audience to experience things through their own eyes so that, if they are to be persuaded, they will be so on their own terms, from a perspective they have helped construct and see as plausible, rather than one imposed on them. This feature of invitation better describes their argumentative practices than the caricature that sees them only as advocates of persuasion at any cost, and this might also be seen to describe their rhetorical practices generally.

Attributing this feature to Sophistic argument may strike some readers as controversial, given some of the assumptions made in important contemporary work on invitational rhetoric, particularly by Foss and Griffin (1995). Foss and Griffin describe different types of rhetoric, which they label as "Conquest," "Conversion," "Advising," and "Invitational." Each of the first three involves an attempt by a rhetor to change the behavior or views of others. By contrast, the invitational is characterized by openness. It protects the integrity of the other person by creating space for growth and change through self-persuasion. Drawing largely from feminist theory, the resulting perspective has a cooperative focus lacking in earlier models. This is clear to the authors who write that "as far back as the discipline of rhetoric has been explored, rhetoric has been defined as persuasion" (1995, 2). This, as we have seen, is a description habitually applied to the rhetoric of the Sophists, and there is no reason to expect that Foss and Griffin think differently. Their view of Conquest rhetoric in particular, as the securing of one argument as the best and the winning of a rhetorical prize, seems an apt description of the activity of the Sophists in the *Euthydemus* and the standard leveled against Sophists of making the weaker argument (or case) the stronger one.

The point here is not to detract from the significance of contemporary invitational rhetoric and the important things its employment has achieved. Rather, the point is to stress ways in which the rhetoric of the Sophists shares several of these positive attributes and so qualifies as legitimately invitational. We have already seen some of the case for this insofar as the goals of rhetoric extend beyond mere persuasion, and in the ways some Sophistic arguments, like those of Gorgias and Antiphon shown above, invite audiences to experience their evidence for themselves. By now returning to the work of Antiphon we can further appreciate the constructive use of rhetoric by Sophists in situations where no argument is prima facie strong or weak and each case must be presented in terms that allow the audience to experience it and persuade themselves of its merits or demerits.

As may be gathered from the discussion of the previous section, Antiphon himself is a controversial figure. Commenting on his material, de Romilly (1992) goes so far as to cast a negative pall over his accomplishments:

> It was heady stuff, no doubt, but alarming too. Such an ability to defend both points of view suggested a disconcerting unconcern for the truth. If it was a matter of defending opposite points of view equally well, justice was left with no role to play. Besides, the art of twisting arguments rendered the very principle of argumentation suspect. In fact, it made the reasoning of the Sophists look like precisely what we today would call "sophistry." (80)

These are serious charges, particularly as they affect "the very principle of argumentation." But they are drawn from a perspective that recognizes an underlying objective truth, the kind of truth that Aristotle's syllogism will later be designed to discover. And these comments also understand "justice" as the means or institution by which such a truth is recognized and upheld. This view, while consistent with a reading of such matters that runs down to us through Plato and Aristotle, is not one that would seem to be shared by Antiphon and the other major Sophists. Gorgias, in his work *On the Nonexistent or On*

Nature, disputed whether Being existed; and if it did, whether it was knowable; and if it was, whether it was communicable (Sprague 1972, 42). Hence the importance and freedom of rhetoric to act on the listener and help modify what appears to be.

To clarify this claim with respect to Antiphon, I need to say something about his relationship to Protagoras. The latter is important to this discussion because there are clear reasons for reading the rhetoric of Antiphon as consistent with the Protagorean perspective. Antiphon, for example, employs discourse very similar to that which Aristotle associates with the name of Protagoras in the *Rhetoric* (Bk. 2, Chapter 24).[22]

De Romilly herself makes the case for seeing Antiphon's speeches as reflecting the spirit of Protagoras's influence, particularly with respect to the technique of double arguments, an elegant trick, the secret of which "lay in knowing how to turn to one's own advantage the facts, the ideas, and the very words of one's opponent, making them point to altogether the opposite conclusion" (1992, 78).

In the *phusis* vs. *nomos* (nature vs. law) debate of fifth-century Athens, Antiphon aligned himself clearly with the forces of *phusis*. The fragments we have of Antiphon's *On Truth* show that he had serious reservations about the value of justice as it was defined by the laws of the state. "For the demands of law are artificial, but the demands of nature are necessary" (frag. A, Col. 1; Sprague 1972, 219). In fact, the division is so strong that many of the things that are just according to law he deems to be at variance with nature (frag. A, Col. 2). This is shown vividly in Fragment B in the discussion of harming those who are innocent. Justice sometimes requires that a person be called upon to give evidence against a neighbor, even though that neighbor has done no wrong to the individual in question. Even if the evidence is accurate, the neighbor is being harmed and left open to suffering. So the witness wrongs someone who has done that witness no harm, and justice requires this. "Indeed," writes Antiphon, "it is impossible to reconcile the principle that this conduct is just [i.e., giving evidence against one's neighbor] with the other principle, that one should not do any injustice nor suffer it either" (Sprague 1972, 221).

Given this view of justice, it is quite understandable that he would carry the attitude over into the speeches he wrote for the law courts (or to teach the writing of such speeches).[23] Fragment A of *On Truth* ends with the observation that "justice" is on the side neither of the sufferer nor the doer, but on the one who can persuade the jury. If there is no "truth" behind the laws of the state, then recourse must be made to nature—a "truth" known through experience. In working with experience, whether his own or that of the jurors, Antiphon must look to probabilities, to what is probable given what we know from experience. On these terms, there is no attempt at "twisting" an argument, as de Romilly suggests. The strength of an argument lies not in its independent "truth" but in its plausibility. Likewise, there is no prima facie weaker argument or case. There are the details that can be presented in various ways by the arguer. But any presentation of details is an interpretation, as Antiphon's *Tetralogies* show. And as those details are presented in different ways, the audience is brought to see the events from different angles. Ultimately, the audience is forced to make a decision, and its only resource is what has been made to seem *most* probable.

This understanding accords with the way Plato presents the practice of Protagoras, particularly in the *Theaetetus*. While we might have concerns over how Plato interprets the Sophists, much of his basic presentation of them fits with what we learn from other sources and from their own fragments. As with the other Sophists who have been engaged in the dialogues, Protagoras represented a threat to Socratic/Platonic methodology. His "measure maxim" (that the individual is the measure of all things, those that are that they are, and those that are not that they are not) acts as a great leveller among people (152a).[24] People can think for themselves, reflect on their own experiences and be brought to view those experiences (the ways things appear to them) with a degree of clarity. It is a direct challenge to philosophical discussion in the Platonic vein: "To examine and try to refute each other's appearances and judgments, when each person's are correct—this is surely an extremely tiresome piece of nonsense, if the *Truth* of Protagoras is true" (161d). It also has a public accessibility which, although something shared with other Sophists, is at odds with Platonic practices presented throughout the dialogues, where the private and interior argumentative dialogue is opposed to the public and exterior argumentative speech.

Perhaps the most revealing passage in the *Theaetetus* is one that evokes the presence of Protagoras himself, summoned to his own defense. What Plato has Protagoras explain serves to fill in the picture of the argumentative practice that we have been exploring here and that Plato would find so problematic. Consider something of this when "Protagoras" says, the man whom I call wise is the man who can change the appearances—the man who in any case where bad things both appear and are for one of us, works a change and makes good things appear and be for him. (166d)

It's clear that for Protagoras all that can be changed are the appearances, for these are all that are known to us, and he must reserve scepticism for any way that things might actually *be* since we have no access to them. Bringing people to change their perspectives involves leading them to think differently about their experiences, to see them in different ways. And this, of course, would be done through argument. It is not a matter of changing the experiences themselves, since these are always correct for the individual; but it is a matter of changing how they view their experiences, a matter of how they develop good judgment. By extension, to deliberate about the experiences of others is to think about what is probable given what one has experienced oneself. Plato, and Aristotle, and a tradition that holds there must be an underlying truth to things—one that argument might be used to bring to light—will not countenance this approach. But those who think differently, as the Sophists clearly did, will not share those concerns, and they will use argument for much different ends, explained here by Plato's Protagoras, and illustrated by Antiphon.

Given Protagoras's "measure maxim," so understood, his rhetoric is also an invitational rhetoric, giving people the skills to perceive experience in different ways. And his argumentation, like that of Gorgias and Antiphon, is a rhetorical argumentation, at least in the sense that it is constructed from the perspective of the audience. "Argument" then, for the Sophists, aimed at much more than persuasion: it sought to create insight and understanding, and to provide an invitation to modify one's views.

This sense of rhetorical argumentation does not disappear with the Sophists, though it may have become overlooked in favor of "richer" treatments of their descendants. As we will see in subsequent chapters, it is found in the dialogues of Plato, expressed through a Socratic rhetoric that will not impose a view on his interlocutors, but strives to bring them to a point where they see themselves reflected in the statements they put forward. They are invited to take ownership of those statements and follow their consequences, both with respect to the meanings of the terms involved and the consequences of such "knowledge" on the lives of the participants. This is the most telling explanation for Socrates' claim that because he knows nothing he cannot say what he knows, and therefore that the statements and beliefs to be investigated must be those of his audience.

An invitational rhetoric, when adapted to the features of Aristotle's account, also best describes that of the *Rhetoric* (Tindale 1999a). Certainly, Aristotle's remarks are influenced by his study elsewhere of demonstration and proof, and his account framed by an interest in the structure of the syllogism. But Aristotle's rhetorical enthymeme, unlike the syllogism, is determined by the audience, by what they can understand (Kennedy 1991, 42). McCabe (1994) takes this further: "Unlike pure syllogisms, they [enthymemes] cannot be purely formal, because they are embedded in the possibilities *that interest us. . . .* Enthymemes, that is, cannot be formalized away from their context in the easy way that syllogisms can" (155). Moreover, the mind that "sees" the validity of the syllogism is passively engaged, situated apart from that which it reviews. Rhetorical argument assumes and requires an active mind, contributing to its makeup and development, engaged through its interests, and acting on its insights. The dynamism suggested here will be explored in Chapter 4.

In this chapter, we have seen something of the emergence of "argument" in the Greek world, taking on different guises here and there as *logos* began to lose its early ambiguity and take on form and structure. The emergence of argument as logical proof alone is far from an adequate account of the richness of argumentation as it was beginning to be practiced, and is more a reflection of a retrospective imposition, much like that which Schiappa identifies in the case of rhetoric. For looking at the origins of argument has also led us, unavoidably, to look deeply into the similar appearance of rhetoric as a subject and tool of interest to practitioners of discourse. As much as we could tell a fuller story about argument as dialectic and argument as logic, what has been important for the early stages of this study is to tell a full and suggestive story of argument as rhetoric, and some of the different ways even that single type might be conceived.

❖ NOTES

1. See also Cole (1991) and Johnstone (1996).

2. A May 1989 search of the Thesaurus Linguae Graecae (TLG), a computer-based data bank of all available Greek texts, confirmed Schiappa's

hypothesis that the *Gorgias* contained the earliest instance of *rhētorikē* (see Schiappa 1991, 207–213).

3. Consider also Quintilian's discussions of the definition of "rhetoric" in his *Institutio* (2.15.32). Those who approach rhetoric as a techne only are inclined to view it as a means to achieve victory, and therefore see argument as eristic. Quintilian proposes more constructive goals, particularly the achievement of a practical wisdom together with the skill to declaim (2.15.38).

4. This is not such a surprising result regarding rhetoric when one considers the similar suggestion from Kerferd (1981) that it was effectively Plato who invented the "Sophists."

5. Aristotle's rhetorical enthymeme is discussed in more detail in Tindale 1999a, 8–12.

6. The next chapter will take up some of the argumentative strategies that might fairly be attributed to the historical Socrates.

7. See Vlastos (1991) for a detailed discussion and defense of this distinction, particularly as it emerges in the *Meno*. The hypothetical method of later dialogues violates at least one important principle of the earlier "Socratic Method": Say only what you believe to be the case.

8. I have in mind here those dialogues in which Plato introduces the Sophists on their own terms and often with some imitation of their styles and ways of arguing. This is in contrast to the *Sophist* itself, which proceeds purely from Plato's own perspective. The "Sophistic Dialogues" include the *Euthydemus, Protagoras, Gorgias, Republic I, Hippias (Lesser* and *Greater)*, and parts of the *Meno* and, importantly, the *Theaetetus*.

9. The question of authenticity that has haunted both of the Hippias dialogues at some point in the tradition seems answered in my judgment by internal consistencies between the two regarding features of Hippias's perspective, as well as their similarities to other Sophistic Dialogues.

10. The same point is made in the *Lesser Hippias* (369b–c).

11. A notable exception is Poulakos (1997), whose views I discuss below, and Mendelson (2002).

12. This agreement will be fundamental to Walton's notion of fallacy, noted below.

13. Elsewhere, Walton (1992, 124) contrasts eristic argument with the collaborative, pragmatic models of Grice (1975) and van Eemeren and Grootendorst (1984), clearly indicating a preference for these latter-day accounts.

14. I'm not suggesting here that Protagoras and Gorgias did employ eristic argument.

15. See in particular, Woods and Walton (1989) and Hansen and Pinto (1995).

16. This, it will be observed, is a definition of fallacious argument. It leaves open the question of whether all fallacies have to be arguments, a question

prompted by an instance like "Complex Question," which is not an argument (see Grootendorst 1987). Since this study is restricted to argument, the problem is not one I intend to pursue at this juncture.

17. Although, as noted, Hamblin has observed that the *Gorgias* and *Protagoras* relate more than just debating competitions, he has not qualified this in any way. Moreover, we may be hard pressed to see either dialogue as offering anything of a debating competition.

18. Even Sprague (1972, 294–295) hesitates to attribute the arguments of the *Euthydemus* to the Sophist himself, preferring to call the material "Euthydemian." Euthydemus is mentioned twice in Aristotle (*Rhetoric* II, 24, 1401a26; *Sophistical Refutations* XX, 177b12), and Dionysodorus is mentioned independently by Xenophon *(Memorabilia* III 1,1).

19. References to the fragments of Gorgias and Antiphon are from Sprague (1972).

20. A close modern parallel to this strategy would be the use of defeasible argumentation, or appeals to normal expectations. The Sophist strategy depends upon an experience of the normal, but also seeks to expand it, to modify an audience's experiences in some respect.

21. That there is a story of Pericles discussing such a case with Protagoras suggests that this may have been a set case about which speeches were written for the purposes of pedagogy.

22. For a discussion of the ways in which Protagoras and Antiphon can be deemed close, as well as ways in which they are distant, see Decleva Caizzi (1999).

23. In fact, among the arguments supporting the thesis that the Antiphon of the speeches, including the *Tetralogies*, is the same Antiphon as that of *On Truth* is this consistency of attitude toward the courts and speech itself.

24. To explore the "measure maxim" in any adequate sense is obviously beyond the scope of this chapter. I intend only to lift a core sense of how Plato understands it that fits with what has been understood so far about Sophistic practice. At the same time, though, the reading here would address the self-refutation charge levelled at Protagoras on the basis of this maxim (see Burnyeat 1976). For a more detailed, but somewhat different, discussion of the maxim in relation to argumentation, see Mendelson (2002, Chapter 1).

3

. . . And
Rhetoric as Argument

❖ INTRODUCTION: RHETORICAL
FIGURES AND ARGUMENTS

The last chapter explored argument as rhetoric. Now we want to turn
things around and ask whether rhetoric, or at least traditional rhetorical devices like the figures, can serve as argument. Reboul (1989) raises
just this question when he asks: "Can a figure of rhetoric be an argument? Can it be an element of argumentation?" (169). A recent study
of rhetorical figures in the domain of science by American scholar
Fahnestock (1999) suggests a very deep relationship between figures
and arguments to the point where figures can be seen to play important argumentative roles. In this chapter, we will look closely at the
work of Reboul and Fahnestock, as well as that of Perelman and
Olbrechts-Tyteca. In drawing on what these scholars have to say about
the place of figures in a theory of argument, we will look to push their
proposals a little further. Certainly, there are many ways in which
figures contribute to the success of arguments. But we can go further
than Fahnestock and show that figures do not just facilitate arguments;
in some cases they *are* arguments. The issue is then whether they work

as patterns of argument like other traditional types of argument, and whether they have corresponding conditions that can help us evaluate them. In some cases, we will see that they can.

Rhetorical figures are devices that use words to make some striking effects on an audience. We have already encountered some rhetorical figures in this book. Van Eemeren and Houtlosser drew on several figures in their development of rhetorical dimensions within the model of pragma-dialectical argumentation. For example, at each stage of a critical discussion appropriate presentational devices can be exploited by an arguer. Here, rhetorical figures are used to impress moves upon the mind, thus compounding their effect. As a case in point, their study of William the Silent's discourse identifies the figure *praeteritio* being used at the confrontation stage: "I will not repeat the perjuries and deceits of the Duchess [of Parma], nor of the King on behalf of My Lords the Counts of Egmont and Horne . . . nor the baits and allurements which they prepared for me" (1999b, 169–170). Here, the claim that the speaker will not repeat things is followed by the mention of what will not be repeated, effectively doing the very thing that he claims not to do.

Elsewhere, van Eemeren and Houtlosser take the common tack of employing a rhetorical figure themselves when they write "all derailments of strategic maneuvering are fallacious, and all fallacies can be regarded as derailments of strategic maneuvering" (2001, 23). The figure of interest here is the *antimetabole*, which involves the reversal of pairs and can serve, as it does here, to emphasize a point. Here, then, the rhetorical figure seems much more than a mere stylistic procedure (Reboul 1989, 169).

Part of the difficulty in explaining and categorizing rhetorical figures lies in the 2,500 years of accounts that may be as noteworthy for their differences as for their agreements (Fahnestock 1999, 6). Early catalogues, like that of the first century *Rhetorica ad Herennium,* distinguish figures of speech and thought while mixing figures with tropes. It seems to have been Quintilian who made the firm distinction between tropes and figures that has survived down to Perelman and Olbrechts-Tyteca's groundbreaking work, *The New Rhetoric* (1969).[1] Here, a "trope" is distinguished as an "artistic alteration of a word or phrase from its proper meaning to another" (Quintilian in Perelman and Olbrechts-Tyteca 1969, 398). On the other hand, Perelman and Olbrechts-Tyteca significantly modify the traditional distinction between figures of speech and thought, which refers to a speaker's intention, and stress rather the effect on an audience (169). This is because a specific figure, recognized as such by its structure, may not have the same effect in different situations. I will return to this below.

What this discussion does point to is an important feature of any definition of the rhetorical figure: its structure. Reboul explains this in terms of it being codified, "because each figure constitutes a known structure which is transferable to other contents: *the* metaphor, *the* allegory" (1989, 169). In this feature, at least, figures resemble the equally codified and transferable types of argument to be discussed below. Perelman and Olbrechts-Tyteca see the presence of a discernible structure to be a necessary, but not sufficient, condition for there to be a figure. A second condition is required, which is "a use that is different from the normal manner of expression and, consequently, attracts attention" (1969, 168). At least one of these requirements characterizes most definitions that have come down through the centuries.

The effect of attracting attention will be important for any argumentative value that figures have. But the sense of a "use" is at this point ambiguous. Reboul refers to "the great tradition going back to Aristotle," which sees the essence of rhetoric as persuasion through discourse. Thus, a figure is rhetorical only "to the extent that it contributes to persuading" (1989, 169). However, as we saw in the last chapter, this image is very much a caricature of rhetoric. Or perhaps we might charitably observe that it is an accurate description of the "great" tradition going back *to* Aristotle. But if we begin from the roots of rhetoric that precede Aristotle, and then trace an understanding and practice that includes him, the use of rhetoric (and in particular rhetorical argument) to persuade is but one use, and a minor one at that. This is something to bear in mind as our discussion continues. It is the case that we see in Gorgias the power of words to evoke emotions, and this has often been seen as the desired effect of rhetorical figures (Herrick 2001, 112), but we will see them doing much more.

In her review of the history of rhetorical figures, Fahnestock observes how Quintilian chooses figures (*figurae*) for the Greek term *schemata*. This term captures, in a way, both senses of rhetorical figures that have interested us:

In the first it is applied to any form in which thought is expressed, just as it is to bodies, which, whatever their composition, must have some shape. In the second and special sense, in which it is called a *schema*, it means a rational change in meaning or language from ordinary and simple form, that is to say, a change analogous to that involved by sitting, lying down on something or looking back. (Quintilian 1921, III:353)

Interestingly, the schema (or schemes) that now most occupy argumentation theorists are the schemes used for arguments. Argument schemes are understood in different ways in current theory (Garssen 2001; Walton 1996a), but in general they capture the structure of inference underlying an argument. As Garssen describes their function, "the link between the argument and the standpoint is adequate if the acceptability of the premise is 'transferred' to the standpoint by means of the 'argumentation scheme' that is being used" (2001, 81). Argumentation schemes are, then, also identified by distinct, transferable structures, but they don't possess the changes of language use that characterize many rhetorical figures. The scope of argumentation schemes is extensive, from the appeal to authority to the argument from analogy. And some would even include the argument patterns of formal reasoning as schemes.

To see how they are understood to work, consider one of Walton's schemes that has obvious relevance to our investigations of rhetorical argument. Ethotic argument, for Walton, involves an appeal to the arguer's character.[2] He sets out the argumentation scheme, with a general first premise (indicated by the x) and a specific second premise (indicated by the a), as follows:

If x is a person of good moral character, then what x contends (A) should be accepted (as more plausible).

a is a person of good moral character.

Therefore, what a contends (A) should be accepted (as more plausible). (1996a, 85)

As we see, it is how acceptability is transferred within the pattern that is at issue.

One clear way in which the identification of argumentation schemes is useful is with respect to the evaluation of arguments, since associated with each scheme is a set of critical questions by which to assess the appropriateness of a particular argument expressing a scheme. In his presentation of the scheme for ethotic arguments, for example, Walton offers the following set of critical questions:

1. Is *a* a person of good moral character?

2. Is the question of *a*'s character relevant, in the context of dialogue in the given case?

3. How strong a weight of presumption in favour of *A* is claimed, and is that strength warranted by the case? (1996a, 86)

Such argumentation does not prove a conclusion; rather, in Walton's term, it "enhances" the conclusion, thereby creating a presumption in its favor.

There is a real danger, though, that we will confuse the sense of scheme here with that used by Fahnestock above to describe a change in meaning or language from ordinary and simple form. That is the sense of scheme that came to be called "figure." Clearly, the same meaning is not at stake now with argument schemes. In order to avoid such confusion, I will discuss ways in which some figures might be seen to serve as arguments or even types of argument (given that they have a regular pattern) rather than argument schemes. What matters to us is the specific ways audiences are moved from considering reasons to considering conclusions. Some rhetorical figures, on some occasions, work in this way. Sometimes they will merely facilitate the argument (but even this is significant for a device that many have seen as no more than stylistic), but on other occasions they are the argument.

This brings us back to the unresolved question of what counts as "rhetorical argument." Indeed, what we will see in figures are strategies that arguers may employ, that serve as ways to communicate with an audience in an argumentative situation. In Chapter 1, it was noted that the key to understanding rhetorical argument is to focus on this argumentative situation and its components of arguer, audience, and argument, with the last being determined by the others. An "argument" here is the discourse of interest that centers, and develops in, the argumentative situation. Insofar as rhetorical figures form such discourses, they are devices of argument.

Like rhetorical figures, types of argument have also already made an appearance in this text. The *ad baculum*,[3] or appeal to force, arose in the discussion of Johnson's dialectical model of argument, and types were evident in the reasoning of the Sophists, including the argument from probability. In its basic structure, and ignoring its other features, an argument has a claim or conclusion and some support presented for that claim. The variety of argument types points to the many different conventional relationships that can exist between the claim and support, or ways in which arguers attempt to encourage an audience to adopt a position or thesis.

❖ REBOUL ON FIGURES AND ARGUMENTS

In the course of his study, Reboul explores the relationship between figures and argument by means of several crucial questions: "in what ways do figures facilitate argumentation? . . . can the figure itself constitute an argument? . . . is not argument itself a figure, more or less?" (1989, 170).

The ways in which rhetorical figures may facilitate argumentation can be seen in the cases of figures of thought like allegory and irony. Here, the figure pertains not to a part of a discourse, but to the discourse itself. Of relevance are the multiple readings that arise from allegorical or ironic discourses, since "double meaning has argumentative value" (173). How Reboul understands this value is perhaps best seen in the case of irony and a related figure of pretense, the *apostrophe*. The latter involves the pretense of addressing an audience other than one's actual audience, or "in imagining a fictitious audience in order to better persuade the real one" (174). Like irony, this reinforces the link between speaker and public. Clearly, from a rhetorical point of view, such reinforcement is important and does have argumentative value. But Reboul is less forthcoming concerning the details of this reinforcement. In the case of irony, however, assuming it is recognized, we can imagine the speaker or writer fostering a commonality with an audience who, seeing the irony, appreciates its power and is more predisposed to receiving the arguer's principal claim (Tindale and Gough 1987). Likewise, with apostrophe, we can imagine particular cases (and much would depend here on the specifics of the case) in which an arguer addresses an absent party, perhaps the ancestors of the real audience, in whom that real audience places some particular value. The strategy is commonly used when a group that has some common specific interest publishes an "open letter" to a government leader or organization. The aim is not to persuade the government leader of anything (at least not directly) so much as to influence the public readership. Likewise, television debates between political candidates are actually intended for the audience, and a lawyer's remarks addressed to a witness are intended really for those interested parties that are listening, like the jury and the media.[4]

When it comes to the question of whether a figure can constitute an argument, the relationship is now internal, as the figure "inserts itself in the web of argumentation" (Reboul 1989, 178). Here, Reboul makes the clearest case through considering metaphor, which is viewed as an argument insofar as it is a condensed analogy. While metaphor is probably the figure that has received the most recent scholarly attention (and thus may least reward further study), Reboul's examples are less than clear. Consider his case of proving that one good piece of news does not guarantee happiness from its similarity to the proverb (courtesy of Aristotle–*EN* I, Ch. 7) "one swallow does not make a summer."[5] The two analogues being compared are identified as *theme* and *phore*, and set out as follows (176):

Theme	*Phore*
A One good piece of news	C One swallow
B does not guarantee happiness (is like)	D does not make a summer

As Reboul explains this, "in our proverb, we prove B given A, C, and D, since the relation between A and B resembles that between C and D" (176). The metaphor is an argument in the sense that it "draws its strength from the analogy that it condenses." But that analogy itself is not clearly an argument, at least not a clear argument from analogy, where a conclusion is drawn that an analogue has a feature, x, on the basis of its similarity to another analogue known to have feature x. Reboul's "proving" of B does not proceed this way. In fact, as a "proof" this seems very weak in the persuasive sense that Reboul understands argument. Alternatively, if we see argument having wider goals than just persuasion, goals like contributing to understanding and insight, then the sense of a metaphor operating as a condensed analogy does have argumentative value in the way it can bring about a change in the audience's perspective by having them view a situation in a different light. That, at least, is how Reboul's example works.[6]

However, Reboul's most interesting discussion is reserved for his last question: is not argument itself a figure? His principal claim here is that "argumentation is indissociable from the figures it uses," although this does not show up in most post-Perelmanian studies of argumentation because they invent fictitious arguments rather than using real ones. This claim is supported by identifying several key features of argumentation: (i) to be effective, argumentation must build on the consensus it establishes with its audience, taking into account features of that audience; (ii) argumentation uses natural language, which is naturally figured; (iii) argumentation does not have the rigor of demonstration (a point that has been emphatically made by Perelman and Olbrechts-Tyteca); and (iv) argumentation is always opposed to another argumentation and thus is polemical in its essence.[7] These characteristics of argumentation, we realize, are also features of the rhetorical figures. And it is because an argument "possesses the same status of imprecision, intersubjectivity, and polemic" (181) that it can be viewed as a figure.

There is much, then, of value in Reboul's treatment. But as I have suggested, its drawback is the restrictive way in which it views the goal of argument as persuasion, at least indirectly. For in Reboul's view, "the essence of rhetoric is persuasion through discourse," and hence a figure is only rhetorical to the extent that it contributes to persuading and, hence further, as soon as it is rhetorical it contributes to argumentation (169). Thus, a link is established between persuasive discourse and argumentation. This, we have seen, is too limiting a goal for rhetorical argumentation and one that is supported neither by the origins of the tradition nor by current models. Reboul further suggests that it is in this way that the authors of *The New Rhetoric* understood the figure. It is the case that they consider a figure to be argumentative if it brings about a change in perspective (Perelman and Olbrechts-Tyteca 1969, 169) or gains the audience's adherence (Perelman 1982, 39), but such an effect was also shown in the previous chapter to involve more than mere persuasion. Perspectives change through insight, understanding, and agreement, and rhetorical argumentation contributes to all of these.

❖ PERELMAN AND OLBRECHTS-TYTECA

However, Perelman and Olbrechts-Tyteca's study of rhetorical figures is an important source for the focus of this chapter, even if they are admittedly more concerned with the techniques of persuasive discourse (1969, 168). The emphasis they give to the figures is on their effects, because although they may be recognizable by their structures, they do not always produce the same effects. A consequence of this is that, for them, the argumentative nature of a figure cannot be described in advance. It is because of this relativity that they turn away from a traditional categorization of figures as those of thought or speech—a division that Aristotle did not recognize, but which seems to have become obligatory since the *Rhetorica ad Herennium* (Fahnestock 1999, 7)—and instead focus on three types of effect: choice, presence, and communion.[8] This is not to propose families of figures, but to show that "the effect, or one of the effects, certain figures have in the presentation of data is to impose or to suggest a choice, to increase the impression of presence, or to bring about communion with the audience" (172).

The argumentative effect of an *oratorical definition* can reveal it to be a figure of choice in a case where the structure of a definition is used not to give the meaning of a word but to bring forward aspects of a case or situation that would otherwise be overlooked or ignored (172–173). Focus shifts from the definition itself to its effect on the audience. Only in this sense does the figure appear as argumentative. Likewise, *prolepsis* can be a figure of choice when it does not just anticipate objections and respond to them, but indicates also a range of possible objections from which the ones addressed have been particularly chosen.

Gross and Dearin find the effect of choice in Perelman and Olbrechts-Tyteca "too obscure for exposition" (2003, 117), and focus their attention on communion and (in a later chapter) presence. There is some ground for their concern, particularly in the sense that if arguers choose those figures that best fit the audience they have in mind, then this seems already a matter of communion. One response to this is suggested in the use of van Eemeren and Houtlosser's similar effect of "topical potential" discussed in Chapter 1. As they define this dimension, it involves not so much fitting one's discourse to the audience but to one's own interests and to the issue at hand. Choice (or topical potential) in these senses involves the attempt of the arguer to control the discourse from the outset by choosing figures that present an issue as the arguer sees it and wants the audience to see it; it also involves selecting those figures best suited to discussing the issue in question. This interpretation of "choice" is suggested by Gross and Dearin's own earlier discussion of the relation between reality and language as Perelman viewed it. In "Rhetoric and Philosophy" (1968, 16–17) Perelman writes,

> The choice of a linguistic form is neither purely arbitrary nor simply a carbon copy of reality. The reasons that induce us to prefer one conception of experience, one analogy, to another, are a function of our vision of the world. The form is not separable from

the content; language is not a veil which one need only discard or render transparent in order to perceive the real as such; it is inextricably bound up with a point of view, with the taking of a position.

If language is so inextricably bound up with our view of the real as this suggests, then it makes perfect sense to recommend that an arguer choose the linguistic vehicle that best fits the view of the real that is at issue. This is a further reason for appreciating why the line between tropes (meaning) and schemes (form) is so blurred for Perelman and Olbrechts-Tyteca, effectively eliminating the value of such a distinction in particular instances.

In the case of figures of presence, the effect, as we also saw in the treatment of van Eemeren and Houtlosser, is "to make the object of discourse present to the mind" (Perelman and Olbrechts-Tyteca 1969, 174). An arguer should begin from premises acceptable to the intended audience. But this rote prescription can overlook the difficulties often involved in an audience actually recognizing what is acceptable to them. Employing devices that make something present actively engages an audience and encourages recognition required for the acceptability of premises. An example may forcefully illustrate a principle that an audience then recognizes as acceptable to it as a basic premise. This is really where the use of an expression different from the norm comes to the fore. Among the various figures that might fulfill this function that Perelman and Olbrechts-Tyteca choose to discuss are *onomatopoeia* (where a word is used in imitation of the thing meant), *repetition,* which seems superfluous in a demonstration but has the valuable rhetorical effect of emphasizing so as to attract attention, and *amplification,* in the sense of the oratorical development of a theme.

Figures that relate to communion are those in which "literary devices are used to try to bring about or increase communion with the audience" (177). On the face of it, "communion" is a vague term, but in the context of *The New Rhetoric* and the examples that Perelman and Olbrechts-Tyteca use, the sense of connecting with an audience on that audience's terms comes through. We see this, for example, in *allusion,* where something is evoked without being expressly named, and that something involves knowledge that is peculiar to the audience concerned. Thus an intimacy is created, a connection that might be built upon. Insofar as arguers try to reason from basic premises that are shared with an audience, then ways to establish such connections that make audiences more inclined to accept premises are essential. Allusion also has ethotic import insofar as such connections increase the audience's appreciation of the arguer.

Similarly, in what Perelman and Olbrechts-Tyteca call *oratorical communication* (178), a speaker invites an audience to enter into deliberation with her or him and think through the issue together, as if they were a common mind at work. Consider how the following discourse on the issue of human cloning works upon an audience concerned by the claims of a scientist (Dr. Seed) that he would open cloning clinics in suburban malls: "Our horrified initial reaction to Dr. Seed's proposal ought now to be critically scrutinized. Thoughtful people will recognize that our strong feelings are sometimes mere prejudice or ignorance masquerading as reason" (Schafer 1998). By introducing the category of "thoughtful people," from which members of the audience are unlikely to believe themselves excluded, the writer establishes the atmosphere of a shared investigation.

In ways like these, Perelman and Olbrechts-Tyteca indicate how such figures can facilitate argumentation. We might also see in the examples of several figures ways in which a figure becomes a part of an argument in the sense of providing the link between premise material and a claim. This is something to be explored further in subsequent sections. Also of value is Perelman and Olbrechts-Tyteca's recognition that a figure becomes argumentative when it brings about a change of perspective (1969, 169). That they see this measured in the principal goal of persuasion (179) does not diminish the value of the insight.

❖ FAHNESTOCK'S FIGURAL LOGIC

The most impressive treatment of rhetorical figures to have appeared in a long time is Fahnestock's (1999). As she explains her purpose, employing a figure she will later analyze, "rhetoric is used in this study to illuminate scientific arguments, but, more important here, scientific arguments are used to illuminate rhetoric" (viii). She goes beyond the well-harvested soil of the metaphor to examine a handful of other figures, like *antithesis, gradatio, incrementum, antimetabole, ploche,* and *polyptoton,* all of which can be identified with arguments or reasoning. In doing so, she lays "bare the cognitive heart of figuration generally" (Harris 2001, 1) and constructs the first truly overwhelming case for figures as arguments (2).

Important to her study is a feature of argumentation generally, and rhetorical argumentation specifically, that is often overlooked because of our habitual fixation on arguments as products that might be "analyzed" in isolation from the contexts in which they arise. The feature in question is that arguments are *experienced:* "whether heard or read, in time, it makes sense to think of them [arguments] as ebbing and surging, now at a 'lower' point of restatement or elaboration and now at a 'higher' point of succinct and epitomizing summation" (Fahnestock 1999, 30). This captures something of the dynamism at the heart of argumentation that will be investigated further in the next chapter's consideration of Bakhtin's suggestive contributions to the study of argument. The experiential aspect is also vividly seen, of course, in the notion of *presence,* of foregrounding objects of a discourse so that the mind attends to them. And a further feature of the experiential aspect that is important at this point lies in the nature of the rhetorical enthymeme, discussed in the previous chapter and elsewhere (Tindale 1999a). The rhetorical enthymeme is an invitation to an audience to become active in the reasoning and its development, and an important part of this is when an enthymeme has the type of "incompleteness" that the audience can remedy.[9]

Fahnestock's study captures the appreciation of the enthymeme insofar as she sees figures invoking the collaboration of audiences. She follows Burke (1969) in considering figures to be able to "express a particular line of argument and simultaneously to induce an audience to participate in that argument simply by virtue of their form" (Fahnestock 1999, 34). How does this work in the case of figures? As Harris (2001) suggests in his critical study of her book, a reader or listener will simply follow the pattern (even if it is against their inclination) "sometimes running ahead of the rhetor and pressing its completion" (3).

This sense of collaboration is brought out most forcefully in Fahnestock's treatment of *antithesis,* the figure that sets contrasting or opposing terms in parallel or balanced cola or phrases. For example: "You have everything to win/and nothing to lose" (1999, 50). Most effective are the double cola, seen for example in Aristotle (*Topics* Bk. II, Ch. 7): "good to friends and evil to enemies." Fahnestock writes of this,

> If it is right to help or do good to one's friends, it is also right to do evil to one's enemies, and if it is wrong to do evil to one's friends, it is wrong to help one's enemies. Here "opposite [good/evil] lies with opposite [friend/enemy]," and therefore either of these statements can be used in support of the other. (52)

What Fahnestock stresses is how this pattern is experienced, how it encourages an active audience to follow the pattern, "fulfill its predictions and even to feel its force" (69). As relevant as such an antithesis would be where the opposites already are accepted by the audience, its greater effect may arise when this is not the case and the argument is constructed so as to set in opposition terms that the audience would not have viewed as such beforehand.

The *antimetabole* (turning about) has a similar predictive aspect to it. In fact, Fahnestock considers that it may be the most predictive because it is easiest to complete following its first clause (124). It is also, like the antithesis, a "premise-gathering machine" (132). The antimetabole involves inverted parallelisms or word reversals. We would recall in this respect President Kennedy's famous antimetabole: Ask not what your country can do for you, but what you can do for your country. The simplicity of its pattern makes it easy to recognize and complete, and Fahnestock shows scientific reasoning to be rife with this figure, from Pasteur to Newton, Faraday to Lamarck (137–154).

The antimetabole frequently characterizes arguments proposing reciprocal causality, or reverse causality, and given the relation between the verbal form and substance of such reasoning, Fahnestock believes we can predict the appearance of the antimetabole in such arguments on the grounds of what she calls "figural logic" (141). This is the kind of reciprocity we see, for example, in Newton's Third Law of Motion.[10] Thus, when Newton comes to clarify and illustrate his law, he does so, predictably, with antimetaboles:

Whatever draws or presses another is as much drawn or pressed by that other. If you press a stone with your finger, the finger is also pressed by the stone. If a horse draws a stone tied to a rope, the horse (if I may say so) will be equally drawn back to the stone; for the distended rope, by the same endeavour to relax or unbend itself, will draw the horse as much towards the stone as it does the stone towards the horse. (Newton 1822, 16; 1952, 14, cited in Fahnestock 1999, 142)

The ways in which the antimetabole works as an argument will be considered in the next section.

Fahnestock also looks at examples of what was earlier identified as *amplification,* but through figures that construct series like *incrementum* and *gradatio*. An ordered, ascending series that builds praise is the kind of thing that exemplifies the former, while the *gradatio* series builds by repeating something of each preceding phrase or claim. Examples of the latter, many drawn from Darwin's *The Origin of the Species*, serve to show the argumentative nature of these types of figure (114–121). We see it also in William Paley's famous: "Design must have had a designer. That designer must have been a person. That person is God" (Paley 1963, 44). Fahnestock takes a more contemporary piece from the *New York Times*, about the reintroduction of wolves to Yellowstone National Park in the winter of 1994–1995, and adds italics to emphasize the overlapping terms:

> 1. Carcasses of large prey, like elk, slaughtered by wolves will add nutrients and humus to the *soil*. 2. The more fertilized *soil* will support lush vegetation, probably attracting snowshoe *hares*. 3. The presence of *hares* will likely prove a lure for *foxes* and other predators. 4. The *foxes* will also prey on rodents like *mice* in the area. 5. A misplaced *mouse predator*, like a weasel, is likely to fall prey to an owl. (1999, 109)

In fact, this verbal *gradatio* is accompanied by illustrations that create a visual *gradatio* as well, thus increasing the argumentative force. Fahnestock assesses this as a clear presentational choice on the part of the experts who produced the text, deciding that "a gradation would most persuasively express the causal reasoning for the large, mixed audience of the *New York Times*" (109). What the *gradatio* does is lead the audience through reasonable, causal steps towards the position of supporting the reintroduction of the wolves. It also anticipates and addresses concern that the wolves might disrupt the ecology. From this perspective, the *gradatio* itself works as a *prolepsis*.

As a last set of examples illustrating her work, we might consider the figures of repetition that Fahnestock provides in *ploche* (a single word or its variants reappearing throughout a discourse like a braid) and *polyptoton* (repeating a word in different grammatical cases). *Ploche* stands out from the other figures we have discussed because it lacks a detectable pattern (and so does not fit Perelman and Olbrechts-Tyteca's first condition for a figure). But this very invisibility is what, Fahnestock finds, makes it potentially so effective. Undoubtedly, an idea can be made present to an audience through such repetition. But what is difficult is the attribution to an author of any clear intention of use. Still, if our interest lies primarily in the effect a discourse has on an audience, then such an intention is less significant. As Fahnestock indicates, *ploche* serves to suggest interconnections among different phenomena. Thus, Franklin uses *ploche* for "electric," "electrical," "electrified," and "electrised" to make connections throughout his experiments (190). Much of the same in terms of value and difficulty holds for *polyptoton*. As Fahnestock notes, while the creation of premises from grammatical shifting seems far removed from modern ideas of good argumentative practice, "[i]t is sometimes the goal of an argument to take a concept accepted by an audience in one role or category of sentence action and transfer it to others, an agent becoming an action or an action becoming an attribute and so on" (171). Indeed, there seems nothing to preclude an arguer from using such a strategy to move her audience through premises to a conclusion. And Fahnestock illustrates this with further verbal and visual examples, like those used to show changes in fossils. It is a measure of the success of her treatments that she can make her case even with such difficult and overlooked figures.

What Fahnestock's work certainly undermines is the traditional view that a figure is just a stylistic adornment to discourse, added for effect. She shows it instead to be woven into the very structure of a discourse, determining its scheme and effect. As Fahnestock notes, the way figures have been schematized has been reelaborated for almost 2,500 years (6). A further consideration of some of them as kinds of argument seems both timely and, in light of what Fahnestock has shown, appropriate. Pouncing on her remark about "figural logic," Harris emphasizes how her work amply illustrates the interdependence of figuration and argumentation (Harris 2001, 6), while she stops just short of drawing the conclusion about that interdependence that her work supports.

❖ FIGURES AS ARGUMENTS

To recall the earlier explanation, the feature of arguments relevant to the present discussion is that they are regularized patterns, or codified structures, that transfer acceptability from premises to conclusions. The ways in which they do this are varied and range from the simple to the complex. If any of the figures are to be recognized *as* arguments, then on the occasions that they function as such they will need to encourage the same movement within a discourse, from premise to conclusion. The similarities between arguments and figures have been well presented by Reboul and Fahnestock. Reboul (1989, 181) shows how an argument "possesses the same status of imprecision, intersubjectivity and polemic" as a figure. Fahnestock takes us much further in laying bare the cognitive heart of figuration. But she has done much more than this by identifying within key figures crucial features of rhetorical argument like collaboration and experience. As part of the latter, she shows how readily figures with their atypical employments of language capture the movements that take place within discourses.

Perelman and Olbrechts-Tyteca reinforce a further important feature: arguments aim at a change of perspective, whether this involves persuasion as their account suggests, or the insight, understanding, and agreement seen elsewhere. Related to this is Perelman and Olbrechts-Tyteca's lesson of case-by-case assessment. As they explain it, a figure can be argumentative or not, depending on the case in question, so a figure functions as an argument when it meets certain conditions.[11] I will specify these as follows:

A figure serves as an argument when

(i) it has a recognized structure (is codified);

(ii) its inner activity promotes the movement from premises to a conclusion;

(iii) it has one of the goals of argumentation.

Beyond this, we must bear in mind that we are looking at arguments from a rhetorical, rather than a dialectical or logical, point of view. Thus, certain features become more important to us, and we ask questions that would not be asked, say, from a logical perspective: questions like "How is this discourse *experienced*?" "How does it invite collaboration?"

Our investigation of figures as arguments cannot be exhaustive. The aim is rather to look at some common patterns that fit the requirements here and learn more about rhetorical argument through their analyses.

As already noted, one of the most common sets of figures are those based on similarity, figures like allusion, analogy, and metaphor. This will be an easier place to begin and make some brief points. In a recent defense of the novel, Rushdie (2002) includes the following:

In America, in 1999, over five thousand new novels were published. Five thousand! It would be a miracle if five hundred publishable novels had been written in a year. It would be extraordinary if fifty of them were good. It would be cause for universal celebration if five of them—if one of them—were great.

Publishers are over-publishing because, in house after house, good editors have been fired or not replaced, and an obsession with turnover has replaced the ability to distinguish good books from bad. Let the market decide, too many publishers seem to think. Let's just put this stuff out there. Something's bound to click. So out to the stores they go, into the valley of death go the five thousand, with publicity machines providing inadequate covering fire. This approach is fabulously self-destructive. (55)

In this piece, we see at least two figures in use: *incrementum* in the first paragraph, and *analogy* through an *allusion* in the second. Both are used argumentatively in Rushdie's criticism of the publishing industry, both are used to encourage the audience to hold a certain perspective on the issue. And they are effective in doing this. I want to focus on the second figure here because it relates directly to Rushdie's charge that the industry is self-destructive. How is it self-destructive? In the way that the infamous Light Brigade was self-destructive at Balaclava during the Crimean war, and with the associated sense of folly. And this is made present through the allusion to Tennyson's poem, explicitly invoked through the phrase he uses, referring to the valley of death.

This is an easier example to begin with because we already recognize the argument from analogy as a type of argument with a specific pattern. So analogy, in this sense, is a crossover device, doing double duty in the repertoires of both rhetors and arguers. Rushdie's use here, though, is made denser, richer by the addition of allusion. Given the forum involved, Rushdie expects literary savvy in his audience. The piece first appeared in *The New Yorker,* and makes assumptions about the background of the audience. In fact, if we do not see the allusion, the piece loses much of its force (for which one must then fall back on the *incrementum* of the first paragraph). When we ask our question, "how is this argument *experienced* by its audience?" we recognize how effective it is at making present the theme of self-destructiveness. Moreover, the allusion requires collaboration in an essential way. The audience must complete the analogy, draw the link between premises and conclusion that the analogy embodies.

Can we step beyond the argument from analogy itself and identify allusion as an argument when used in such ways? I think this example allows that we can. Allusion has a codified structure, it involves something being evoked without being expressly named, a knowledge that we expect the audience to have. We see a movement from the premises to the conclusion, from a recognition/understanding already shared between arguer and audience to a recognition/understanding that it is proposed they should share. And it works here to achieve an argumentative goal: to bring the audience to see the publishing industry as self-destructive. It may also have the further ethotic element noted by Perelman and Olbrechts-Tyteca (1969, 177) and Leff (2003), insofar as the intimacy created by the allusion increases the audience's appreciation of the arguer. When allusion is used as an argument, it would have conditions like the following:

x is evoked by a discourse

x involves a connection with A that when made present increases the plausibility of A.

Therefore, A is plausible.

In the example under question, x is represented by Rushdie's allusion to Tennyson's poem (and perhaps Tennyson's own deeper allusion to *Psalms*), or more particularly to the self-destructiveness of the actors in that poem, and A by the self-destructiveness of the publishing industry. In assessing such an argument from the point of view of its effect on an audience, certain questions come to the fore:

- Does the audience recognize what has been evoked (do they see the allusion)? This is a question about audience relevance. If the author misjudges this point, the argument is not effective.
- Is the connection between x and A sufficient to increase A's plausibility? This requires a judgment on the part of the evaluator, as assessing plausible reasoning often will.

The next example is less contemporary and comes from Socrates' speech in Plato's *Apology*. This example requires more discussion than the last because it involves the figure *praeteritio*, or pointing to what one claims not to mention, and what is pointed to in this way is a recognized type of argument. At 34b–e, Socrates tells his audience that he will not use an *ad misericordiam* argument.

> Perhaps one of you might be angry as he recalls that when he himself stood trial on a less dangerous charge, he begged and implored the jury with many tears, that he brought his children and many of his friends and family into court to arouse as much pity as he could, but that I do none of these things, even though I may seem to be running the ultimate risk. Thinking of this, he might feel resentful toward me and, angry about this, cast his vote in anger. If there is such a one among you—I do not deem there is, but if there is—I think it would be right to say in reply: My good sir, I too have a household and, in Homer's phrase, I am not born "from oak or rock" but from men, so that I have a family, indeed three sons, gentlemen of the jury, of whom one is an adolescent while two are children. Nevertheless, I will not beg you to acquit me by bringing them here. Why do I do none of these things? Not through arrogance, gentlemen, nor through lack of respect for you. Whether I am brave in the face of death is another matter, but with regard to my reputation and yours and that of the whole city, it does not seem right to me to do these things, especially at my age and with my reputation.

The *ad misericordiam*, or appeal to pity, attempts to further a case (support a position or conclusion) by bringing in some reference or aspect that is designed to provoke an emotional response in the audience, thus making them more sympathetic to the arguer's point. Insofar as such an appeal has been viewed as a diversion from the matter in question, and hence not strictly relevant to establishing it, it has been judged fallacious (Hamblin 1970). Many current textbook accounts will treat it in this traditional way. But what really comes into question when reviewing such an argument is what we mean by "relevant" and the role that such appeals are deemed to have in argumentation. Images of starving children accompanying a text proposing that we ought to assist in some way may well actively increase our reasons for accepting such a claim (and acting on it) by awakening appropriate moral sensibilities in us. That is, an argument that aims at action addresses us as complete individuals and so needs at some level to relate matters to beliefs we hold. Hence, when performing such a contributory role, and depending on the context in question, an *ad misericordiam* may indeed be relevant. This is the way more balanced recent accounts have come to view the matter, allowing legitimate uses for it (see Walton 1997).

But, of course, the thrust of this example is Socrates' *refusal* to employ the *ad misericordiam*, thus apparently anticipating the sensibilities of modern logicians who find it fallacious. This is how most commentators have tended to approach the passage, largely taking Socrates at his word. Burnet (1924) notes, for example, that Socrates refuses to make what was a customary appeal but not, as Xenophon had suggested, because the *ad misericordiam* would be illegal, but because it is unworthy of himself or Athens (144). Reeve (1989), in noting the similarity between Socrates' speech in the *Apology* and Gorgias's *Defense of Palamedes*, sees Socrates rejecting the appeal to the *ad misericordiam* and resting his case on truth and justice (7). Others, like Taylor (1956, 166), place their interpretation on this latter point—a direct reading of what Socrates says. Brickhouse and Smith (1989) note how this refusal to adopt a common ploy in his speech seems calculated to undermine his defense since it is likely to enrage some of his jurors who have engaged in a practice he is now calling shameful (206). But given his principles, they conclude, he cannot choose otherwise and still reason rationally (208).

Interestingly, and from a slightly different perspective, Walton identifies this passage as employing a rhetorical strategy of *omission*. He writes: "By saying he is not going to appeal to pity, Socrates is actually (in effect) bringing the subject of pity up, reminding the audience of it, and thereby having the rhetorical effect of putting the subject of pity (implicitly) into the argument" (1997, 47). In Walton's view, this is in keeping with Socrates' penchant for staying silent on certain points, thereby requiring his interlocutor to discover what is at stake. More ominously, it is described as a strategy of deception, of disguising what he is doing. Walton interprets this as an indication of how negatively the appeal to pity was viewed at the time, compelling Socrates to, at least ostensibly, distance himself from it (48). However, in the context of our current investigation a more constructive reading of Socrates' rhetorical aims can be suggested.

What Walton identifies as omission we might more traditionally call the figure *praeteritio*. We saw this figure referred to earlier in van Eemeren and Houtlosser's discussion of the discourse of William the Silent (1999b). I want to explore how Socrates uses this figure as an argument, which is to say that he does appeal to pity, but he does so through the use of a *praeteritio*.

We can, indeed, approach this passage from the perspectives given to us by logical or dialectical argument. In the case of logical argument, as I have suggested, Socrates indicates that the *ad misericordiam* is a regular (even common) argumentative strategy that the audience knows and would expect in this situation. Thus his breaking with conventions by refusing to use this particular appeal supports the view that he deems it fallacious. Socrates is refusing to engage in fallacy. From the perspective of dialectical argumentation, with its interest in the procedures involved, we might consider that there may well have been a dialectical procedure that Socrates alluded to by rejecting it: a procedure that members of the jury expected as part of the speech in such a circumstance. We cannot reconstruct such a procedural approach, but we can find instances of *ad misericordiam* appeals in speeches that are available to us from contemporary sources, like Antiphon. Consider, for example, the opening of his "Against the Stepmother" (Gagarin and MacDowell 1998, 10): "I am still so young and inexperienced in legal matters." The young prosecutor (of his father's alleged murderer) goes on to establish a case on the basis of pity. If we find this strategy in speeches of Sophists, then the refusal to use it could be viewed as another part of Plato's general attempt in the *Apology* to distance Socrates from that group.

However, it is only when we turn to consider his argument from the rhetorical perspective that the real complexity of his strategy emerges. In saying that the use of such a move as the *ad misericordiam* would discredit him (as well as the jury and the state), Socrates introduces the rhetorical move of increasing his credibility by "not" using it. His argument here is what I earlier identified as *ethotic*, and bears resemblance to Leff's treatment of rhetorical *ethos* that was considered in Chapter 1. It is aimed at improving his status or *ethos* and thereby supporting his cause.

As defined by Brinton, "*ēthotic argument* is the kind of argument or technique of argument in which ἦθος is invoked, attended to, or represented in such a way as to lend credibility to or detract credibility from conclusions which are being drawn" (1986, 246). Widely used in argumentation, with both legitimate and illegitimate varieties,[12] ethotic arguments look to add weight to the individual that is saying something (or take away weight) by drawing attention to aspects of his or her character and building (or diminishing) that. Hence *weight* is the criterion of strength in ethotic arguments, occurring when the threshold of strength is high. Weight shifts the presumption in a speaker's favor and makes it more difficult for an opponent to raise doubts. In this instance, Socrates shows himself both reasonable in what he will advance and respectful of the jury and the state.

Yet in a further rhetorical twist, as Walton observed, Socrates actually uses the very strategy he claims to be avoiding by employing a *praeteritio*. His statement *invites* the audience to construct such an appeal to pity for themselves. In saying he will not bring his children before the court and invoke a response of pity, he effectively does bring his children into view. This serves to draw the audience into the account in an intimate way. Since he is talking to them of their expectations and beliefs, he invites a construction from their perspective. Thus producing the children orally but not physically gives license to the imagination of his audience to create the spectacle for themselves. The sense of *spectacle* is important here, because it underlines the way the figure brings objects of the discourse (in this case the absent children) to the attention of the audience; it makes them *present*. Or rather, in the spirit of rhetorical collaboration, the audience makes them present. At the same time, not *actually* producing them supports the appeal to his own *ethos* that is directed to that portion of his audience who will have taken what he says at face value and not have seen the *ad misericordiam* present.

So, we might conclude, Socrates' double strategy of decrying yet still invoking an *ad misericordiam* is deliberate (or, we might say, was an actual aspect of the original speech, whether or not it is a strategy that Plato would have encouraged). Rather than improving on the "current rhetorical commonplaces" then, as Burnet (1924, 67) has suggested, or adopting a deceptive strategy of omission, as Walton suggested, we see Socrates here employing the rhetorical figure *praeteritio* in a quite standard way. In the very process of claiming not to do something, he actually does it. He even supplies his audience with the details of his family in order for them to complete the appeal. But the argument belongs to the audience, not to Socrates. In this case, the strategy meets an important expectation of good rhetorical argumentation in that it creates the opportunity for the audience to become actively engaged in the argument, to complete the reasoning in some way.

The question remains as to the wisdom of adopting this strategy of denial or *praeteritio*. Historically, we know the outcome of the trial to not be favorable to the defendant. Yet from the point of view of strategy alone, one with a combination of features, each aimed at a different part of the audience, might be expected to be better than a solitary strategy. If we measure success against the accomplishment of what it sets out to achieve, then we might say this fails. But, on the other hand, that is the cumulative goal of his complete speech. The piece being reviewed here has the intermediate goal of winning support from his audience and is part of those aspects of his speech that aim at increasing his credibility. To this degree it may well have "worked." Given the closeness of the vote for conviction, which seems to surprise even Socrates, then we can only speculate as to whether the passage had an effect on that vote. But we can judge it in the terms that we have been employing here: we value argumentation that speaks to more of an audience over that which speaks to less of it, when it evokes the experiential element and invites collaboration. Socrates' *praeteritio* does all of this.[13] More importantly, in this example, the *praeteritio* serves as an argument, to which we can attribute the following conditions to govern such cases:

An arguer, *a*, draws attention to *x* while professing to avoid it.

The audience is invited (implicitly) to construct *x* for themselves.

x, so constructed, increases the plausibility of *a*'s position.

Again, these conditions suggest critical questions that would be appropriate for exploring any argumentative use of a *praeteritio*:

Is *x* sufficiently suggested that the audience in question would be likely to see it?

Are sufficient details provided for the construction of *x* by the audience?

Does plausibility transfer from *x* to *a*'s position?

As was the case with allusion, these questions must be put to a case in context and can never be posed in an abstract way (as the question of an argument's validity might be). Nor do they suddenly render the argument clearly strong or weak. But they serve as tools to enable the evaluators to explore the strength or weakness of an individual case and draw a weighted conclusion for themselves.

The two figures discussed so far both involve some crucial element that is left implicit in the argumentation, and so might be seen to more readily lend themselves to the requirements of experience and collaboration. A few examples of figures that do not rely on hidden elements in the way that allusion and *praeteritio* do will strengthen the thesis that rhetorical figures can serve as arguments.

Much is made by Fahnestock of the figure antimetabole, and we have seen it used earlier by van Eemeren and Houtlosser (2001, 23). Consider how antimetabole works in the following piece of reasoning that addresses the ethics of human cloning and research on embryos:

> [C]reating multiple embryos from the same embryo damages respect for human life itself—even if it does not contravene respect for any one human individual—and for the transmission of human life. It turns a genetically unique living being of human origin into just an object and one that is replicable in multiple copies. It changes the transmission of human life from a mystery to a manufacturing process. It fails to recognize that we are not free to treat life in any way we see fit, that we do not own life. Rather, we have life and, more importantly, life has us. Recognizing that we owe obligations to life can provide a basis on which to establish respect for life in a secular society. (Somerville 2000, 69)

The antimetabole is phrased with the classic reversal, "We have life and, more importantly, life has us." It comes at the end of three amplifying sentences that up the ante on bad consequences of creating multiple embryos. The antimetabole is a change in strategy; it breaks the rhythm of the amplifying statements as the discourse turns back upon itself. The approaching statements corroborate ways in which, indeed, we have life. But the author's point lies in the second clause of the antimetabole, that life has us. It reverses the power relationship, inviting the reader to think not of the human as the agent (who manipulates life), but as the beneficiary, and hence the one who owes something, that something being respect. It is, then, the figure that carries the argument, that argues the point. And it does this through bringing the reversal to the attention of the audience, altering the audience's perspective on the issue.

In other instances, the antimetabole may indeed serve different functions, like simply emphasizing a point. That seems to be how van Eemeren and Houtlosser used it in stressing the relationship between derailments in strategic maneuvering and fallacies. But when functioning as an argument, it reverses relationships in an audience's mind so as to support a conclusion. It awakens an insight in an audience that the arguer would expect them to accept, and thus increases the plausibility of the conclusion that insight supports. In Somerville's case, we might suggest, it is basic humanity that is being appealed to and in which the assumed acceptability would be grounded. When used as an argument, the following conditions would capture the move from reasons to conclusion:

> An arguer reverses a relationship, x to y, to suggest y to x.

> The reversal supports a conclusion related to one or the other of the relationships, making that conclusion more plausible.

Again, we have here the requisite elements of experiencing the rhythm of the discourse, "seeing" the reversal, and the invited collaboration of the audience. Critical questions for assessment would include the following:

> Does the reversal work in the argumentative way the author suggests?

> Is plausibility appropriately transferred from the suggested relationship to the conclusion?

As a fourth and final example here, I look at *prolepsis*. This is a figure identified by Perelman and Olbrechts-Tyteca (1969, 169) as involving an argumentative move. Its significance lies in its importance to dialectical argumentation, models of which will often require something very like *prolepsis* in the procedural rules (or dialectical obligations) it proposes for good argumentation. *Prolepsis* in the sense I use it here is the anticipation of objections to one's position and preemptive response to those objections. To identify this as itself a type of argument seems really to do little more than push the dialectic on this in a direction it is already heading.

In a very controversial article, May (2002) advances the position that regular American citizens bear responsibility for the killing of Palestinians by Israelis. The argument for this is developed by means of an analogy between a drowning child and a passerby who could save the child, but chooses not to. "Palestinian civilians are no more able to resist their killing than the child could resist the waves. And Americans, through our taxes, are helping to stir the water." May then turns to defend the analogy: "Some will say there are important differences between the killing of Palestinians and the drowning child," that the average American citizen is really like a passerby who could not swim. But May counters this by insisting that there are other ways of providing assistance to the drowning child. He then considers a further response, "But suppose one doesn't know what is happening?" And, again, May counters this by considering the options open to the passerby who is unsure whether the child is drowning. Then he considers a third objection—that the analogy itself is misleading.

> Rather than seeing the Israeli invasion as a destructive wave and Palestinian civilians as helpless children, they would offer an analogy of the following type. You're walking along the street and you see a larger kid beating up a smaller one. You learn that the smaller kid has beaten up the larger kid's little sister. Do you have responsibility to stop the beating? And here they would answer, not necessarily.

May attacks this analogy as itself inaccurate (Palestinian *citizens*—my emphasis—have attacked no one), and even if it were accurate, he proposes, there is an obligation to help the smaller kid. One final objection is considered: "But suppose you don't know who really started it?" This is similarly addressed before the main conclusion is reiterated.

At the heart of the argumentation here is an argument from analogy, but by far the most prevalent strategy used is that of *prolepsis*. The point is made by a series of imagined objections and counters to those objections. This is not just the strategy of counter-argumentation that many theorists already promote in any arguer's repertoire; this is the countering of imagined objections, and so success depends to a large extent on the quality and appropriateness of such imaginings. Once again, the audience is able to "experience" the reasoning insofar as *prolepsis* presents to the mind the semblance of an exchange into which that audience enters. In a similar way, it invites collaboration. Unlike previous figures surveyed, *prolepsis* seems better suited for an audience not predisposed to the position being advanced. Hence, if the arguer is to establish some commonality of acceptance from which to move toward a conclusion, that must be done in more creative ways. Successful *prolepsis* depends on the acceptability of the objections. The ones introduced need to be ones that the audience, even if they had not thought of them themselves, could imagine making or could see it appropriate to make. Again, like other figures, successful use of this also has an ethotic payoff, since using *prolepsis* gives the argumentation an air of objectivity, shows the arguer trying to conceive things from the other point of view and treating that point of view in a reasonable fashion. So there is much to recommend *prolepsis* as an argument. The following captures the conditions for it being used:

Arguer *a* imagines objections to her or his position and counters those objections.

Such objections and counters, appropriately conceived, increase the plausibility of *a*'s position.

As my discussion has indicated, critical questions aimed at assessing *prolepsis* as an argument must address an audience's reaction to it:

Are the objections raised, although imagined, "real" in the sense that they are plausible objections in the context, and thus acceptable to the audience?

Are the objections adequately countered so as to increase the plausibility of the position being advanced?

❖ CONCLUSION

Many rhetorical figures are particularly suited to serve as arguments in rhetorical argumentation because of the ways in which they are constructed to engage the audience through their experiential nature and collaborative invitations. The work of Reboul, Perelman and Olbrechts-Tyteca, and Fahnestock all point in this direction, and I hope through these few but, I believe, representative examples to have shown the appropriate conclusion to which that work leads. The point has not been to make a general claim about all figures, but rather to show that some figures, on some occasions, can function as arguments, and to provide identifying conditions and questions of assessment for such occasions. In a similar way, I suspect we could approach this from the other end, starting with some traditional types of argument and showing how they serve primarily rhetorical ends and function like figures. The "ethotic argument" from Walton (1996a) is a clear example of this, as the elaboration of this argument in discussions of this chapter would indicate.

This is not to deny that there is something distinct about the arguments drawn from figures. It is their rhetorical nature that makes them most effective, not just in persuading an audience, but engaging them at a quite deep, often emotional level, before reason moves in as an organizing force. They relate to a level of engagement that grounds the argumentative situation, and thus they further demonstrate why the rhetorical is the primary, most influential layer in any model of argument that seeks to integrate the logical, dialectical, and rhetorical. Those who limit the rhetorical to matters of style have missed this and failed to see how it conditions and determines the organization of the logical choices and dialectical procedures. Ways in which this deep engagement constructs the context will be explored further in the next chapter.

❖ NOTES

1. The seminal role of these two thinkers in rhetorical argumentation was acknowledged in Chapter 1. While Perelman has attracted more scholarly attention and been judged the originator of the principal ideas, recent work on Olbrechts-Tyteca has come to challenge this view in interesting ways (see Warnick 1997).

2. For a more developed definition of "ethotic argument" see the discussion of Socrates later in this chapter. (See also Tindale and Welzel, forthcoming.)

3. I treat this not as a fallacy but as a legitimate argument scheme.

4. I am grateful to Randy Harris for these examples.

5. The analogy Reboul draws is not exactly Aristotle's meaning in using the statement, but that is beside the point here.

6. A better discussion of Perelman and Olbrechts-Tyteca's treatment of metaphor is provided by Gross and Dearin (2003, 121–122).

7. Here, "opposition" should not immediately suggest conflict: opposing opinions can invite discussion aimed at understanding and involve a variety of agreements; conflicts may be such as to invite no discussion at all.

8. As this discussion proceeds, the influence of this division on van Eemeren and Houtlosser's similar triad of topical potential, presentational devices, and audience demand should become apparent.

9. This is not necessarily incompleteness in the traditional sense associated with the enthymeme (Tindale 1999a, 9–11), but in the sense of the enthymeme as a probable argument, the details of which must be matched against, and confirmed by, the audience's experience. Some of Antiphon's arguments in the previous chapter were seen to have this feature.

10. To every action there is always opposed an equal reaction; or, the mutual actions of two bodies upon each other are always equal, and directed to contrary parts.

11. The title of the relevant chapter in Gross and Dearin's (2003) study of Perelman, "The Figures as Argument," suggests a thesis similar to the one I am expounding here. But with the exceptions of irony and metaphor, their discussion and examples are actually intended only "to demonstrate the pervasiveness of figures as a component of arguments" (130).

12. Under this very general term of ethotic argument, or person as argument, we can include the *ad verecundiam* (appeal to authority or expertise) and the *ad hominem* (argument against the man). But there is also a very general sense of appeal to *ethos* that involves just calling on the good character of someone to support a conclusion. While ethotic appeals may rarely be sufficient to establish a conclusion, the point here is that they serve as a type of reason for conclusions. Aristotle extended great importance to them (*Rhetoric*, 2.1.5–7).

13. With regard to the ethotic move, Socrates does successfully give himself weight in this passage. On any objective reading we can see him attending to his character, as this appears to the audience he wishes to influence, and saying the correct things to strengthen the image of his character in their eyes. His expressed desire not to discredit himself, his audience, or the state, is aimed at thereby making himself more credible.

4

Rhetorical Contexts and the Dialogical

❖ INTRODUCTION: DIALOGUE AND DIALOGUES

Our uncovering of the rhetorical argumentation in early Greek texts in Chapter 2, and the last chapter's assessment of the role that rhetorical figures play in argumentation, have one very important feature in common—the centrality of *audience*. Our focus has shifted quickly from the argument and its source (the arguer) to its destination (the audience). Now we must ask what kind of relationship best captures the interaction between the agents in an argumentative situation. Everything that has been said so far certainly indicates that it cannot be a passive relationship. The participants in argumentation enter into an active communication: they enter into an argumentative dialogue.

Rhetorical argumentation is dialogical. That is, there is a dynamic sense of dialogue alive in the context. The existence of this has already been suggested by previous discussions that indicated the types of communication, beyond persuasion, that are involved in argumentation, and explored the way rhetorical figures are experienced by an audience and rhetorical argument itself invites the collaboration of audiences. Thus we have seen how much the rhetoric of interest here is to be characterized as an invitational rhetoric. Recent research on this notion, like Foss and Griffin's (1995) work that has already been noted in Chapter 2, or Makau and Marty's (2001) introductory text on cooperative argumentation, has done much to draw attention to, and advance the interests of, an argumentation that is not adversarial. The current chapter furthers this initiative by drawing on the fertile ideas of Bakhtin. Here we will draw from Bakhtin's work the theory of argumentation implied there, laying bare its dynamic nature. We will explore the terminology he uses, indicating its suggestiveness for understanding the argumentative situation. And we will apply what we learn to several examples that show the value of this model even for texts that seem to express only one voice.

In the first chapter's exploration of Johnson's theory of dialectical argument, we saw him make the following remark:

> Genuine dialogue requires not merely the presence of the Other, or speech between the two, but the real possibility that the logos of the Other will influence one's own logos. An exchange is dialectical when, as a result of the intervention of the Other, one's own logos (discourse, reasoning, or thinking) has the potential of being affected in some way. (2000a, 161)

In saying this Johnson moves toward a notion of argument that actually challenges his own bipartite model with its illative and dialectical tiers, in which the former grounds the latter. However, the next two sentences undermine the promise of what has preceded them when he writes: "Specifically, the arguer agrees to let the feedback from the Other affect the product. The arguer consents to take criticism and to take it seriously" (161). Here Johnson reverts to the idea of argument as a finished product, *after which* feedback and criticism of it can be considered. The previous suggestion for "genuine dialogue" promised something far more interactive in the very composition of the argument. This is the place to follow the direction in which Johnson was pointing, toward a model of argument that can be drawn from Bakhtin's work.

The argumentation that we find implied in Bakhtin's writings is consistent with the terms of his dialogism (explained below), and thus it will be referred to as "dialogical." By so identifying this model, and its relevance to rhetorical argumentation, it is important to show how it succeeds over recent advances in argumentation theory that have an interest in "dialogue" or "dialectics,"[1] primarily because of its unique features. These are what recommend it for the rhetorical rather than the dialectical and save me from an apparent *volte-face*, in that I could now be seen to be advocating a dialectical model after all. This would be a mistake. What will emerge from the ensuing discussion is a model that is much richer than those implicated in current dialectical models, in the ways that it captures and describes the depth of the rhetorical context. Thus we will see from Bakhtin how the rhetorical underlies and conditions the dialectical, while at the same time completely recasting it.

For the most part, current interest in dialogue models pays attention to the two-sidedness or turn-taking nature of argumentation. Johnson's (2000a) innovative introduction of the dialectical tier for arguments has already been discussed in detail. Walton's (1996b, 40–41) centralizing of "dialogue" in his pragmatic account means that the dialogue provides the context that will determine the argument by telling us how the set of inferences or propositions at its core is being used. And Barth's (2002) exhaustive discussion of the history of dialogue logic ends with a plea for the application of such a model to encourage greater cooperation between parties.[2] Yet with these senses of a dialogue model it is still possible for dialogue-focused or dialectical argumentation to involve no more than an exchange of distanced, monological positions (perhaps through turn-taking, perhaps in whole), where each side presents its argument for acceptance or rejection (Shotter 1997). Were such to occur, the drive for a more genuinely interactive or "involved" perspective might be lost. Hence these models do not appear to be strong candidates for the kind of relationship between arguer and audience that we are seeking in this chapter.

There is no better illustration of what I would call a "distanced dialogue," one that is not genuinely interactive, than the conversations between Socrates and his interlocutors, conveyed to us through the works of Plato, as these are usually interpreted.[3] An example of such a conversation is the one we find in the *Euthyphro*, one of the more widely read Platonic dialogues.

This is a typical "Socratic" dialogue between a Socrates who does not know the key idea he is interested in and an expert who can offer knowledge of that idea, in this case Euthyphro. The idea or concept in question is "piety," or what is "holy," of interest to Socrates because he has been accused of acting impiously, and also of significance to Euthyphro who is prosecuting his own father and so may himself be acting impiously if he is wrong in his prosecution. Socrates is happy to have found an interlocutor who claims to know what Socrates needs to know, and it should be a simple matter for the expert to communicate his understanding. Having agreed with Socrates that piety, or holiness, will always be the same in every action and that this is what they seek, Euthyphro proceeds to explain what it is.

> I say that holiness is doing what I am doing now, prosecuting the wrong-doer who commits murder or steals from the temples or does any such thing, whether he be your father or your mother or anyone else, and not prosecuting him is unholy. (6d–e)

As a "sure proof" for this claim, that is, as a reason in support of it, he offers the example of Zeus, who put his father in bonds because he devoured his children.

While Socrates, in his turn, has doubts about the reason and the claim, he can accept the reason—from stories about the gods—on Euthyphro's say-so because he is the expert, after all. But he cannot accept the claim because it is not what was asked for: Euthyphro has presented examples of holiness, when what he was asked for was the standard, or definition, by which he can recognize such things as being holy (6d).

Now the dialogue has shifted to a different level. Euthyphro finds himself in a situation where he must defend his point of view, rather than simply dispensing wisdom. He tries again: "[W]hat is dear to the gods is holy, and what is not dear to them is unholy" (6e–7a), and he agrees to show that what he says is true. But this he cannot do, because they have agreed that the gods quarrel, and so what is dear to some may not be dear to others, particularly on an issue like this. When asked what proof he has that what he is doing is an act of which the gods will approve, he responds: "But perhaps this is no small task, Socrates; although I could show you quite clearly." To which Socrates replies: "I understand; it is because you think I am slower than the judges; since it is plain that you will show them that such acts [like the killing of which he has accused his father] are wrong and that all the gods hate them." To which Euthyphro in turn replies: "Quite clearly, Socrates; that is, if they listen to me" (9b).

The confidence that Euthyphro reveals here he is soon to lose. Socrates points out that what amounts to their revised definition (what all the gods love is holy) still does not give them what they want. He shows this by raising a pivotal question (it is pivotal because it is about to shift the discussion out of Euthyphro's domain of expertise and so quite beyond his control): "Is that which is holy loved by the gods because it is holy, or is it holy because it is loved by the gods?" (10a). We can understand Euthyphro's plight when he responds to this: "I don't know what you mean, Socrates."

Essentially, leadership in the conversation has shifted to Socrates at this point. Euthyphro's failure to defend his claims, to know his own mind, has led him to lose control of the dialogue. Socrates' answer to the question just posed, put succinctly, is that the gods love the holy because it is holy and not that it is holy because they love it. That is, the gods are not the source of the holy, but they recognize it for what it is and love it. On this they are on par with humans, and Euthyphro's expertise (restricted to knowledge of the gods) has been surpassed. He has lost his status within the dialogue.

Socrates, we might imagine, is well aware of this, but still he persists: "But tell me frankly, what is holiness, and what is unholiness?" (11b). To which Euthyphro famously responds: "But Socrates, I do not know how to say what I mean. For whatever statement we advance, somehow or other it moves about and won't stay where we put it." Euthyphro's statements have run away from him. This is emphasized in the exploration of a final attempted definition, ostensibly conducted by Euthyphro but now directed by Socrates who has assumed control of the discussion, where the investigation leads them back to the (failed) definition that they have just left. Lost in this labyrinth of words, Euthyphro has nowhere left to turn, except away from the discussion.

This interpretation of the dialectical exchange between Socrates and Euthyphro makes very traditional assumptions about how dialogues proceed: that the source of a position is the best person to know and explain that position; that one ought to be able to provide reasons for one's position; that there are, as it were, separate roles in a discourse of this type, quite distinct from each other; and that while the participants might change roles, they do so completely (moving from knowing to unknowing, from control to no control). While the dialogue presents a picture of two people cooperating on a venture, that cooperation is less than clear to both parties and, ostensibly, unsuccessful. Interpreted this way, we have a "distanced dialogue" in that the parties manage to retain a clear distance between them. They don't see themselves working together, and the dialogue is more than a little adversarial, sometimes overtly so.

Still, the exchange exhibited in the Socratic dialogue at least retains the essence of a dialogue. Dialectics itself, as Bakhtin (1986) views it, is judged to have lost that fundamental structure:

> Take a dialogue and remove the voices (the partitioning of voices), remove the intonations (emotional and individualizing ones), carve out abstract concepts of judgments from living words and responses, cram everything into one abstract consciousness—and that's how you get dialectics. (147)

The sense here is that the value of dialogue has been lost; it has been depersonalized, replaced with artificial and static concepts, and robbed of its essential sense of "otherness." These ideas, among others, will characterize Bakhtinian conceptions of "argument" and "argumentation," conceptions that in a sense beckon from a distant point on the path on which much current argumentation research is traveling. But before we can fully engage those ideas, I need to prepare the ground by discussing some of Bakhtin's basic ideas that are relevant to this enterprise.

❖ BAKHTIN'S TERMINOLOGY

Bakhtin anticipated so many trends and developments in twentieth-century thought, from literary theory to linguistics to philosophy, that it should be no surprise if his work holds promise for some of the central themes in argumentation and communication and even anticipates some of the current ideas. One of the few writers to have recognized this is Rühl (2002), who integrates a discussion of Bakhtin's approach to literature into what he calls a "dialogic rhetoric." Rühl's sensibilities are clearly in line with rhetorical argumentation, as we see when he writes: "Dialogic rhetoric is dialogic, and it is rhetoric, in that it does not assume the argumentative situation to be characterized by a discourse segment having a well-defined beginning and end and to be regulated by dialectical rules, but to be an interaction in which the interactors are subject to the coercions of everyday life" (152). Hence, Rühl advocates paying serious attention to Bakhtin's work because of the way communication is conceived there, as a matching of individuals' fundamental assumptions and the reactions of addressees to speakers (27, 143). While Rühl limits his study to authority and appeals to authority, and mines Bakhtin principally for his insights into literary dialogues, his promotion of rhetoric, and his recognition that an argumentation drawn from it has multiple goals, are all welcome moves. More significantly, he identifies Bakhtin's work as something to be taken seriously by the argumentation community (30). The adaptation of Bakhtin's concepts developed here, while not following Rühl's path, originate in a similar belief.

When we think of "argument" as a product with premises and conclusion, we focus on the sentences or propositions involved. The tradition that harbors this model conceives the logical proposition in the case of the well-formed sentence as the basic linguistic unit. But for Bakhtin, these sentences are impersonal, they tell us nothing about the relations between speakers or arguers. As the tools of the logician, they communicate *their* own relations, the relations of statements themselves as they are set out on the page. Moreover, dialogic relationships exceed logical relationships and are not reducible to them. For example, we may offer two identical judgments, "'Life is good,'" 'Life is good'" (Bakhtin 1984, 183). In so repeating the judgment, it is embodied twice, and while we can speak of the logical relationship of identity between two judgments, "if this judgment is expressed in two utterances by two different subjects, then dialogic relationships arise between them (agreement, affirmation)" (184). It is these relationships that should interest us, and not simply (if at all) the identity relationship.

Hence in contrast to the sentence (and such logical relations), Bakhtin advocates the utterance as the basic linguistic act, where spoken utterances acquire their meaning only in a dialogue. To become dialogic, logical relations must enter into another sphere and become discourse: "that is, an utterance, and receive an *author*, that is, a creator of the given utterance whose position it expresses" (1984, 184).

Mention of "utterance" evokes the familiar work of the philosopher Grice (1989), whose investigations of utterances and implicatures have had an enormous influence on the development of pragmatics. Part of the richness of his writing has to do with the developed distinction between what is said in an utterance and what is implicated by it. Thus a speaker may "intend" several integrated things by an utterance, creating a layering of meanings, and the success of communication lies in the degree to which a hearer captures and correctly unpacks those layers. But as influential as it has been, Grice's work has also received criticism for its reliance on suggestions rather than detailed analysis, and for the most part, his work on implicatures was left largely incomplete (Blakemore 1992, 26). Bakhtin's approach to the "utterance" is on essentially different lines.

For Bakhtin, the utterance gives us the boundaries between different speakers. The sentence cannot do this: "The boundaries of the sentence as a unit of language are never determined by a change of speaking subjects" (1986, 73). Second, the sentence is not "correlated directly or personally with the extraverbal context of reality (situation, setting, prehistory) or with the utterances of other speakers" (73), and is quite unlike the utterance in this respect. Third, and importantly, the sentence "has no capacity to determine directly the responsive position of the *other* speaker, that is, it cannot evoke a response" (74). This last point captures a key feature of the utterance: it is marked by "its quality of being directed to someone, its *addressivity*" (95). Hence it is directed toward a response and accommodates that response in its very structure. An utterance then, has essentially both an author and an addressee; it cannot exist in isolation.[4]

Moreover, the utterance arises within the context of a particular situation. Or, to put it in Bakhtinian terms, the situation is a constitutive element of the utterance. As Todorov (1984) notes, this nonverbal element that corresponds to the context was known prior to Bakhtin. The difference to note is that Bakhtin did not treat it as external to the utterance, but integral to it. The extraverbal does not influence the utterance from the outside. "On the contrary, *the situation enters into the utterance as a necessary constitutive element* of its semantic structure" (Todorov 1984, 41).

So understood, "utterance" can help us to appreciate how Bakhtin employs the term "dialogism" and its conception of the "word." This is another term that may evoke the understandings of other authors. Perelman and Olbrechts-Tyteca (1969, 176) use "dialogism" simply to refer to a group of people engaged in a conversation. In her empirical study of how well people use the skills of argument, Kuhn (1991) describes her approach to argument as "dialogic," defining this as "a dialogue between two people who hold opposing views," and which involves justifications of these views and rebuttals (12). Such an understanding could easily take its place among those mentioned earlier in the chapter, which convey the normal sense of a two-person dialogue, while not explicitly avoiding the scenario of distanced, unintegrated positions. For Bakhtin, on the other hand, "what gives dialogue its central place in dialogism is precisely the kind of *relation* conversations manifest, the conditions that must be met if any exchange between different speakers is to occur" (Holquist 1990, 40). Bakhtin himself marvelled at the way that linguistics and the philosophy of discourse had valued an artificial, preconditioned notion of the word, which was lifted out of context and taken as the norm. By contrast, "[t]he word is born in a dialogue as a living rejoinder within it; the word is shaped in dialogic interaction with an alien word that is already in the object" (Bakhtin 1981, 279). In this dynamic conception the word finds its meaning. Bakhtin continues,

> But this does not exhaust the internal dialogism of the word. It encounters an alien word not only in the object itself: every word is directed toward an *answer* and cannot escape the profound influence of the answering word that it anticipates.
>
> The word in living conversation is directly, blatantly, oriented toward a future answer-word: it provokes an answer, anticipates it and structures itself in the answer's direction. Forming itself in an atmosphere of the already spoken, the word is at the same time determined by that which has not yet been said but which is needed and in fact anticipated by the answering word. (280)

This, he tells us, is understood for all rhetorical forms, and he stresses the importance for rhetoric of having the relationship with the listener enter into the structure of rhetorical discourse. But by and large, he believes, those who have turned to the study of rhetorical forms have looked at the question of style in order to understand and clarify the effects of discourse. In doing so, they treat the listener as passive. By contrast, Bakhtin points to the *active* role of the listener, or audience. In saying this, he takes his place in the tradition of rhetoric that I have been explaining since Chapter 1, a tradition coming out of the Greeks into the modern day, which stresses the activity of the audience in completing discourse and arguments. But, as the remarks already presented would indicate, he takes the listener/audience's contributory role much further:

> Responsive understanding is a fundamental force, one that participates in the formulation of discourse, and it is moreover an *active* understanding, one that discourse senses as resistance or support enriching the discourse.
>
> Linguistics and the philosophy of language acknowledge only a passive understanding of discourse, and moreover this takes

place by and large on the level of the common language, that is, it is an understanding of an utterance's *neutral signification* and not its *actual meaning*. (280–281)

This clarifies, or furthers, the essential notion of addressivity mentioned earlier. The word is directed toward a reply; it "anticipates it and structures itself in the answer's direction." The reply, and hence the replier, is already "there" in what is being replied to. This is not just (or even!) the completion of an idea or argument, as we might expect from a traditional understanding of an enthymeme. Rather, this suggests involvement in the composition from the start.

In contrast to this rich and vibrant model, Bakhtin places monologism. From the point of view of traditional rhetorical argument (1986, 150), we can recognize the monological in the attempt to determine in advance an audience's response by closing debate and ending further discussion. Bakhtin thus sets victory (seen in monologic rhetoric) against mutual understanding (dialogism) (150).[5] The contrast can be seen in what he has to say about the Socratic and Platonic discourses. One sense in which the Socratic dialogue (and here Bakhtin is speaking of the genre in general, which includes works, mostly lost, of people like Antisthenes, Phaedo, and Xenophon, and not just those of Plato) (1984, 109) is dialogic is insofar as Socrates asserts no truth. His conversation is not closed off, but is an open dialogue, with members working together to determine what is true. Plato's work, particularly in the final period when "the monologism of the content begins to destroy the form of the Socratic dialogue" (110), asserts a fixed, closed, truth. Hence the sense of the monological discourse as involving words that expect no answer because it is "closed-off discourse" (63).

In this way, the monological involves the whole of a single consciousness that absorbs other consciousnesses into itself, whereas the dialogical involves "a whole formed by the interaction of several consciousnesses, none of which entirely becomes an object for the other" (18). As it has been described earlier, the traditional concept of argument certainly fits the monological mould.

❖ DIALOGIC ARGUMENT

I turn now to the crux of our investigation: what conception of "argument" can we derive from Bakhtin's ideas? Shotter (1997) turns to

Bakhtin's views for an understanding of dialogical communication and argument within actual communities. I want to take this further and look for an implicit notion of argumentation, one that really captures the cooperative nature of dialogue. Given the richness of his ideas, I will pursue this through separate discussions of "argument," "arguer," and "audience," since Bakhtin provides suggestive remarks relevant to each of these.

The first thing to determine is whether argumentation qualifies as what Bakhtin calls a "speech genre." It is my contention that it does. A "speech genre," as defined by Bakhtin (1986, 60), is a sphere of communication that has its own relatively stable types of utterances. I take it as uncontroversial that argumentation fits this description. Later in the same work, he writes: "We learn to cast our speech in generic forms, and, when hearing others' speech, we guess its genre from the very first words" (79). Certainly, argumentation with its particular locutions expressing claims and reasons fits here as well. Bakhtin himself includes a wide variety of discourses as speech genres, beyond the frequently studied literary genres: the "short rejoinders of daily dialogues . . . everyday narration, writing (in all of its various forms), the brief standard military command, the elaborate and detailed order, the fairly variegated world of business documents," (60) as well as scientific statements. The types of utterances specific to arguers, and identifiable as parts of arguments such that "we guess its genre from the very first words," given the kinds of contextual considerations mentioned earlier, clearly delineate the sphere "argumentation."

A traditional model of logical argument, conceived in terms of the set of statements involved, conveys the monological assumptions that Bakhtin challenges. Primarily, they are impersonal. As they are presented for evaluation in the typical logical analysis, such sets reflect the understanding discussed earlier of arguments as products. They appear here as residues of arguments, as visible remnants. But even this way of talking makes it sound as if the argument is finished, decided. Bakhtin would view such an "argument" as something torn from the flow of arguing itself, incomplete and inadequate for learning anything about the actual process involved.

The closest Bakhtin comes to talking about argumentation *per se* is when he discusses polemical discourse, hidden or overt. Practical, everyday speech is full of the words of others. We react to these in different ways, assimilating some, or using those we take to be authoritative to reinforce our own words, or injecting some with our own aspirations. With respect to this last variety, Bakhtin writes: "Another's discourse in this case is not reproduced with a new intention, but it acts upon, influences, and one way or another determines the author's discourse, while itself remaining outside it. Such is the nature of discourse in the hidden polemic, and in most cases in the rejoinder of a dialogue as well" (1984, 195). Here both discourses retain their identities, yet *determine* each other (assuming a polemical exchange). Polemic, then, is the strongest kind of discourse for Bakhtin, reflecting the adversarial nature of traditional argument. It treats the other's words antagonistically and, in the case of overt polemic, it openly refutes it (196). But even this discourse is dialogical at heart in the sense that each party's utterances are acted upon, influenced, and determined by the other. The involvement here is not cooperative, but it reveals the ground from which cooperation can be developed. And certainly it suggests a deeper understanding of the dialogical nature of argument.

A concept of argument conceived along Bakhtinian lines will not pull discourse from reality and treat it as a series of statements (premises and conclusions) disconnected from arguer and audience/respondent. In this Bakhtin would not differ from some of the more innovative approaches to argument that I have outlined in earlier chapters. But Bakhtin again stands out in stressing the uniqueness of meaning that a sentence has within an utterance, to the extent of insisting that the repetition of the sentence makes it a new part of the utterance (1986, 109). A sentence changes its meaning (or has it added to) in the course of an utterance. In fact, Bakhtin specifically excludes logical relations, like negations and deductions, from those relations that are dialogical (Todorov 1984, 61). Dialogical relations are "profoundly specific" (cited in Todorov 1984, 61), logical relations are not. This sets a Bakhtinian model of argument quite beyond the boundaries of traditional formal deductive logic, a point that cannot be stressed too strongly. This is not to say that logicians present only a static concept of argument. In fact, and interestingly, some form of agency is often attributed to the set of statements involved. Traditional logicians, and indeed even argumentation theorists more contemporary in their outlook, will still speak, perhaps unwittingly, about how "the argument shows . . . ," "the premises support . . . ," "the evidence warrants . . . (or speaks for itself)," or "the conclusion claims . . ." Simply put, with the participants ignored, or deemed not relevant to the assessment of the argument, there is no other source for its agency than the argument itself.

In the Bakhtinian model, the arguer is co-agent and an essential component of the argumentative situation. In this we again have a richer conception, this time of the arguer.[6] Traditionally, the arguer is distinct from the argument, able to distance herself or himself from any integral involvement. This is the monologic perspective, one that "denies the existence outside itself of another consciousness with equal rights and equal responsibilities," and one that is "deaf to the other's response, does not expect it and does not acknowledge in it any *decisive* force" (Bakhtin 1984, 292–293). This is consistent with that aim of persuasion that desires the "complete victory and destruction of the opponent" (Bakhtin 1986, 150). But from the Bakhtinian perspective, with its stress on the addressivity of dialogue, such separation is neither accurate nor possible. The arguer as the "author" of a position in argument, or discourse, depends on the interlocutor for the direction and details of the utterances involved. In fact, the arguer as arguer exists only in relation to the other involved, and hence only in relation to the argument.

This idea points to another interesting feature of the account that further distinguishes it. As we have seen, in traditional models of rhetoric and argument we find talk about the way the arguer or argument aims to persuade the audience. The movement of expected change is centrifugal, from arguer to audience. Where change does take place, it is in the audience. Overlooked is the way in which the act of engaging in argument can change the arguer herself or himself. One of the assumptions left behind with the monological model is that of the self-knowing author of a discourse, who fully forms ideas before they are communicated, and possesses authoritative control over their meanings.

The concept of "person" has been given little attention by argumentation theorists. Exceptions to this are Walton (1998b) and Johnstone (1978). Walton's study of the *ad hominem* considers what notion of "person" lies behind the strategy of personal attack in argumentation. He offers the following definition: "*Person* in this sense means a participant in argument who is capable of arguing in a coherent, consistent sequence of reasoning and who has commitments and obligations to other persons by virtue of a role that the person has in these relationships" (1998b, 105). Johnstone took this idea a little further when he emphasized ways in which argument can actually establish the self, insisting that "argument is a defining feature of the human situation" (1978, 112). A being that could not argue would lack a self.

Such recognitions of the connections between the persons and argument are welcome contributions and suggest a fruitful direction for further research. But they do not hint at a role argument and discourse may play in the development of persons in quite the way that Bakhtin does. "Person," for Bakhtin, "is a dialogic, still-unfolding, unique event" (Holquist 1990, 162). The "I" of the other is affirmed, not as an object, but as another subject (Bakhtin 1984, 11). The Bakhtinian person lives on the boundary between self and other, a product of interaction. As such, "a person has no internal sovereign territory" (Bakhtin 1984, 287), no authoritative control over a meaning conceived in advance and in isolation from a context. Rather, situated at the boundary, introspection involves looking "*into the eyes of another or with the eyes of another*" (287). That is, we learn to see ourselves as others do and come to exist for ourselves as a result of that understanding. Shotter (1992) puts this well: "There is no preformed, orderly, and constant relations between thoughts and words but only ones that we 'develop' or 'form' as we attempt to express them to others in some way" (13). Here Shotter expresses the idea that we come to discover what we mean as we listen to ourselves, along with others, and not prior to them. This is an idea Merleau-Ponty (1962, 178n, 194) suggested in distinguishing between a second-order speech, a "spoken speech," which gives us the illusion of an inner life and which leads us to believe in a thought that exists for itself before it is expressed, and "primitive" or "authentic" speech, which does not translate prior thought but accomplishes thought and is the real phenomenon of speech itself.

This learning about ourselves from what we say in dialogue with others has instructive implications for the notion of the arguer. As an arguer, I must consider my audience in order to orient my speech toward them. And when I consider my audience, I consider how "I" appear to them; I look at myself through their eyes. I search for beliefs and attitudes that are implicated by the utterance between us, which is the product of our discourse, and of which we are a product. In turn, those beliefs and attitudes come to be understood and changed *in light of* the argumentative exchange. Argument is the occasion of change not just in the audience but also, and perhaps foremost, in the arguer. In articulating my position for my audience, I also articulate it for myself. The dialogic construction of meaning draws dialogue with another, and all that this entails, to the center of my consciousness (Maybin 2001, 70). Accordingly, we have suggested here a model of argument that takes us far beyond the adversarial tension of the polemic. Or, rather, it promises an understanding that is not restricted to that way of conceiving argument. Here we can find the metaphors of war that have been the subject of a number of critiques (Cohen 1995; Berrill 1996) replaced by the virtues of understanding and agreement.

Bialostosky (1995), in comparing Bakhtin's ideas to the work of Billig (1987/1996), makes the interesting claim that the two positions are similar in "not shaping the context of discourse to the audience of that discourse but [in giving] precedence to the 'counter-opinions' that the discourse must answer" (90). As correct as this insight is, it may lead us to lose sight of the way in which the addressee (second party or audience) is a constituent of the utterance involved. In this sense, and also recalling the essential addressivity of the utterance, there seems no distinction (for Bakhtin) between the audience and the "counter-opinions" that a discourse must answer. Like the arguer, the addressee/ audience is personalized in the argument and contributes specific actual and anticipated responses to a unique situation. Bakhtin's work captures this responsiveness. But this is more than the accommodation of a reply, the anticipation of objections to one's position. Here, again, addressivity conveys the way an argument is always *addressed to* someone, and thus needs to include an understanding of that other (audience/respondent) in its structures or organization. Hence the argument, while having the arguer as its principal author, can be said on this level to be co-authored by the addressee. For Bakhtin, we recall, "every word is directed toward an *answer* and cannot escape the profound influence of the answering word that it anticipates. The word in a living conversation is directly, blatantly, oriented toward a future answer-word: it provokes an answer, anticipates it, and structures itself in the answer's direction" (1981, 280). We can imagine here two people in a dialogue, anticipating and responding in a way that makes their argument a common discourse, and in a way that precludes the isolation of positions, speaking back and forth across a gulf.

❖ REFLECTIONS ON A BAKHTINIAN MODEL

Perhaps the most notable feature of a Bakhtinian model of argumentation would be its context dependency. Generally, it is context that enlivens rhetorical argumentation and recommends its primacy in any integrated model of argument. Important features of context include locality, background, arguer, and audience, all of which require detailed attention (Tindale 1999a). The Bakhtinian model emphasizes argumentation as a site of response and anticipation, of co-voicing and unconscious collaboration. Before the argument has arisen to the level of product, it is already infused with the characters of its participants— their beliefs, attitudes, and understanding. Its meaning is inseparable from those in whom it originates. And hence the unpacking of that meaning must, fundamentally, include an understanding of these participants. Directing a discussion of language or words in terms of voices personalizes it in a way that a traditional model of argument would not. The focus upon the utterance rather than the sentence means that an associated concept of argument cannot be understood in terms of mechanistic rules, because the relations between utterances are too rich and varied. This in turn is to affect the shift from form to the exigencies of everyday argumentation that recent attempts have striven to capture.

The essential ideas this dialogic argumentation contributes to our understanding of context are involvement, anticipation, and response. Involvement stresses the interweaving of the participants' perspectives, or the growth of a shared view, rather than the traditional product of their encounter. Reading the argumentation in this way requires resisting the temptation to see the participants as separate and looking more for the commonalities of view that grow between them. This should hold for both the dialectical and monological arguments that were illustrated earlier. Facilitating this process of involvement is the sense of anticipation at work in the model. At its deepest level, there is the "addressivity" of which Bakhtin speaks. For our purposes, we would look at the ways in which the speech of each participant anticipates the other's perspective in its very structure and in the meaning of the words within the discourse. On the same terms, but worth keeping here as a separate thought, is the way an argument *already* responds to its objections: participants think ahead of themselves, project themselves into the minds of the other, and draw that counter position into the construction of their own.

This is also a model of argument that would appear to aim for agreement. Even polemical discourse is constructed, and can be unpacked, in the way just indicated. Thus it contains at its heart the prospect of agreement, given the commonalities that influence it. And, of course, polemical discourse would be only one type of discourse, its aims only one among the aims of argument that we have already recognized. Goals of mutual understanding and agreement motivate the practices of many arguers of a rhetorical persuasion. On the question of agreement, Todorov (1998, 7) writes that for Bakhtin "[t]he goal of a human community should be neither silent submission nor chaotic cacophony, but the striving for the infinitely more difficult state: 'agreement'." The word used here means, at root, "co-voicing," reminiscent of the "double-voiced discourse" of which Bakhtin also writes (1981, 324). There is an intuitive appropriateness about this suggestion, given the unifying nature of the utterance and the allowances that must be made by arguer and respondent.

But at the same time, not all commentators interpret Bakhtin this way. Some stress the sense of social struggle rather than agreement (Hirschkop 1986, 73–79). Others, like Shotter (1992), stress the way that speakers in a discourse always occupy different "positions" and "can never completely understand each other; they remain only partially satisfied with each other's replies" (12). Again, it might be insisted, Bakhtin's central project is a rejection of the sameness of mind that affects monological discourse, and sameness is too clearly associated with agreement.

A close consideration of these points of view will indicate that they do not have to preclude each other, and while an agreement wrought from sameness of mind and outlook is antithetical to Bakhtin's project, the kind of agreement considered by Todorov is not. An agreement, where achieved through dialogical argumentation, does not mean an identity between positions; it does not involve a winner and a loser who gives up her or his position. Rather than the holding of the same position, agreement stresses an understanding of the position involved. As Todorov (1984, 22) recognizes, understanding is a type of reply, it is that to which both arguer and respondent move through the utterance. In this sense, understanding is dialogical and can be seen as a goal of argumentation within the perspective being extrapolated from Bakhtin's statements.

Among Bakhtin's final notes we find the denial of a last word: the dialogic context has no limits and each meaning gives birth to more (1986, 170). Argument, like dialogue, is ongoing. Conversations and disputes may seem to end, but they always reappear anew or slightly changed, building on what has been developed or established.

❖ EXAMPLES

I turn now to consider some examples from the perspective on argumentation that Bakhtin encourages. The first one is the dialogue between Socrates and Euthyphro. As previously noted, Bakhtin views the Socratic dialogue as an open discourse in which individuals work together. Such a sense of cooperation did not arise from the more traditional reading given to this exchange earlier in the chapter. Approached now in the light of our subsequent discussion, different aspects of the dialogue between Socrates and Euthyphro come to light. The goal first and foremost is no longer to seek a definition of piety or holiness but to reach an agreement of understanding—to reach a common point of insight into the nature of what they are investigating and the enterprise of that investigation itself. And yet, the question of piety or holiness is still important because it frames the context or situation out of which the utterances arise. As the model suggests, the context is a constitutive element of the utterance. The meaning of piety is crucial to the very self-understanding Socrates and Euthyphro each has of himself. It haunts their discourse at every turn. Each exchange is textured by the urgency of knowing what they seek: Socrates will die for lack of this, and Euthyphro's father may die. This context cannot be shed from their utterances.

Still, the example I have chosen here does not fit my interests in every sense, because it is clear that differences of inequality exist between the two participants. Those differences, however, are not simply as they appeared in the earlier reading. They are differences that force Socrates to work at the dialogical level I have suggested.

At the start, he and not Euthyphro is in control, insofar as it is Socrates and not Euthyphro who sets the conditions for the agreement that will govern their inquiry. Socrates says: "Tell me what you just now asserted that you knew so well. What do you say is the nature of piety and impiety, both in relation to murder and to other things? Is not holiness always the same with itself in every action, and, on the other hand, is not unholiness the opposite of all holiness, always the same with itself and whatever is to be unholy possessing some one characteristic quality?" To which Euthyphro answers: "Certainly, Socrates" (5d).

This is the point on which Euthyphro quickly founders, since his attempts at definitions do not reveal this standard that they agree they need. And Euthyphro will be reminded of this agreement as the dialogue proceeds. It is a commitment that he may have cause to regret, but within the parameters of which he agrees to stay. It is a commitment that connects him to the statements explored.

Beyond this, as the dialogue proceeds, the two participants become as one. Or rather, Socrates, who has established control of the discussion, loses himself in Euthyphro. Because what they argue about are Euthyphro's statements: his beliefs expressed in words. If power is source, then Euthyphro, who is the source of each definition, never gives it up completely. Instead, he shares it in a common venture, since for most of the discussion Socrates has no words of his own, but works with those of Euthyphro.[7] Socrates becomes Euthyphro in this sense: He thinks his thoughts with him and lives his statements to see where they will lead them. And he does this well, often thinking ahead, anticipating what will come next and adjusting to accommodate it, while allowing Euthyphro still to "lead" the dialogue through to its terminal points, from which it needs to restart.

Most explicitly, this comes after that earlier point of perplexity in Euthyphro (11d) where they have picked up a further definition, which leads them back to their previous (inadequate) point, that holiness is what all the gods love. At that point, the exchanges are as follows:

Socrates: "[Y]ou remember, I suppose, that a while ago we found that holiness and what is dear to the gods were not the same, but different from each other; or do you not remember?"

Euthyphro: "Yes, I remember."

Socrates: "Then don't you see that now you say that what is precious to the gods is holy? And is this not what is dear to the gods?"

Euthyphro: "Certainly."

Socrates: "Then either our agreement a while ago was wrong, or if that was right, we are wrong now."

Euthyphro: "So it seems." (15c)

Euthyphro has come to see what Socrates had already grasped. But as earlier, it is an insight they must share before they can move on. They think together, through the terms that they will use, through their understanding of the gods and the kinds of things they would dispute among themselves about, and arrive in each case at a common way of seeing that allows them to move on. Dialogical argumentation here aims at agreement, required to move it forward, maintain its flow. The insight of such agreement is itself valuable beyond any subsequent achievement.

After this last failed definition, the dialogue breaks up. Socrates proposes that they start again, but Euthyphro confesses to being in a hurry and rushes off. The dialogue is identified by commentators as one that ends in *aporia*. That is, it is unsuccessful, since it fails to discover what it sets out to discover—a definition of piety. But much else has happened: the participants have been transformed. Socrates has become Euthyphro, has lived through his words and experienced the failure of those words to deliver the knowledge claimed. Euthyphro, who claimed he knew, has discovered himself to be the one who does not know—the position Socrates always claimed for himself. He has become Socrates. This is not a simple shift of roles between them. Rather, it is the reaching of a commonality. They both come to understand what it is they do not know, and thus need still to learn. One likes to believe that this is a successful dialogue, that such an agreement of understanding has been achieved through this dialogical exchange, and that when Euthyphro rushes off at the end, it is to withdraw the charges he had laid against his father. Through this rushing off, the dialogue remains open-ended.

The dialogue in general ways expresses features of the dialogical model. We see the flow of the conversation toward understanding. Each utterance expects a response and, as we have seen, anticipates that response and is so framed to express that anticipation.

Socrates: "For surely, my friend, no one, either of gods or men, has the face to say that he who does wrong ought not to pay the penalty."

Euthyphro: "Yes, you are right about this, Socrates, in the main." (8e)

Each statement is forward looking, moving the discussion along, as they think together through language, developing common understandings. And as this flow proceeds, the participants change their views and perspectives. Or at least, Euthyphro does, but in this dialogue his is the only perspective that is revealed—the one being investigated. He shifts, revises, recants, and repeats. And at the end he is not the same as the discussant who began. He has, at the least, understood something important about himself.

If Euthyphro has been "persuaded" of his own ignorance, that persuasion comes from self-recognition. The discourse has developed on his terms, he influences the structure of Socrates' contributions, his responses are what Socrates' statements anticipate. If Euthyphro has been "persuaded," it has been by means of an invitational, rather than adversarial, rhetoric.

It must be conceded, though, that the lessons to be drawn from this example are limited because the dialogue is artificial. It is not a piece of live discourse between two participants, speaking naturally and without forethought. More worrying, perhaps, is that while it is a dialogue and fits the Bakhtinian perspective that has been developed, the texts we encounter in everyday situations are not so explicitly "dialogical." Interestingly, though, it is with this further kind of text that Bakhtin's prompting may be of greatest value, because such texts invite us to think of the ways in which they work as dialogues in the deeper senses explored in this chapter. The key to this lies in what Bakhtin calls "hidden dialogicality":

> Imagine a dialogue of two persons in which the statements of the second speaker are omitted, but in such a way that the general sense is not at all violated. The second speaker is present invisibly, his words are not there, but deep traces left by these words have a determining influence on all the present and visible words of the first speaker. We sense that this is a conversation, although only one person is speaking, and it is a conversation of the most intense kind, for each present, uttered word responds and reacts with its every fiber to the invisible speaker, points to something outside of itself, beyond its own limits, to the unspoken words of another person. (1984, 197)

This is profoundly suggestive because it implicates the way we read what we might have taken to be nondialogical texts: argumentative texts produced by one author that do not contain the explicit responses of an audience. The suggestion is that these responses are there, but hidden. This is how we in fact read an argumentative text when we read it from a rhetorical perspective, looking for the presence of the audience, for the way it is recognized, accommodated, and anticipated by what the arguer says.

To illustrate this, a second example comes from a speech delivered by George W. Bush to the American people after he sent troops into Afghanistan in October 2001.[8] I will select a few paragraphs of this speech, where we have the visible words of the first participant (Bush), and look for the invisible words of the second.

The opening paragraphs of the speech give a simple "what, who, and why." Bush starts with a statement of authority by explaining that, on his orders, the United States military had begun strikes against Al Qaeda terrorist training camps and military installations of the Taliban regime in Afghanistan. The reason he gives for this action is to disrupt the use of Afghanistan as a terrorist base of operations and to attack the military capability of the Taliban regime. The "who" consists of a number of "friends," as cumulative support for the claim: "We are supported by the collective will of the world." And the "why" is effectively presented in the form of an "Appeal to Force" that had failed to be effective: "More than two weeks ago, I gave Taliban leaders a series of clear and specific demands: Close terrorist training camps. Hand over leaders of the Al Qaeda network. And return all foreign nationals, including American citizens, unjustly detained in their country. None of these demands was met. And now, the Taliban will pay a price."

The remainder of the piece consists of various explanations and justifications, along with supporting information. He is aware of his audience, as is seen in the rhetorical use of patriotic appeals and demonizing of the enemy, and the creation of himself as a figure of justice and peace (in contrast to those who oppose him). Not only does his speech demonstrate control, but it is designed to do so manifestly: that is, he is seen in control of events. This, too, should reassure his audience.

As with our first reading of the Socrates/Euthyphro dialogue, the argumentation appears to be cooperative: he is addressing people with whom he wishes to cooperate, or who he wishes to cooperate with him. But also like our first judgments of Socrates and Euthyphro, these are what we might call "isolated cooperations"; they do not explicitly work together. To this end, Bush's argumentation lends itself to an adversarial reading.

However, while we appear to have just a monological text, there is much more involved. Bush is not just addressing his audience, he is reasoning with them as a participant in a dialogue. Read dialogically, his speech is a response to the points contributed by that participant, the concerns and fears that the people share. His text is filled with anticipation and response. Those he addresses are as much authors of the speech as he is.

After providing the clarifying statements of what, who, and why, obvious points that the audience will require to be first addressed, Bush goes on in the following three paragraphs,

By destroying camps and disrupting communications, we will make it more difficult for the terror network to train new recruits and coordinate their evil plans.

Initially the terrorists may burrow deeper into caves and other entrenched hiding places. Our military action is also designed to clear the way for sustained, comprehensive, and relentless operations to drive them out and bring them to justice.

At the same time, the oppressed people of Afghanistan will know the generosity of America and our allies. As we strike military targets, we will also drop food, medicine, and supplies to the starving and suffering men and women and children of Afghanistan.

From the first of these paragraphs to the second there is a shift, a hesitancy even. What the second paragraph does is address the effectiveness of the operation, allowing that it will not be straightforward. In this Bush anticipates a response from his participants, who would want to know the prospects for quick success. Again, we can imagine the question: Will this be a war on the people of Afghanistan? This question the third paragraph promptly answers.

The speech proceeds like this in subsequent paragraphs, taking up the anticipated question of whether this is a war on Islam, and responding in the negative; taking up the anticipated question of whether war was necessary and the United States the aggressor, and responding: "We're a peaceful nation." And, importantly, taking up the anticipated question of whether there will be reprisals with points about security and the measures he has enacted.

These are points the participant in dialogue requires him to address. In this sense they are not his alone; he shares them with this co-contributor who through its expectations and known values has played a role in the construction of what has been said. As Socrates becomes Euthyphro, so Bush, to be effective, must become the American people and think through them. The power and control that he might seem to have over this discourse is thoroughly diluted here.

This audience is also instrumental in the way things are said. He responds to their emotions and character. He assesses them to be angry and indignant, and responds with harsh words and indignation that the United States has been attacked and forced into this position. He senses their fear and answers with reassurances tempered with realism. He judges them compassionate in character and speaks early on to the ways in which the people of Afghanistan will receive aid. He judges them peaceful and responds accordingly. He knows them to be deliberative and logical, and so does not simply speak to incite emotions (this also comes through in his tone of delivery, absent from the transcript), but answers the need for deliberation with remarks on risks and costs. He understands their own sense of their role in the world and brings that out in his remarks on freedom and Americans' responsibility to protect it at home and abroad. These are beliefs already held by his audience. He is recalling them and focusing them so as to reach a common agreement on what is happening, what is at stake, and why it must be done.

One of the values of argumentation is that it brings people to see the obligations that they inherit by interacting with others in this way. In order to fully understand one's own position, one needs to have thought carefully about the alternatives to it. To understand how strong a case we have for a position we hold, we need to be able to conceive what would count as evidence against our position. That leads us to enter a dialogical sphere of thought, where we imagine what our position looks like to others, particularly those who do not hold it. What objections would they raise? What clarifications would they require? The ability to imagine counterarguments is synonymous with the ability to evaluate one's own arguments. All the better if the dialogical encounter is real (as in the case of actual dialogues) and not simply monological.

Through such exercises, participants can come to discover their beliefs and preferences. Even when we are aware of our responses to certain issues in a general way, it is through the specific challenges of dialogical argumentation that those responses become fully realized beliefs with accompanying reasons, and the choices and decisions made become identified preferences that may be applied to other contexts. Arguers come to discover themselves through the exercise of arguing, and develop themselves through what builds power of thinking and character. And obviously, through such argumentation we come to discover the thought patterns of others and appreciate the positions they hold and their reasons for holding them.

This, then, can allow for the kind of agreement of understanding discussed in this chapter. While there are still other positive features of the process in general, the achievement of such shared understanding must count as an important measure of success of any such argumentation. And that agreement will be seen through how people respond, what choices they make in light of argumentation. This is, arguably, a better measure than the correctness of arguments gauged through the instruments of validity and soundness.

It might be objected that this is simply persuasion delivered under a different guise: the arguers never completely lose sight of their desire to convince the audience of some position or claim, and immersing themselves in this dialogical process just allows them to achieve it more efficiently and, perhaps, ethically. The empirical measure of adherence to an idea seems the same in either case.

But this loses sight of the transformative powers of argumentation with respect to both (or all) participants. The process allows for the modifications of all perspectives, including the arguer's, and this makes it possible to reach a result not first anticipated by the arguer, but agreeable to all parties. Besides, persuasion in the traditional model is marred by the passive role of an audience subject to the aggression of the arguer. In what we have discussed, the audience is an active participant, and if conclusions are persuasive it will be because the parties involved come to persuade themselves of their merits. And this will result if the arguer has appropriately accommodated the audience by anticipating and responding to its contributions so as to achieve a joint understanding.

❖ CONCLUSION

This chapter has taken us deep into the argumentative context, and has aimed at further understanding the rhetorical features that make up that context and establish it before dialectical procedures come into operation or any argument product emerges. I have done this by exploring key elements in Bakhtin's work and thus introduced him as an important figure for argumentation theory from whom we can derive a full and fertile model of argumentation. Such a model awaits further development. But aspects of that model also enter the discussions of the next chapter, where we turn our attention to the perplexing problems that plague our notions of the rhetorical audience.

❖ NOTES

1. Blair (1998) laments a proliferation in the literature of terms that appear to be employed without discrimination or distinction: "dialogue," "dialogical,"

"dialectics," and "dialectical." While all these terms relate to a basic sense of dialogue as exchanges between one or more participants, "dialogical," in the sense in which it will be developed in this chapter, describes ways in which the differences of those participants are lost in the commonalities that underlie exchanges.

2. See also Lodder (1999, Chapter 6) for a discussion of further dialogical models of argumentation.

3. An alternative reading will be suggested later in the chapter. We should also recognize the positive reading that Bakhtin gives to the Socratic dialogue (1984, 110).

4. Where an actual interlocutor is not present, "one is presupposed in the person of a normal representative, so to speak, of the social group to which the speaker belongs" (Todorov 1984, 43). I do not want to overlook the kinds of problems that can come with such a projected "objective" standard. This will be addressed in the discussion of objectivity and audiences in the next chapter.

5. In this mention of "victory" Bakhtin invokes a more traditional view of rhetoric, perhaps one tainted by Aristotelian and Platonic reading of the Sophists noted in Chapter 2. Still, he does identify this as "the lowest form of rhetoric" (1986, 152), and allows that there are more positive, higher forms, as we have just seen him indicate.

6. In a sense, speaking about an arguer may be strange when we recognize the mutuality involved and the way in which the initiator becomes respondent as her or his utterances are formed by those they anticipate and respond to. But here I will employ the conventional understanding of speaking of the initiator of the discourse, or promoter of the primary position in a dispute, as the "arguer" so as to distinguish this role from the role of the audience.

7. Even when he makes contributions, after the point seen earlier at which Euthyphro becomes completely perplexed, he does so only insofar as he can solicit the agreement of Euthyphro. They work together in this way throughout.

8. The transcript of this speech is available at www.cnn.com/2001/US/10/07/ret.bush.transcript/

5

Martians, Philosophers, and Reasonable People: The Construction of Objectivity

<hr>

❖ INTRODUCTION

Bakhtin's theory of dialogical relationships opens up our ways of thinking about how arguers anticipate and incorporate the ideas of their audiences and how the argumentative context is alive with the contributions of two (or more) parties. Each of two apparently opposing views is influenced by the view that it opposes. Thus dialogism enriches not just our understanding of contexts but also of the contributions of rhetorical audiences. But such audiences themselves present us with a plethora of challenges. In particular, they raise a central question of assessment, of how argumentation ought to be evaluated and judged. The next three chapters will take up this issue in different ways. Audiences also raise questions of exploitation, prejudice, objectivity, and relativism. In many respects, these questions can reduce to the central one of objectivity: When dealing with audiences and attempts to gain their adherence or bring them to a position where they persuade themselves of the value of what has been presented to them, how do we insist on some measure of objective standards of reasonableness? Or to put the problem in its most acute form: From where do we derive the principles that govern good argumentation?

This turn in the investigation may strike some readers as odd. I have been stressing the subjective and intersubjective in the previous chapters, and now I seem to be turning to a more traditional sense of objective standards that somehow govern us. Argumentation and communication must always confront this tension in some way. We want to give free reign to audiences in their evaluations and decisions, and the invitational stance of the rhetorical argumentation discussed in this text accommodates as much. But at the same time, theorists worry whether this means "anything goes" as long as it meets the goals of anticipation, involvement, and response between arguers and audiences. Should we not feel uncomfortable, for example, at the license this may seem to give to the propagandist who strives to manipulate, or the promoter of hate whose discourse is welcomed by a like-minded audience? At a certain level we want to say that some standards of reasonable argumentation must be able to influence, and perhaps govern, the argumentative situation. But, importantly, we want an answer to this concern that is consistent with the model of argumentation advanced here: one that meets the requirements of cooperation and Bakhtinian co-construction.

This chapter approaches the above question by exploring some of the different attempts that have been made to put forward standards of reasonableness to help us judge what is right or wrong in situations, particularly argumentative ones. As we will see, standards like the Martian appeal are problematic in ways that bring to light some of the concerns that have just been expressed. But in studying these, we begin to see what it is we do need. The logical and dialectical perspectives on argument have their own responses to the question of how we determine principles of good argumentation, unsatisfactory in various ways, couched in notions of self-evidence or agreement between parties.[1] But the answers suggested by rhetorical argumentation again show why this perspective needs to underlie the others in any integrated model of argument. Within that rhetorical perspective, Bakhtin's work has its own way of responding to this question, phrased in terms of what he calls a "superaddressee" who bridges the internal dialogism of a situation and what lies outside of it. I will explore this idea later in the chapter. In a further twist to the historical development of ideas in the twentieth century, we will see that in its substantial form Bakhtin's superaddressee anticipates the most promising proposal for providing the standard we are seeking, one that has been advanced by argumentation theorists of a rhetorical disposition—namely, Perelman and Olbrechts-Tyteca's universal audience. Importantly, as we will see in Chapter 6, this standard is rooted in the actual audiences who co-construct and freely assess argumentation and thus offers a solution to the tension presented above.

As promising as the idea of a universal audience is, it is also notoriously difficult to interpret and apply, giving rise to quite diverse understandings of it. It is also appropriate to note that no really adequate explanation of this idea has yet been forthcoming, including my own attempts to provide one (cf. Blair 2000; Willard 2002).

After considering the parallels between the universal audience and Bakhtin's superaddressee in this chapter, Chapter 6 will take up directly the criticisms of the universal audience and show in response to those criticisms how it offers an adequate and useful standard of what is reasonable. Prior to this, though, we need to investigate the problem of objectivity as it arises in argumentative contexts and some of the devices arguers use to suggest, if not achieve, such objectivity. That is the task of the bulk of this chapter.

We will approach the problem by looking at one of the more extreme devices used to suggest objectivity in argumentation. This is not an explicit standard that is openly evoked with credentials laid bare. Yet it is the lack of this openness that lends it a certain rhetorical force, while at the same time indicating the problems of its use. The device in question is what I will call the "Martian standard."

❖ HOW MARTIANS REASON

On the morning after the announcement of a government's financial statement, an economist on a radio show proposed the following: "If you came to this country from another planet, you would think that the debt had been eliminated." This was by way of commentary—criticism, even. The reference to someone from another planet might amuse us. But why has the speaker chosen to phrase things this way? What role does it play in the discourse?

Another example, from a Canadian magazine article, gives more details of the device. In "What a Visitor from Mars Would Discover," Fotheringham (1998) writes: "A visitor from Mars, you see, arrives in Canada and can't figure out this debate on whether Quebec is going to separate or not. On examination, the puzzled visitor would find . . ." Fotheringham then proceeds to detail the number of high Canadian officials who hail from Quebec, gives his version of the country's history from 1759 to the current political situation in the country, in which the leader of the Federal Conservative party was being pressured to resign and take up the leadership of the Liberal party in Quebec and oppose the Parti Quebecois government in the next Quebec provincial election in order to "save the country." He concludes, "The visitor from Mars would find this a very funny country. The visitor from Mars would be right." Again, why has Fotheringham chosen to draw on this device? What advantage does he see in it, or is it just a flowery image to give his prose character?

Other examples reveal similar features. Consider the *Los Angeles Times* editorialist who observed, after the O. J. Simpson verdict, that a Martian would wonder about the state of the American justice system. Or the column by Davis (1999) in Britain's *The Daily Telegraph* that begins: "If Martians landed in California—apart from feeling at home—they would think that cigarettes were deadlier than cruise missiles."

Such discourses should lead us to wonder how these Martians reason (and how the person making the appeal is in a position to know). In almost every case, we find it used in the context of a critique, usually characterized by strong disagreement. No one with only a mild complaint sees need of this device; it is an argumentative trump card played down on particularly serious occasions. It represents an expression of shock or puzzlement, the observation of absurdity. But the reasoner or speaker doesn't explicitly make this expression or observation. While they are presumably prepared to be associated with it, they solicit the agreement of another perspective. Hence the criticism itself is transferred to the Martian or alien perspective. This gives it rhetorical force, it emphasizes the complaint. The implicit claim that X is wrong is made in a more powerful way through the mustering of this "support." The economist believes that the government is on the wrong track in its fiscal policies, that they don't make sense. We see this because the person from another planet can see that the policies do not make sense. Fotheringham claims his is a "very funny country" *because* the visitor from Mars would find it so. The clever circularity of the reasoning is hidden by the device used. We are quite distracted by it. Again, the situation with which Fotheringham is at odds does not make sense to him. Presenting it from a totally "other" perspective emphasizes that. And the O. J. Simpson decision made a mockery of the American justice system, according to the editorialist, because it would even move a Martian to wonder about it. In each case, the appeal stands in lieu of giving concrete justification for a position. In each case, we can see that the Martian represents the sensible, or what is deemed the "reasonable," position.[2]

So, Martians reason reasonably. But that is no answer at all. Rather, Martians reason reasonably according to a human standard. And here "a human" is nicely equivocated upon, because what might appear a general standard of human reason is in fact a particular one—that of the person making the appeal. Somehow, in the transition to the Martian perspective, the particular view of the speaker is exchanged for an "objective" standard. The Martian appeal is an attempt to create the appearance of objectivity. Even though we might *think* we know how the Martian reasons and agree with the point, the standard, as a standard, has no substantive content and thus is not accessible to real critique.

The tack I am exploring here should not be confused with that taken by adherents of the "Martian" school of poetry, popular in the later 1970s and early 1980s, in spite of a basic similarity of presenting an alien perspective (cf. Morrison and Motion 1982, 17–18). The name of the school is taken from the British poet Craig Raine's "A Martian Sends a Postcard Home" (1979). In this poem, everyday things are themselves made to appear "alien" when viewed from a perspective that is innocent of all cultural, social, even "human" meanings. Thus Raine evokes the strangeness of automobiles by describing a Model T as a room with the lock inside, the key to which frees the world to run past the window like a film; and the strangeness of a telephone by describing it as a haunted apparatus that sleeps in homes, snores when lifted, and occasionally cries in order to be soothed to sleep with sounds.

This is a positive, constructive use of a Martian strategy that invites us to rethink familiar things and relationships we take for granted. For the most part, this is not presented as a strategy of reason and judgment in the ways that interest me in this chapter. It does show, however, that all Martian appeals are not as negative and deceptive as might be implied here.[3]

As has been noted often in earlier chapters, every audience has a set of beliefs and presumptions that a speaker or arguer is wise to take into account in inviting them to reason to a specific conclusion or position. In a deeper sense, we might allow that there are underlying "truths" that are shared by audiences. While these may change over time, they are more resistant to such forces and form the basis for constructive discourses between audiences. When a speaker or arguer interacts with an audience, the question of what is "reasonable" in any case must surely arise. We feel, for example, that some prejudices held by specific audiences are unreasonable. That is, they are not well-grounded or justifiable in the sense that the holders could not give an account that would gain a sympathetic review from others. Likewise, the speaker or arguer will be judged according to some similar standard of what can be justifiably supported. But this really just pushes the question farther back: What grounds such a standard of justification? That is, to repeat the question behind this chapter, from where do we derive a standard of reasonableness that we take to be "objective" such that it can be used as a measure in judging the merits of argumentative discourse and will be widely recognized as such?

As we saw in Chapter 1, Johnson (2000a, 166) argues that the standards of good argument can be determined by looking at the behavior of the best practitioners of the enterprise. Johnson's ideal of best "practitioners" is philosophers and logicians. These are dedicated rather than casual participants in the practice. They set the standard. By contrast the casual practices of everyday arguers and their audiences are secondary. Johnson believes that philosophers produce not just better arguments, but products that more truly reflect the nature of argument. And he draws the analogy between the project of recognizing and appraising arguments and what goes on when we reflect on the paintings of skilled artists or the novels of the better novelists. But, as I noted earlier, while we may agree that philosophers produce better arguments (generally) and recognize exceptional novels, when we are interested in the *nature* of the novel, or of argument, surely it is important to look at the *range* of things that pass for each without prejudging what is central and what is not? I leave aside the more thorny question of how we decide philosophers produce better arguments without already having a standard (philosophers' arguments) to assist in such judgments.

Perelman and Olbrechts-Tyteca (1969) talk about the ways an elite audience can supplement the universal audience for many thinkers. But the two audiences are quite distinct, since the elite audience lacks the commonality of the universal audience (34). Perelman and Olbrechts-Tyteca recognize that what the elite audience often represents is a model to which people should conform; it is the ideal of knowledge and opinion. But on these terms it is difficult to see such an elite audience arising from particular audiences in the way that we will see a universal audience doing so for them. Perelman and Olbrechts-Tyteca recognize this, noting that the "elite audience embodies the universal audience only for those who acknowledge this role of vanguard and model" (34). Otherwise (and this is how Perelman and Olbrechts-Tyteca consider it), it is no more than a particular audience.

❖ THE MARTIAN STANDARD AND
   THE PROBLEMS OF EVALUATION

Johnson's standard of philosopher-logicians has the merit of being recognizably objective, even if we might disagree about what features make up that objectivity. The Martian standard is not so obliging. It stands as a subjective first-person perspective masquerading as an objective third-person one. Why is it employed? From what has been said so far, I can make the following suggestions: (1) It masks a circularity, (2) it creates an aura of objectivity such that the speaker can feel immune to some kinds of criticism, and (3) it gives the speaker control over that standard. The last point is important, because unlike the kind of third-person standard provided by Johnson, the Martian perspective is not subject to any preformed content such that we could respond that, actually, it doesn't allow this or that case or has been misinterpreted. There is nothing to misinterpret since the speaker has granted herself or himself free license to create the perspective.

As it happens, the Martian appeal is just a subspecies, although an admittedly strange one, of a general strategy reasoners employ of appealing to third-party objective sources for support for their positions. As a strategy of argumentation, it has close affinity with the "appeal to authority." One of the older and, perhaps, more ill-traveled forms of argument, the appeal to authority is the simple strategy of using the say-so of a recognized authority (person, source, or institution) as evidence in support of a claim or belief. I call this "ill-traveled" because for many people the appeal to authority has been judged inherently fallacious. "Be wary of the argument from authority," warn Sokal and Bricmont (1998, 178) in their attack on intellectual imposters, because it encourages a mental laziness where we allow others to do our thinking for us.

Textbook treatments, however, have argued successfully that such appeals can be reasonable *if* they meet certain criteria. For example, the authority's credentials must be stated; those credentials must be relevant to the claim or case in question; the authority must be free from bias in the case; there should be wide agreement among relevant experts; and the claim must concern an area of knowledge wherein such consensus would be possible (Groarke and Tindale 2004, Chapter 14). While they are not without their problems,[4] such criteria work well up to a point, helping students develop reasoning skills and recognize the better ways to proceed. But in the case under consideration, we are thinking about an *abstract* authority or "expert," one never, to my knowledge, considered in treatments of the appeal to authority.

Judged by the criteria just presented, the Martian appeal fails miserably, lacking credentials and infected with the biases of the user so as to preclude any achieved agreement. Yet the appeal clearly belongs under this rubric, since the strategy is one of marshaling the support of an authority. Admittedly, as we have seen, it is far more complex than that, because the aspects of exaggeration and absurdity are also important to it, but the specter of an authoritative third-person source cloaks it entirely.

In asking how the Martian reasons, we could also ask how the American taxpayer reasons, or the "man" on the street, or how the "reasonable person" reasons, since these are similar "devices" we may have heard used by arguers to support their positions. Sometimes, we might determine, there actually is an objective standard to which an appeal is being made, and sometimes it is the creation of the person making the appeal.

A challenging case in point involves Lord Patrick Devlin's response to the "Report of the Committee on Homosexual Offences and Prostitution," released in Britain in 1957. Named after the committee chair, the Wolfenden Report recommended that homosexual behavior between consenting adults in private should no longer be a criminal offense, and made a similar recommendation on prostitution. In his Maccabean lecture in jurisprudence titled "The Enforcement of Morals," Devlin begged to differ.[5] He investigated the relationship between the moral law and the criminal law and concluded that there are certain standards of behavior or moral principles that form the basis of the criminal law. His argument is long and complex, but having decided that society is founded on collective moral judgment, he had to confront the question of how such judgment is ascertained. His answer is instructive. "It is surely not enough that [the moral judgments of society] should be reached by the opinion of the majority," he writes; "it would be too much to require the assent of every citizen."

Instead, Devlin turns to a standard evolved through English law that "does not depend on the counting of heads," that is, the standard of "the reasonable man." It is what he has to say about this standard that is particularly interesting: "[The reasonable man] is not to be confused with the rational man. He is not expected to reason about anything and his judgment may be largely a matter of feeling. It is the viewpoint of the man on the street ... He might also be called the right-minded man" (1965, 38).[6]

We should observe that there are some odd categories at work here. The reasonable person is contrasted with the rational person. It is not precluded that the rational person might also be reasonable, but what Devlin wants is someone who does not think (only "feels") and the rational person thinks. Hence "reasonable" is equated with feeling, not thinking. But this shift from reason to emotion is then undermined by referring to the (hypothetical) individual as the "right-minded man." That is, presumably, the individual thinks correctly. If such a standard ever worked, it seems unlikely to be effective in the less homogenized societies of today. But what kind of randomness is really behind Devlin's standard? He goes on to observe that: "This was the standard the judges applied in the days before Parliament was as active as it is now and when they laid down rules of public policy. They did not think of themselves as making law but simply stating principles which every right-minded person would accept as valid" (1965, 38). That is, if any random individual might be expected to espouse these correct views, then judges themselves might be expected to hold them. Thus they could confidently espouse the principles of the right-minded person. Anyone who disagreed would prove themselves by virtue of that disagreement not to be right-minded.

Something of this circularity pervades Devlin's treatment of the Wolfenden report and its recommendations, which he takes to be wrong-headed because they try to establish a sphere of private morality. Devlin recognizes only the public domain, which gives his standard its currency. Thus, in the context of Devlin's argument, when we ask how the representative of his "objective" standard reasons, the answer depends on the kind of access Devlin has to the source and his accuracy in interpreting it. Immorality is "what every right-minded person is presumed to consider to be immoral" (38).[7]

The "reasonable man" would appear to be a Martian. The case possesses the defining characteristics of the Martian case: a context of critique marked by strong disagreement; an underlying circularity; an aura of objectivity that immunizes the speaker from criticism; and, as far as we can see, control of the standard lying with the speaker.

The authoritative voice here can take on a frightening aspect, and I do not want to speculate too much on our general propensity to do something similar: that is, to assume we are representative of how others generally think (even though such a propensity contradicts our pride in our own individuality). Hume (1964), for example, who makes a lot of "uniform experience" in his essay on miracles, doesn't really address the question of *whose* "uniform" experience is involved. That is, he uses it as a standard to judge what kinds of things would be deemed astounding, without asking how his knowledge of the "uniformity" of experience is acquired. Is it a projection of his own experience, or is it a collation of others' testimony?[8]

The Martians of the early examples reason like Devlin's "reasonable man" in that they must reason after the manner of their creator or instigator. As a supposed "objective" source of evidence (only implied in such cases) they represent merely the avoidance of admitting the subject's ownership. There may be some rhetorical force to the appeal: it shows *how clearly wrong* the challenged position must be, in the reasoner's view. But there is no means of evaluating it, except as the reasoner's view. In this sense, and crucially, it becomes part of their case and not contributory evidence for it. Hence the circularity of its employment.

What marks these as problematic is the lack of accessibility anyone has to the "source." Yet I would not wish to completely dismiss Devlin's initiative in approaching things the way he did. There are features that do distinguish his case. He is making a concerted effort to draw a notion from what he understands around him. In the terms of the discussion yet to be developed, he makes a real attempt at universalizing. Also, in terms of how the "reasonable person" standard has developed in Anglo-American law, judges are not immune from criticism when they use the standard, and an individual's decision will only have precedential force if other judges concur.[9] Still, in this example we witness the kinds of problems of which we should be wary in any such exercise. As I suggested at the start of this chapter, both Bakhtin and Perelman provide standards that avoid the problems infecting the Martian appeal and its ilk, but without all the details and drawbacks of scientific polls. I turn now to the question of how these standards avoid the problems of subjectivity and nonrepresentativeness.

❖ BAKHTIN'S SUPERADDRESSEE

Bakhtin's dialogism seems to recognize two types of audience: one the immediate and personalized audience, the other more abstract. To the speaker and respondent (first and second parties) he adds a third consideration: "Each dialogue takes place as if against the background of the responsive understanding of an invisibly present third party who stands above all the participants in the dialogue (partners)" (1986, 126). This third party has a special dialogic position (because, of course, there can be an unlimited number of participants in a dialogue, so this is not simply a third member). As Bakhtin further explains this role,

> [I]n addition to this addressee (the second party), the author of the utterance, with a greater or lesser awareness, presupposes a higher *superaddressee* (third), whose absolutely just responsive understanding is presumed, either in some metaphysical distance or in distant historical time (the loophole addressee). In various ages and with various understandings of the world, this superaddressee and his ideally true responsive understanding assume various ideological expressions (God, absolute truth, the court of dispassionate human conscience, the people, the court of history, science, and so forth). (126)

These "just" or "true" responses suggest that we have here an objective standard conceived by the audience of the utterance as an active participant possessing various degrees of awareness. On the other hand, Bakhtin's reference to the way this "ideological expression" has been viewed suggests it is no more than a very traditional notion of universality. Yet a reliance on such a traditional model seems inconsistent with what we have understood of Bakhtin's project. Bakhtin uses the analogues of "including the experimenter within the experimental system . . . or the observer in the observed world in microphysics" (1986, 126), to stress that there is no *outside* position (which is how a traditional notion of universality is usually understood—and is part of the grounds on which traditional universality is criticized by Perelman and Olbrechts-Tyteca). Likewise, we cannot expect the superaddressee to stand outside of the utterance, unaffected by it. Insofar as the superaddressee represents responsive understanding, and understanding cannot be from the outside, then the superaddressee is internal to the utterance. Furthermore, this superaddressee is "presupposed" by the author of the utterance; it is controlled by the author.

What is less clear is how integrally the third party superaddressee is related to the second party respondent (as we will see, Perelman and Olbrechts-Tyteca's universal audience is related to the particular audience). But here again, a remark of Bakhtin's is instructive: "The aforementioned third party is not any mystical or metaphysical being (although, given a certain understanding of the world, he can be expressed as such)—he is a constitutive aspect of the whole utterance who, under deeper analysis, can be revealed in it" (1986, 126–127). Like the first and second parties (and other features discussed in the last chapter), the third party is a constitutive aspect of the utterance. As presupposed by the author, this party must be understood in some essential relation to the second party who is being addressed and who is, as we have seen, coauthoring the utterance itself.

Later, Bakhtin makes two important qualifications that further clarify the ideas involved. In the notes of 1970–71, he introduces a more restrictive sense of the third party. Here he refers to it as an abstract position identified with the objective stance of "scientific cognition" (1986, 143). This third-party perspective is justified only when the "integral and unrepeatable individuality of the person is not required" (144). There are, after all, generalities to existence and, in our context, these will often become the subject of, or be drawn on for, argumentation. But the vital experienced life knows no generalities, and here "*my word* and the *other's word*" are irreducibly personal (144).

Second, in "Toward a Methodology for the Human Sciences," Bakhtin criticizes the notion of an "ideal listener." Of this he writes:

> It is an abstract ideological formulation. Counterposed to it is the same kind of abstract ideal author. In this understanding the ideal listener is essentially a mirror image of the author who replicates him. He cannot introduce anything of his own, anything new, into the ideally understood work or into the ideally complete plan of the author. He is in the same time and space as the author or, rather, like the author he is outside time and space (as is any abstract ideal formulation), and therefore he cannot be *an-other* or other for the author, he cannot have any *surplus* that is determined

by this otherness. There can be no interrelations, for these are not voices but abstract concepts that are equal to themselves and to one another. Only mechanistic or mathematical, empty tautological abstractions are possible here. There is not a bit of personification. (1986, 165)

Lest we think this in some way contradicts earlier remarks about the superaddressee, we might note how impotent this entity is: it is not another voice, but represents the pure extension of the author. As such it performs a function very much like Blair and Johnson's (1987, 50) community of model interlocutors, a community which mirrors the author. It is too subjective, and it is a notion of universality that is *brought to* an argumentative situation. By contrast, what Bakhtin had proposed earlier in the remarks on the superaddressee is a model that is *found in* the argumentative context, a constituent of the essential utterance and not merely a reflection of the author or arguer.

❖ PERELMAN AND OLBRECHTS-TYTECA'S UNIVERSAL AUDIENCE

Bakhtin's criticism of the ideal listener is one with which Perelman and Olbrechts-Tyteca in their context would be likely to agree. They were aware of the problems involved with objective audiences, writing in *The New Rhetoric:*

Does a person suppose that there is really objective validity in what convinces a universal audience, of which he considers himself the ideal representation? Pareto has made the penetrating observation that the universal consensus invoked is often merely the unwarranted generalization of an individual intuition. (1969, 35)

As we saw, Devlin's universalizing seems to have this kind of objectivity, where it is difficult to distinguish it from the writer's own position. But it is a step beyond the Martian cases insofar as there is the sense that an attempt is being made to find real objectivity, recognized as such.

Perelman and Olbrechts-Tyteca's "model" audience, the "universal audience," has been criticized as if it had the characteristics we have seen to apply to the Martian category—ideality and inaccessibility

(Ray 1978; Ede 1989). But, contrary to this, it actually has the best kind of objectivity we can hope to achieve in such situations.

There are a number of audiences recognized by Perelman and Olbrechts-Tyteca (1969, 30), but an important distinction is made between the particular audience being addressed and the universal audience somehow lying within, or framed by, or participating in, that particular audience. The relationship between the two audiences has occasioned considerable debate, and several key criticisms have been brought against it.

Briefly, we should understand the following: Perelman and Olbrechts-Tyteca's universal audience is not an abstraction but a populated community. It derives from its conceiver, conditioned by her or his milieu (Perelman 1989, 248). The universal audience is a concrete audience that changes with time and the speaker's conception of it (Perelman and Olbrechts-Tyteca 1969, 491). It is far from being a transcendental concept borne out of a rationalism (Ray 1978). But although the universal audience will change, the test of universality goes on—*it* transcends a milieu or a given epoch.

While being a hypothetical construction, the universal audience is not, on this reading, an ideal model. What this allows us to do is to keep our focus on the immediate audience with its particular cognitive claims, while recognizing a standard of reasonableness which should envelop that audience, and which it should acknowledge whenever recourse to the universal audience is required. In this way we can understand Perelman and Olbrechts-Tyteca's repeated insistence that the strength of an argument is a function of the audience, and that in evaluating arguments we must look first and foremost at the audience.

Like Bakhtin's superaddressee, and unlike the kinds of models illustrated in Blair and Johnson (1987), the universal audience is distinguished by the common ground that it shares with the particular audience. The universal audience, as conceived by Perelman and Olbrechts-Tyteca, is not a model of ideal competence introduced into the argumentative situation from the outside. It is developed *out of* the particular audience and so is essentially connected to it.

One may appreciate from this discussion of the universal audience why critics might be moved to charge that Perelman espouses relativism.[10] As van Eemeren and Grootendorst (1995) explain it, Perelman reduces the soundness of argumentation to the determinations of the audience. "This means that the standard of reasonableness is extremely relative. Ultimately, there could be just as many definitions of reasonableness as there are audiences" (124). Introducing the universal audience as *the* principle of reasonableness to mitigate this problem only shifts the source of the concern to the arguer. Since the universal audience is a construct of the arguer, now there will be as many definitions of reasonableness as there are arguers. Such a criticism would seem to view the universal audience very much as if it were of the Martian variety, having only subjective validity. Here though, understanding the superaddressee/universal audience from within Bakhtin's project may allow us to address the concern over an apparent relativism in Perelman and Olbrechts-Tyteca's model. The charge that there will be as many universal audiences as there are arguers misses what a Bakhtinian model of argumentation, as I have developed it, makes clear: that in a very real sense the "arguer" will only exist for us in relation to an "argument" (understood now in dialogical terms). And this argument is a unique event involving the particulars of speakers and their situation and the universal audience relevant to them. It is not a matter of each arguer deciding the universal audience in some arbitrary way, such that there are as many universal audiences as there are arguers. It is a matter of the argumentative context dictating to the arguer how the universal audience can be conceived, and the respondent or particular audience playing a co-authoring role in that decision. The argumentative context imposes clear constraints on the freedom of the arguer.

❖ CONCLUSION

Bakhtin and Perelman and Olbrechts-Tyteca give us standards of objectivity that exceed the limitations of simulacra like the Martian appeal while also avoiding the problems we have seen associated with it. Since Perelman and Olbrechts-Tyteca's is the clearer, more complete model, this is the one I will choose to develop and explore in the next chapter. But its parallels with the superaddressee of Bakhtin's dialogism serve further, I believe, to show the degree to which Bakhtin anticipated the concerns and directions of rhetorical argumentation in the twentieth century.

The universal audience meets the central demands we must make of any third-person objective standard: (1) there must be a real source standing behind the "abstract" standard, and (2) there must be some recognized means of accessing and evaluating that standard. It meets (1) in that it lies in, and is derived from, the standard of reasonableness that is alive in a real particular audience. It meets (2) in the same terms: that a real particular audience can be accessed and its ideas evaluated. Thus it is more than just a projection of the arguer, like the empty standard of the Martian. At the same time, and to this extent like the other standards we have explored in this chapter, the closeness to Bakhtin's notion, with its roots in a shared context, shows a close affinity between the arguer and this standard. They exist only in relation to each other. Or, rather, each exists only in relation to the relevant argumentative context.

This chapter has introduced the universal audience. Given the propensity that exists for appealing to objective standards, of our necessity for doing so, it is important that we have a coherent idea of how such a standard can work in argumentation. Also, the answer to the origin of the standards of good argumentation suggested by the universal audience—that they derive from actual, particular audiences—needs fuller consideration. In the next chapter I turn to this consideration and at the same time attempt to address some of the concerns raised about the universal audience, while further stressing its value and application.

❖ NOTES

1. For evaluations of these, see Tindale 1999a, Chapters 1 and 2.

2. There are other types of "Martian appeal" where the Martian represents the perspective that is not sensible or reasonable. In his biography of Isaiah Berlin, for example, Ignatieff (1998, 85) remarks of a group of Oxford philosophers infatuated with the language of positivism: "To anyone outside the circle, the discussions might have seemed Martian." Our interest, though, is restricted to cases in which it is the perspective of the author and a standard of what is deemed reasonable, as when Conradi (2001, 588) reports of the young Iris Murdoch: "In 1935, a schoolgirl, she had noted, 'If a visitor from Mars were to see this free land. . . .'"

3. I am grateful to Norman Alm of the University of Dundee for drawing this material to my attention.

4. For example, should we distinguish between authorities and experts? How do we appraise competing claims of "authorities" in cases where there is obviously no consensus, but consensus might be in the process of being formed? And how, most importantly, do we deal directly with authorities and evaluate their responses? I cannot take up these questions here.

5. References are to the 1965 version of the paper under the title "Morals and the Criminal Law."

6. He goes on to say that this is the makeup of the jury box and that the moral judgment of society must be something concerning which any twelve men or women drawn at random "might after some discussion be expected to be unanimous."

7. He does allow that tolerance (not acceptance) will vary by generation.

8. In 1999b, I have argued the latter.

9. I am grateful to Jean Goodwin for drawing this point to my attention. As the standard is used, it can be a vivid example of Bakhtinian co-construction.

10. Here the criticism seems aimed at Perelman alone, following the standard view that he is responsible for the original ideas in the project with Olbrechts-Tyteca. Barbara Warnick (1997), however, has gone a long way toward advancing an effective challenge to the one-sidedness of this view. In particular, she shows how ideas and themes in *The New Rhetoric* are discussed and developed in Olbrechts-Tyteca's single-authored works, including her thesis, *Le Comique du Discours*. Warnick's discussion of Olbrechts-Tyteca's own views on the universal audience (1997, 78ff.) suggests it is unwise to assign the device to Perelman alone. Hence, in the discussion here and in the developments of the next chapter, I will assume that the idea of the "universal audience" with which I am working originates with both of *The New Rhetoric*'s authors.

6

Developing the
Universal Audience

❖ INTRODUCTION: WHY
THE UNIVERSAL AUDIENCE FAILS

As a principle of universalization, a universal audience provides shared standards of agreement by which to measure argumentation. It provides the details of what is "reasonable" in any particular case. The task of this chapter will be to explore how this works and is to be understood. To this end, I will first consider some of the more intransigent problems associated with Perelman and Olbrechts-Tyteca's universal audience, before turning to some recent readings of the concept to determine whether those problems have been adequately addressed. The remainder of the chapter will aim to complete that task by developing the idea of the universal audience and suggesting how it can be applied in argument construction and evaluation.

Perelman and Olbrechts-Tyteca distinguished clearly between the rational and the reasonable, matching this to their more fundamental distinction between demonstration and argumentation. Starting from accepted, self-evident premises, demonstrative methods of proof work well in situations where there is nothing to be argued, where everyone will be compelled by the same "evidence." Argumentation arises when things are controversial and in dispute (1969, 13–14; Perelman 1982, 6). In fields such as law and ethics, those not founded on indubitable self-evidence, argumentation is indispensable. At the same time, where questions arise about the axioms underlying proofs or whether something is self-evident, then argumentation is also called upon. So not everything is arguable and there are matters outside of argumentation, *if* the principles of demonstration are agreed upon.

Corresponding to this distinction, what is *rational* characterizes demonstration, or mathematical reason, "which grasps necessary relations, which knows *a priori* certain self-evident and immutable truths" (Perelman 1979, 117). What is *reasonable,* on the other hand, characterizes the domain of the holistic inquirer, who draws on experience and dialogue with others. The rational person, we might say, is subsumed by the aspect of *logos.* The reasonable person supplements this with *pathos*[1] and *ethos,* and the *logos* pursued becomes transformed through its alliance with these other components of the human reasoner. Audiences are made up of such reasoners. Unlike the "rational person" in whom reason is separated from other human faculties, the reasonable person judges reason as only one component within the project of human development, and as something that is instantiated in real audiences. *They,* actual reasoners in real audiences, are the source of the principles of good argumentation.

As the previous chapter demonstrated, the desire to find the grounds for what is reasonable is natural and necessary. The difficulties associated with this desire arise from the complexity of the very problem that it aspires to address. It is tantamount to a reformulated statement of the problem of induction itself, since however we approach this, reason underlies itself, is its own justification in some form or another. Hence the criticisms leveled at proposals like that of the universal audience of Perelman and Olbrechts-Tyteca are as understandable as they are challenging.

Something of the concern over the appearance of a subjective element in determining universal audiences was addressed in the last chapter. Van Eemeren and Grootendorst's (1995, 124) charge that the standard of reasonableness is extremely relative is met with the recognition, courtesy of Bakhtin, that the argumentative situation is unique. The arguer, audience, and argument itself exist in relation to a situation that is defined by them and defines them, and it is among those components that we should look to determine what is reasonable *in that situation*. Still, the criticism here can resonate in other ways. Since we cannot poll the universal audience, how are we to be sure we know its mind (Willard 2002)?

Related to this, we might be concerned by the apparent vagueness of the notion of authority underlying the universal audience: what is the *authority* for identifying characteristics of the universal audience in particular audiences, such that we can judge an audience to be "reasonable" on the one hand, or on the other hand, for determining that something is excluded from the universal audience and so objectionable in a particular audience. This criticism comes closest to identifying the apparent circularity noted earlier of proffering instantiated reason as its own justification.

A third criticism involves a challenge to the general thesis that rhetorical argumentation is the foundation for any integrated model that also includes the dialectical and the logical. A key test of the reasonableness of a claim or position, from the perspective of a universal audience, is whether it can be universalized without contradiction (Tindale 1999a, 118). The reference to "contradiction" here can raise alarms, since this is a logical rather than a rhetorical term (Johnson 2000b). Among the kinds of things that a universal audience would reject as contradictory would be logical fallacies. But how do we see this? Given that one of the problems with fallacies is that they deceive audiences and get believed, why should we think they would be recognized by the reasonable element in an audience? This is to ask how a universal audience really functions as the principle of reasonableness within any audience. How does that principle come alive and operate in specific circumstances? In the absence of such clarification, Johnson (8) draws on his own tools to provide an answer:

> It seems clear that [the universal audience] will be relying on some criteria or standards in making these judgments—that is why they are reasonable people. My suspicion is that while there is no overt appeal to them, logical standards for the evaluation of argument (like relevance and truth and sufficiency) will be imbedded in the way the audience is conceptualized; they are built into the notion of a reasonable person. In that way as well, then, the rhetorical presupposes the logical.

If it seems strange to refer to standards the universal audience might use when *it* is being advanced as *the* standard, the problem lies not so much in the criticism as in the vagueness of the idea that is being criticized.

Finally, we might switch our attention from the construction of such audiences to ask how the idea of a universal audience is useful for the individual who must evaluate arguments. The thrust of the account given so far is from the perspective of one who constructs arguments, who must decide what to say to convince the universal audience. But a comprehensive model of argument must also address things from the evaluator's perspective, particularly when that evaluator is also the target audience for the argument. The evaluator's interests seem far more caught up in matters of cogency than matters of rhetoric. So, again, the universal audience fails to make the case generally for the primacy of rhetoric in argument.

Two general concerns about the universal audience emerge from this discussion. The first has to do with the vagueness of the concept itself, the details of its nature and its relationship to the particular audience. The second has to do with its applicability—its usefulness for a range of matters that occupy those interested in argumentation. In addressing both these general concerns I will also respond to the specific questions that have arisen around subjectiveness, authority, the rhetoric/logic relation, and the construction/evaluation distinction. I will approach these issues first by exploring two recent interpretations of Perelman and Olbrechts-Tyteca's universal audience put forward by American scholars.

❖ READING THE UNIVERSAL AUDIENCE: TWO VIEWS

The readings I am interested in here are both positive and generally try to provide applications of the universal audience.[2] The first of these comes from Gross and Dearin (2003), scholars of rhetoric who place an examination of the universal audience within a rich study of Perelman's overall thought. It is their contention that explanations of the universal audience have suffered for not being understood within the complete theory of rhetorical audience that can be derived from Perelman and Olbrechts-Tyteca, and it is this complete theory that they are concerned to detail. To this end, they focus on a core distinction—that between facts and values. Facts and truths constitute the real, whereas values embody the preferable (Perelman and Olbrechts-Tyteca 1969, 66). Facts are things that stand fast; values change. Facts relate to the universal audience, values to the particular audience.

> Philosophy and science are the paradigm examples of discourses in which facts, truths, and presumptions are central; these are discourses that aim at a universal audience, the imagined community of all rational beings. On the other hand, public address is the paradigm example of a discourse aimed at an imagined community of particular beings: Americans, the Elks, the elderly. (Gross and Dearin 2003, 31–32)

This passage sets the rationale for Gross and Dearin to explore ideas in their later chapters through discourses drawn from philosophy, science, and public address. Of more significance, though, is the claim indicated here that all rhetorical audiences are constructed, whether universal or particular.

Crucial to the interpretation involved is a passage early in *The New Rhetoric* in which Perelman and Olbrechts-Tyteca distinguish between argumentative structures and the effects they may have on real audiences. Were we to judge arguments only by the effects they have, it is suggested, then we would be in the realm of experimental psychology, "where varied arguments would be tested on varied audiences" (1969, 9). Instead, Perelman and Olbrechts-Tyteca propose to proceed by examining the different argumentative structures, since this must happen prior to any experimental tests of their effects. Gross and Dearin understand this passage to mean that Perelman and Olbrechts-Tyteca have no interest in studying real audiences, since this is beyond the reach of rhetoric (2003, 32). Hence the complete shift to constructed audiences.

Granted, Perelman and Olbrechts-Tyteca do write that the audience is "always a more or less systematized construction" (1969, 19), but neither this claim nor the passage from *The New Rhetoric* that Gross and Dearin cite precludes a study of real audiences in relation to what is constructed out of them, and the interpretation they develop fails to give sufficient weight to the ways in which the construction of audiences always begins with real auditors or readers. If we look for a balance between the speaker (or writer) and the audience in question, then Gross and Dearin's account has significantly shifted things to the position of the speaker or writer, who must guess the audiences' views of the real and preferable, even though they never deny that there are real people standing before the arguer (2003, 36). So this does seem an interpretation that would lend itself to the criticism that the universal audience is *no more* than a product of the arguer.

Given that both universal audiences and particular audiences are constructed on this reading, the difference lies in the focus of the discourse—on the real or the preferable. In addressing the real, a speaker or writer considers the men and women of the audience not in terms of their nationality or religion, for example, but as rational human beings. Discourse focused on values can never appeal to the universal audience because particular values do not bind all humans.

Ede (1989) criticizes the universal audience as too ideal (and inconsistently presented) because Perelman and Olbrechts-Tyteca write: "Argumentation addressed to a universal audience must convince the reader that the reasons adduced are of a compelling character, that they are self-evident, and possess an absolute and timeless validity, independent of local or historical contingencies" (1969, 32). At least one of the ways that this is problematic is in its apparent contradiction of the claim that it is demonstration and not argumentation that aims at self-evidence. Gross and Dearin do not dispute what is said in the passage, instead they defend it against Ede's criticisms as highlighting a natural paradox in the exercise of constructing universal audiences: "speakers arguing for the real in a particular case must assume its existence in the general case. All such arguments are subject to the paradox that speakers presuppose a concept of timeless validity, a concept clearly subject to contingency" (2003, 37).

A far stronger defense of Perelman and Olbrechts-Tyteca on this point, however, is to challenge whether the view presented in the offending passage is one that they advocate. Gross and Dearin are right to point out that Perelman is first and foremost a philosopher and his approach a philosophical one (2003, 14). To this end, his and Olbrechts-Tyteca's position is set against a traditional philosophical account of objective reason with its own notion of a universal audience. At issue, for example, is that "[t]he Cartesian ideal of universally applicable self-evident knowledge leaves no room for rhetoric and dialectic" (Perelman 1982, 159). Perelman wants to separate the traditional philosophical values of guaranteed objectivity and a rhetoric based on the "knowledge of truth" from his view of argumentation. Philosophers, he insists, must broaden their conception of reason (161). Thus there are two notions of the universal audience in Perelman and

Olbrechts-Tyteca's work: the traditional one they are resisting and the one they are advocating. The passage Ede criticizes relates to the notion that is rejected. "[It] links importance to previously guaranteed objectivity and not to the adherence of an audience, rejects all rhetoric not based on knowledge of the truth" (Perelman 1989, 244). It is the familiarity of traditional notions of universality along with the obscurity of the new model that Perelman is advancing with Olbrechts-Tyteca that makes our task of understanding the latter so difficult.

Still, important points emerge from Gross and Dearin's account, particularly given their attention to the paradox between the audience a speaker confronts and the one that he or she addresses. In the first instance, identifying philosophical and scientific discourses as paradigmatic of discourses addressed to a universal audience draws attention to the important content of those discourses. A philosopher like Socrates, for example, imagines every member of his audience embodying universal standards of rationality. This "accounts," write Gross and Dearin, "for the emphasis in philosophical discourse on logical as distinct from emotional appeals" (2003, 38). Thus we have some suggestion of how the universal audience might make judgments—by appealing to principles of logic that, if not timeless, certainly endure over time and transcend particular audiences.

It is also interesting to consider how the idea that all audiences are rhetorical is cashed out. In contrast to philosophical and scientific discourses, those of public address focus on both facts and values. Gross and Dearin illustrate this with the example of Lincoln's reply to Douglas at Galesburg, October 1858. In identifying certain values in Douglas, Lincoln is raising matters of fact and so addressing a universal audience. But in asserting that certain of such values, like the advocacy of slavery, are wrong, he is appealing to values, and hence a particular audience. Yet on Gross and Dearin's terms both of these audiences are imagined, rhetorical audiences, audiences that exist in the discourse. The significance of this arises in the interpretation given to Perelman's remarks about the way an audience changes over the course of an argument: "We must not forget that the audience, to the degree that speech is effective, changes with its unfolding development" (Perelman 1982, 149). We saw such change as a natural result of the dynamism of dialogical encounters. Gross and Dearin, however, see these changes rooted in the rhetorical audiences. At the end of his address, for example, Lincoln imagines his audience to be different from the one at its starting point (Gross and Dearin

2003, 41). Whether the actual audience is affected seems, on this account, beside the point.

The view of Perelman and Olbrechts-Tyteca's treatment of audience as a coherent theory of rhetorical audience governs the way Gross and Dearin read what is said about relations between the universal and particular audiences. And this reading stems from their initial understanding that Perelman and Olbrechts-Tyteca are not concerned with the effects of argumentation on actual audiences. In spite of the insights in the account, this distancing of rhetorical audiences from the real ones that underlie them is troubling because of the gaps it allows. Or, rather, it does not sufficiently make clear how the rhetorical audiences are rooted in the real ones that, in underlying them, also constrain them in serious ways, thereby restricting the "imagination" of the arguer.

The other account that I will explore is a more developed one. In fact, there is much more to what Crosswhite (1996) has to say about the universal audience than I can discuss here. Consequently, I focus on what is most striking or useful for the current discussion.

To say that we belong to audiences is to suggest something that seems merely incidental to us—a casual feature of ourselves, one that could be other than it is. Crosswhite puts the lie to this. Speaking of "invoked" or "addressed" audiences fails to capture what is at stake here. "Audience" is an event: "That is, audience is something that happens in time, as an event in people's lives, in their talking and writing and communicating in general" (139). This begins to move audience from the periphery to the center, from something casual to something essential. More profoundly, Crosswhite recognizes, "audience is a mode of being, one of the ways human beings *are*" (139). Even though we may constantly move among audiences as our allegiances and interests change, we are always "in audience." Crosswhite stresses the ways in which audiences serve as the evaluators of arguments. But his central insight here extends to all aspects of argumentation. Argumentation is part of our essential being in the world of others because it is audience-forming and audience-directed. Inasmuch as we cannot escape from being "in audience," neither can we escape the realm of argumentation.

From the point of view of evaluation, argumentation may address us through our particular involvements, in groups, families, religions, and so on. Here it speaks to a specific audience to which we belong. But if it addresses us simply as reasonable people, without recourse to the values of the group or religion, or other involvement, then we are addressed as a universal audience (141). Thus Crosswhite recognizes the inextricable link between the universal and particular audiences and, combined with his previous insight, we can realize these as two aspects of our way of being as audience—particularly or universally. This is an important observation about the universal audience, which is so often taken as a vague abstraction. It is from the start rooted not only in real audiences, but in our own experience.[3]

Crosswhite mines Perelman and Olbrechts-Tyteca for the various ways of constructing universal audiences, for what he calls "Rules" for such constructions. In each case, one begins with a particular audience on which imaginative operations are performed. Thus we might set aside the local features of an audience and consider its universal features. Or we might exclude from the particular audience all members who are prejudiced, or irrational, or incompetent. Or we might combine particular audiences so as to cancel out their particularity (eventually reaching all humanity). Or we might imagine a particular audience across time, as similar audiences in other times (145). None of these approaches to construction is foolproof, and conflicts can arise. But they point to useful ways to determine what is particular and what is universal.

Crucial to this determination again is the fact/value distinction to which Gross and Dearin drew attention. As we recall, facts are things that stand fast while values change; facts relate to the universal audience, values to the particular audience. "Thus," Crosswhite writes, "there is a rhetorical way to distinguish the domain of the real (what stands fast) from the domain of the preferred, as well as presumptions and hypotheses about the real (about what we can argue without undermining the rhetorical situation)" (147). Values are what define different groups and account for the disagreements between them. Facts are things about which we expect agreement. "Facts have a universal claim on human beings or else they are not facts" (147). And where values have gained the adherence of the universal audience, they have attained the status of facts.

As an implied criticism of this account, Crosswhite notes that it reflects the attitudes of a liberal European of late modern times. But a more significant criticism that takes him beyond the discussion drawn from Gross and Dearin points to a collapse of this fact/value distinction when it comes to the universal audience. As Christie (2000) observes in another important discussion of Perelman's work, the universal audience is essentially interested in what is good, not only what is "true." In the same vein, Crosswhite notes that "[t]he universalizing interest of reason is essentially an ethical one" (1996, 154). Hence universal audiences embody the evaluative rather than the factual.

It is in relation to a universal audience's embodiment of values that Crosswhite reaches the farthest. In viewing the universal audience this way, we are adopting another external perspective, one that assesses and judges universal audiences themselves. Whose perspective is this? Crosswhite argues that the universal audience of *The New Rhetoric* can be better understood as a paragon audience, a model of perfection or excellence. In an implicit extension of Perelman and Olbrechts-Tyteca's work, Crosswhite suggests,

> [f]rom within the rhetorical situation from which a universal audi-ence arises, universality is its defining feature. However, viewed from "outside," relative universality is only one of the features of a paragon audience, and not the only defining feature. From a distance, local concepts of universality are also agreements on concrete values. (151)

He then introduces the concept of an "undefined universal audi-ence," which is mentioned only once in *The New Rhetoric* (1969, 35). This is what is used to judge whether the universal audience drawn from a particular audience is appropriate. *It* is the audience for our construction of a universal audience.

There may seem a danger here of slipping into a kind of "Third Man" criticism that was advanced against Plato's Forms, where each fur-ther "external" audience requires yet another more distanced audience to judge *its* appropriateness. But Crosswhite, like Perelman and Olbrechts-Tyteca, counters this by stressing the different kind of univer-sality involved. It is undefined in the sense that it is not tied to any particular audience. Of course, it is the grounds for its judgments that interest us. Crosswhite argues for the familiarity of such a move of addressing the undefined universal audience, "even if one does not understand exactly what it is." We see it whenever an audience responds to us in ways we had not expected yet we recognize to be legitimate. How do we make this recognition? Because operating in us is an (empty) idea of an undefined universal audience, "which allows us to recognize the legitimacy of its responses once they do find a voice" (1996, 153).

It is from here just a small step to the conclusion that the princi-ples of reason (as seen in logical principles and rules), as we currently understand them, are what we mean by the judgments of a universal audience. Logic gives us real universalizability. "At our current evolutionary and historical-cultural location, we have a relatively well-defined idea of what counts as a competent human being. In its most stripped-down form, it is captured in some basic rules of reason" (159).

Crosswhite, then, arrives at the place where the critic stands who judges the universal audience unnecessary beside the principles of logic. But he arrives there having taken an important journey in order to *explain* the source of these principles of logic in the universal audience, and the universal audience in particular audiences. Thus we see how our notions of what is reasonable can change over time, just as our understanding of the principles of reason changes. Current innovation in informal logic and rhetoric would appear to be an indication of just this point. Thus Johnson was justified earlier in his suspicion that logical standards for the evaluation of arguments are active in the universal audience. But this does not make the rhetorical subordinate to the logical. On the contrary, we see here how the rhetorical is the vehicle for the development and expression of the logical, for the logical is a product of audience and can be nothing more, nor less.

❖ REAPPRAISING THE UNIVERSAL AUDIENCE

In light of the foregoing discussion some clarification on points already expressed is in order. Perelman and Olbrechts-Tyteca's first and foremost audience is the person or group to be persuaded, it is the audience that *personalizes* the argument (Perelman 1982, 3). This personalizing of arguments, in ways that make them a co-venture, is in part what prevents the exploitation and abuse of audiences characteristic of traditional criticisms. Argumentation acts upon an audience, to be sure, and is intended to modify its convictions. But "it tries to gain a meeting of minds instead of imposing its will through constraint or conditioning" (1982, 11). This echoes the invitational rhetoric of early Greeks and recent accounts and reinforces the real nature of the audiences involved. It also reinforces the cooperative nature of argumentation that emerged from Chapter 4. Insofar as I imagine my audience, what I imagine is an anticipation of their likely response, given who they are and what they believe, to what I say or write. I have no license to construct something not rooted in the real. Doing so would be counterproductive to my endeavors. And I must be able to justify the anticipated responses in terms of what is likely, given what is known of my audience. This was graphically demonstrated with the case of the rhetorical figure *prolepsis* in Chapter 3.

Nor is my audience necessarily those who hear or read what I say. If my intention is to reinforce, say, the political views of the majority of those present on a particular occasion, then that there are others present who do not share such views, or that the speech may be printed and more widely disseminated, is incidental to my intentions, with their aim at a specific audience. On the other hand, I may deliberately intend a composite audience, thereby widening my scope so as to encompass all (or more) of those present, and I construct my argument according to this change of intended audience. Either way, my audience is those I want to consider and have work with my arguments (Perelman and Olbrechts-Tyteca 1969, 19; Perelman 1982, 14).

If I envision those I address as a universal audience, then I appeal to reason. I aim to convince them as reasonable people. In this way, my premises are universalizable and should be "acceptable in principle to all members of the universal audience" (Perelman 1982, 18). Now my exercise has shifted focus, while still having as its principal goal the responses of a particular person or group of people. But here the issue or the circumstances lead me to aspire to a firmer conviction and hence my audience's adherence must be consistent with what is acceptable in principle to reasonable people. There is no mystery to this.

It follows that the premises with which an arguer begins are crucial to the success of the outcome. Where convictions are desired, those premises must be acceptable to both the particular audience and the universal audience. But how do we know what is acceptable to a universal audience? Perelman answers this through his discussion of presumptions.

Presumptions are things that, while not having the status of facts or truths, "furnish a sufficient basis upon which to rest a reasonable conviction" (1982, 24). These are agreements that are sufficiently widespread that anyone who wants to reject them must give good reasons for doing so. In other words, a presumption imposes a burden of proof on anyone who wants to oppose it.

While they can be challenged, then, presumptions are well enough established in a community to serve as reasonable basic premises. Perelman and Olbrechts-Tyteca list some common presumptions that might serve in this way:

Let us mention some common presumptions: the presumption that the quality of an act reveals the quality of the person responsible for it; the presumption of natural truthfulness by which our first reaction is to accept what someone tells us as being true, which is accepted as long and insofar as we have no cause for distrust; the presumption of interest leading us to conclude that any statement brought to our knowledge is supposed to be of interest to us; the presumption concerning the sensible character of any human action. (1969, 70–71)

Gaskins (1992) has criticized Perelman and Olbrechts-Tyteca's notion of presumptions as being "simply localized biases or prejudices, characteristic of discrete groups but certainly not binding on the community as a whole" (34). The examples just provided, however, suggest that they are far more widespread and fundamental, and while they may not be "binding," it is not clear that such a constraint is intended, or even consistent with the basic idea.

Beyond such widely shared agreements, we may also draw presumptions from what we know of the relevant cognitive environment, as this idea was discussed in the first section of the present chapter and in Chapter 1. The point here is that we are justified in presuming that something is widely accepted if we know it exists in the appropriate cognitive environment. The test for this, we recall, is not whether everyone in our intended audience is known to share knowledge, but whether they live in such environments that we can attribute certain presumptions to them. Thus we can justify our claims that such and such is a presumption by recourse to an actual cognitive environment.

Presumptions are connected with what is normal and likely. In fact, *this* claim, Perelman and Olbrechts-Tyteca hold, is itself a presumption accepted by all audiences (1969, 71). Our ability to know and appeal to what is normal depends in turn on the concept of inertia as Perelman and Olbrechts-Tyteca explicate it.

For Perelman and Olbrechts-Tyteca, reason is governed by a force that gives it stability and regularity, a force comparable to the effect of inertia in physics. As they explain this,

In science certain propositions are set apart and qualified as axioms and are thus explicitly granted a privileged position within the system. . . . In most cases, however, a speaker has no firmer support for his presumptions than psychical and social inertia which are the equivalent in consciousness and society of the inertia in physics. It can be presumed, failing proof to the contrary, that the attitude previously adopted—the opinion expressed, the behavior preferred—will continue in the future, either from a desire for coherency or from force of habit. (1969, 105–106)

Inertia is what gives value to the normal and habitual. At any point in time, reason, embodied in real communities, has a bedrock of attitudes, opinions, and beliefs that are stable and widely accepted. The soundness of argumentation is supported by this ground of acceptability. The obvious institutional examples of this are the body of legal rulings that constitute precedent in law. They represent a tradition of reasoning that requires no justification and is used to illuminate and judge new cases.

Against the background of tradition, change must be justified, whether by pointing out a modification that circumstances necessitate, or an improvement which, while not necessary, is dictated by various goods that are favored. Argumentation is the tool to effect such change. How this change is justified, how the need for it is recognized, points us to the central idea in Perelman and Olbrechts-Tyteca's account. "The rule of justice," they write, " furnishes the foundation which makes it possible to pass from earlier cases to future cases. It makes it possible to present the use of precedent in the form of a quasi-logical argument" (1969, 219).[4]

The link here is the idea of precedent. Precedents set standards for treating similar cases in similar ways. The rule of justice, likewise, "requires giving identical treatment to beings or situations of the same kind" (218). "Justice," for Perelman, is a principle of action that demands the same treatment for beings of the same essential category (1982, 16). The stress on a principle of *action* here is crucial, because argumentation that is effective in bringing about a change in the minds of an audience "tends to produce action" (155). Furthermore, Perelman believes that the rule of justice is our most fundamental and most widely accepted presumption. No matter how much we may disagree on other matters, we agree in principle that those who are equal deserve the same treatment. This insight is captured in all interpretations of Perelman and Olbrechts-Tyteca's work that I have reviewed. No matter how else they might differ, they regard the rule of justice as central (Gross and Dearin 2003, 24–25).

In *The New Rhetoric*, the rule of justice becomes the standard of judgment for the strength of arguments: "this strength is appraised by application of the rule of justice: that which was capable of convincing in a specific situation will appear to be convincing in a similar or analogous situation" (Perelman and Olbrechts-Tyteca 1969, 464). Who makes this judgment? Since they speak here of convincing, and an early discussion had assigned this to argumentation that presumes to gain the adherence of every rational being (28), then this is a role of a universal audience. In fact, as Crosswhite (2000) also observes, this discussion of the strength of arguments is the only place where the universal audience is identified with the application of the rule of justice.

❖ APPLYING THE IDEA OF A UNIVERSAL AUDIENCE

Let us reflect on what we have gathered in the previous sections: The *ground* (rationale, justification) for Perelman and Olbrechts-Tyteca's universal audience is the particular audience that "anchors" it. I use this term deliberately. As was recognized in the previous chapter, particular audiences are notoriously self-interested and prejudiced. "Effective" rhetoric is often seen to have license (or take license) to exploit such traits. We have seen how Perelman and Olbrechts-Tyteca resist this, and the kind of morality we saw associated with a Bakhtinian model would add its agreement to such resistance. While the success of their rhetoric is the ability to gain the adherence of an audience, they do not sacrifice reasonableness to effectiveness. Any universal audience, as a representation of reasonableness in a specific context, cannot value effectiveness over reasonableness. This would be self-contradictory. The prejudices are still there, but factored out by the particular audience insofar as the universal audience is active in it.

On this model, the particular audience is brought to agreement on its own terms; on terms that are internal to it, that it recognizes and supports. Producing and evaluating argumentation involves learning about what is reasonable, rethinking it, adding to it, and taking from it. The *source* for this is the particular audience and its own values, and it is brought to recognize these and, perhaps, desires to modify them through argumentation. There is no other empirical ground. And the subsequent test of approval of what results is the particular audience. The process is the construction of a universal audience. And the result is the uncovering of what is held to be reasonable, tested and confirmed as such. There is nowhere else to look for our standard of reasonableness other than to reasoners themselves as they self-consciously engage in this activity.

Again from this, we can see how universal audiences must develop over time as our attitudes toward, and understanding of, what is reasonable changes. The degree of change involved depends always on the communities in question and the ways in which they come to agree with or challenge the views of each other. In regulating a dispute between communities (understood in all the variety the term "community" licenses), seen now as particular audiences, we step back and try to derive a common universal audience that reflects their agreements and in light of which we might hope to move them forward. But, as we have also seen, such a procedure is not a panacea for dispute resolution, no matter how much it may contribute to such a possibility. What the universal audience in such a circumstance makes possible is a common insight into the shared aspects of the communities involved, an insight that can foster understanding, and perhaps no more.

Constructing a Universal Audience

As Gross and Dearin rightly observe, the construction of a universal audience is an operation of the imagination. But as we saw also from the rules for such constructions that Crosswhite extracted from Perelman and Olbrechts-Tyteca, this is an imaginative operation *on* a real audience that exists, whether it be the one I want to convince by arguing *with* them and inviting them to recognize a conclusion to which they should adhere, or the one that I need to extract in order to evaluate argumentation that has been addressed to me as an audience, or to some audience in which I have no involvement (where I am purely an evaluator). In the first type of cases, I am an arguer; in the second, I am an evaluator. While much of the procedure would appear to be the same in both enterprises, the different goals elicit some different features in terms of, say, testing the appropriateness of the universal audience invoked.

To take a case in point, I may decide to argue that community service is something we ought to do. Although I may hold this as a general claim, supportable on that level, I will likely in the first instance apply it in a specific circumstance, arguing to people in my own community. Here, I know particular features about them, drawing on local background and information, constructing premises that are acceptable to them because they involve this information. Taking my "ought" in its broadest senses, I can appeal to ways in which a community becomes stronger and richer through such service, hence appealing to the self-interest of the audience in having a better place to live; and I can appeal to grounds that merit certain types of sacrifice, of time and finances, by calling upon values that are shared by members of the community related to indirectly expressed notions of the "good" held in common.

If I wish to aim at conviction rather than mere persuasion, I need to consider my audience as reasonable people and ensure that my argumentation will be acceptable to them on that basis. I am effectively testing my argument for its reasonableness, looking for ways in which it fails to take note of events known in the community that might undermine some of my premises (a service agency, for example, that has received bad publicity for wasting, or worse, the help it received from volunteers), for ways in which it contradicts other values that have been expressed. I test the relevance of its parts to the audience I have in mind. I ensure that my argumentation does not violate rules of language that the reasonable element in my audience would catch. Here, of course, my audience is rhetorical in the ways that concern Gross and Dearin, because I am imagining reactions that might, but have not, occurred and addressing them. Here, also, are principles of logical analysis that were suspected to be at work in the activity of invoking a universal audience. But, as noted earlier, this is logic brought to bear upon a rhetorical situation, activated by it. Abstract principles have no real bearing on argumentation *until* they are brought alive in real situations, used by, or tested against, real audiences. Hence the rhetorical underlies this use.

Addressing a Universal Audience

We have turned for our understanding of what is "reasonable" to real audiences, rather than to the empty standards of devices like the Martian critic or the abstract principles of logic. The latter, indeed important and "real" in their own way, only gain that importance and reality for us insofar as they can be used in argumentation (rather than the principles of self-evidence and the like, which are immune to argumentation and hence outside of it).

Here, then, we can be interested in the reasonable in two ways: in how it informs arguments, validates them; and how it is modified by arguments. In the first case, the reasonable informs arguments insofar as they meet the conditions of the cognitive environment of the audience involved. Successfully doing so ensures that an argument has the important relationship of relevance to the audience. We are relevant insofar as we take into consideration the cognitive environment of the particular audience and construct our reasoning accordingly. Perelman and Olbrechts-Tyteca's principle of inertia comes into play here. In anticipating and acquiring the agreement of my audience about basic premises (those that can be presumed in the ways discussed in the previous section), I engage the universal audience within my particular audience. My argumentation is reasonable to my audience to the degree that the premises are acceptable as basic in this way. Testing for this should not be difficult in most cases: it involves asking where the presumption lies with respect to a specific premise, with me as the arguer who must defend it (to search for a more basic premise that is acceptable), or with any member of the audience who would challenge it.

In the strongest type of effect on an audience, I win the adherence of my audience to the conclusion by modifying their cognitive environment so as to introduce the right kinds of evidence for that audience in the right relations to the conclusion. Again, this is a combination of audience-relevance and premise-relevance, the former relating the argumentation to its context, the latter relating the premises of the argument to its conclusion (Tindale 1999a, Chapter 4). As a logical principle, premise-relevance gains its utility from its relation to audience-relevance in specific contexts.

We have seen in earlier chapters of this book ways in which the cognitive environment may be modified by the evidence so as to bring about adherence to the conclusion, so it would be unproductive to repeat them here. But of central interest in this respect is the way the rhetorical arguer makes *present* various aspects of the cognitive environment so that it registers in the audience's minds, encouraging the drawing of inferences and the conviction an audience brings about within itself. Effective here would be the employment of rhetorical figures *as* arguments in the ways explained in Chapter 3; figures that evoke the experience of the reasoning and invite collaboration.

To a great extent, the process discussed above involves the reasonable within an audience being successfully activated and directed. More difficult is to imagine the ways in which the reasonable itself is brought to change. Perelman and Olbrechts-Tyteca's discussion of inertia emphasizes this difficulty. Still it does change, as we know. My understanding of what is reasonable changes when I recognize that another person's point or response to myself has merit, deserves serious consideration, and is then to be adopted over what I have proposed. In being capable of such recognition, in being able to step out of my own perspective with its attachments and interests and take an "objective" stance on the exchange, I must activate the reasonable within me and then add to it, modifying it. After the exercise I no longer think in the same way. I hold some particular claim or position to be reasonable that I did not hold before. And on a more general or abstract level, my understanding of what is reasonable *per se* has changed. And I have convinced myself of this, moved by my firsthand recognition of the force of good argument.

In a sense, then, the reasonable changes insofar as a different universal audience is addressed and convinced. It changes whenever we modify our ideas about reason itself and the principles that "govern" it. This book, in its modest way, is an attempt in that direction, and to that end imagines a universal audience with the background and interests to engage its arguments and reflect on them. And perhaps, in the manner that Crosswhite suggested, to be arrested and convicted by them.

Of course, it is insufficient to say that sometimes we recognize the correctness of someone's criticisms of our ideas, and that the feature within us that makes that recognition is the judgment of a detached and disinterested reason. But this is at least enough to show that we do change our ideas when we are brought to "see" in this way, and that the process does involve an activity of reason within us that is detached from associations with our particular interests. In an analogous way we can imagine this taking place with larger and larger audiences, experiencing this disinterested reason and "seeing" the need to change because of the incorrectness of their views (even if the actual changes take longer to come about). Part of what warrants such changes must be something like Perelman and Olbrechts-Tyteca's rule of justice that does more than perpetuate the traditions of precedents, but creates those precedents through modifications of analogous, but not identical, cases.

Evaluating a Universal Audience

Among the criticisms of the universal audience paraded at the start of the chapter, one remains as having received scant attention in the ensuing discussions. This is the charge that rhetorical considerations seem rarely pertinent to the assessment of arguments.[5] In particular, while I must consider what an arguer took her audience to be if I want fairly to understand her argument, it is not clear how audience comes into play when I am trying to decide myself whether to change my mind once the argument has been determined.

To a certain degree, this may be a case of failing to see what is closest to hand, for it is tantamount to asking where the audience is when I am the audience. As Crosswhite poignantly instructs us, we are always "in audience." Of course, in light of some of the other things that have been considered in this chapter, we might want to revise our understanding of this insight. For while I may always be "in audience," while this is an essential aspect of my being in the world, I am not always part of an audience directly addressed by an argument, or the intended audience for an argument. Crosswhite's point can better help us here if we recognize that we always can have the perspective of an audience and hence understand what it can mean to be addressed by any particular discourse (even if we do not understand the particularities of that address, that is, those features that render it for a particular audience in which we are not included). Hence we can pick up a text intended for an audience that may have disappeared long ago and appreciate it from *an* audience's perspective. That is, we can see what it demands of them and the kinds of things it is assuming about them; we appreciate what it would mean to be addressed by that text.

To this we need then add a further distinction to cover two types of evaluation: one in which I am part of the intended audience and one in which I am not (or it is not clear whether I am). I will call the first type of evaluation *engaged* and the second *unengaged,* thereby directly indicating how audience must enter into argument evaluation.

Under the dialogical account developed in previous chapters, we can recognize the engaged evaluation as that which characterizes the ongoing activity of argumentative exchange at its most dynamic. This type of evaluation is coextensive with the development of the argument; it is part of the dialogical exchange of anticipation and response. "Evaluation," from an essentially logical point of view, tends to consider an argument as something finished with neatly defined parameters. We have had difficulty with viewing it so cleanly. Arguments are activities in time, defined by their participants and defining those participants. Thus I become an audience for an argument through such engagement. And as I enter into the exchanges, which evaluation can partly invite me to do, I become co-arguer, as we have seen. From this perspective, as I start to review the reasoning, I should see something of myself mirrored there, if the initiator of the argument (the "arguer") has done her job well. For she will have developed her discourse with me in mind, my beliefs and attitudes, such that I should find myself addressed in the discourse, and even my responses anticipated. Where she has not done this well, and I was the intended audience (or part of it), then this argument will likely fail to gain my serious consideration. This is a measure of its weakness. It does not invite me, because it fails to be for me. Once engaged, as a contributor to the exchange, I can look both for what speaks to me particularly and to what speaks to the principle of reason within me. And bringing the skills of a good evaluator to my engagement, I will be particularly alert to the latter. Here, points such as have already been discussed become central: is the discourse relevant to me and does it also exhibit internal relevance between its parts? Have fallacies been committed? And so forth. The question of fallacy is still an appropriate one under this approach to argumentation, even if the notion of "fallacy" changes in a rhetorical account,[6] because these are violations of the principles of good reason. These change over time, and some audiences will always be deceived by them, it seems. But as an evaluator, and particularly an engaged evaluator, these are always a concern for me.

Unengaged evaluation characterizes classroom analyses as well as the aware readings of arguments for which we are not part of the audience—historical arguments, for example. But while these are distinguished in that the evaluator is not a contributor to the argumentative exchange, the unengaged and engaged evaluations are not necessarily so distinct, and the unengaged can be profitably influenced by the hypothetical existence of the engaged. We can perform engaged evaluations because we can participate in argumentation, and we can do this because we stand socially "in audience." Thus, we can bring much that we learn from being engaged to the more abstract exercises of unengaged evaluations. What is lost through not having intimate understandings of the particularities of the case can be compensated for by the stance of objectivity that may be possible when we have nothing at stake in the outcome. Here, more than anywhere, we act like a universal audience for that argument. Not abstractly, though, for we are still asking what is reasonable in this context with its particular circumstances. That is, how should the principles of reason, the questions of acceptability and relevance, have been played out here? If we find the argument (treated as complete, as unengaged readings will tend to do) wanting in any of these respects, we can judge that the arguer failed to construct the appropriate universal audience for the context. How serious a failure we have in any particular circumstance will depend on the specific problems involved, which the details of the evaluation must work out and weigh.

❖ CONCLUSION

Audiences are always at issue, then, and a universal audience particularly so. But as a source of reasonableness in argumentation, a universal audience succeeds where others fail. The key problem with the Martian cases of the previous chapter was the absence of any real objective source standing behind the standard. A universal audience meets this condition insofar as it is anchored by a real, particular audience. This also means that there are recognized means of accessing and evaluating the standard. If difficulties remain in understanding and applying the standard, then the fault lies in our expectation, given the complexity of argumentation itself, that our means of treating it would ever be straightforward. In the final analysis, this seems a better, more legitimately grounded standard than any other available. The standard of the universal audience has the attractive feature of confronting us with the question of what counts as reasonable and the realization that in any particular case it has not been decided in advance. What is ultimately so disconcerting about Martian cases is that they assume otherwise and leave no room for debate. Some of us, governed as we might be by individual prejudice, may prefer a standard that we control and adapt to suit our inclinations. A visitor from Mars, though, would find that quite absurd.

❖ NOTES

1. As Gross and Dearin (2003, 134) observe, Perelman and Olbrechts-Tyteca tend to pay little direct attention to the role of emotion in argumentation.

2. Negative readings such as Ray (1978), Ede (1989), and van Eemeren and Grootendorst (1995) have been addressed elsewhere (Tindale 1999a, 87–89; Crosswhite 1995).

3. Thus Crosswhite avoids the difficulties of those like Habermas and Rawls who attempt to ground conceptions of reasonableness in ideal audiences, because the argumentation directed at such audiences is abstract and formal (1996, 150).

4. Quasi-logical arguments gain their power to convince from their similarity to the formal reasoning of logic and mathematics (Perelman and Olbrechts-Tyteca 1969, 193).

5. I owe the formulation of this criticism to J. Anthony Blair in a paper delivered at the National Communication Association annual conference, Seattle 2000.

6. For a discussion of fallacies of process in rhetorical argumentation see Tindale 1999a, 157–181 and 2004.

7

The Truth About Orangutans: Conflicting Criteria of Premise Adequacy

❖ INTRODUCTION: DEEP DISAGREEMENTS
BETWEEN LOGIC AND RHETORIC

Argumentation aims at action, more than it aims at truth. That, at least, is one of the prominent sub-texts of the previous chapter. If, as Crosswhite (1996, 151) indicates, universal audiences are more embodiments of a concept of good than of what is true or factual,[1] then this raises questions about the nature of truth and its role in argumentation, along with suggestions about the types of evidence that should interest us. This issue is more than incidental to our project. The kind of theory of argumentation being discussed here takes direction from Perelman and Olbrechts-Tyteca's central claim that the theory of argumentation can help develop "the justification of the possibility of a human community in the sphere of action when this justification cannot be based on a reality or objective truth" (Perelman and Olbrechts-Tyteca 1969, 514). This chapter will investigate the claim that "truth" is an important criterion for evaluating argumentation, and will be particularly concerned to inquire into the sense of "truth" involved. Dissatisfied by the outcome of this inquiry, the competing criterion—acceptability—is proposed as the better choice for evaluating rhetorical arguments.

Plato challenged the Sophists for failing to advance questions about the essential truth of things, for exercising their wares in the public arena without caring to have their notions of social good informed by a grounding in objective truth. As we saw in Chapter 2, that dispute can more profitably be cast as one involving conflicting notions of the "true," and the Sophists' treatments and applications of an emerging rhetoric were rich and vibrant and perfectly suited to the ends they envisioned. Those lessons should be recalled now.

The dispute between Plato (and Aristotle) and the Sophists has been rehearsed often in the traditions of Western thought, with the Platonic preference for objective truth holding sway and dominating agendas to such a degree that the Sophists and their ideas were relegated to the shadows and largely ignored. Their rehabilitation is still incomplete, with the task of reconstructing Sophistic argumentation an important part of that unfinished project. We might have thought to be free now from the vestiges of such ancient debates in a time when both logic and rhetoric have been reanimated by fresh breaths of insight prompted by concerns to make them more amenable to everyday use. At root, however, disputes over the appropriate ends and criteria for argumentation still plague us, even as we make advances on other fronts.

As an indication of the kind of disagreement involved, consider again the work of Johnson, one of the more innovative practitioners of informal logic. Johnson (2000a) still finds rhetoric to be the culprit in what he thinks ails theories of informal reasoning: "Many informal logicians," he writes, "have adopted acceptability as a criterion of premise adequacy. In dropping the truth requirement, informal logicians have—so I believe—been persuaded by rhetorical values and concerns" (271).

Instead, insists Johnson, a viable theory of evaluation must include both truth and acceptability. This gives rise to what he calls the "Integration Problem" (191), which asks how a theory of argument evaluation is to include both an acceptability criterion and a truth criterion when they can sometimes come into conflict. What he has to say in this regard is both instructive and important, allowing us to test the merits of the approach advanced in this book against a well-considered alternative.

According to Johnson: "The truth criterion concerns the relationship between the premise and the state of affairs in the world. The acceptability criterion concerns the relationship between the premise and the audience" (2000a, 336–337). From this it follows that many arguments will satisfy both. Moreover, since all arguments are addressed to an audience, the acceptability requirement will have a broader applicability than the truth requirement.

For Johnson, problems arise when it is determined that a given premise is true but not acceptable, or when it is false and acceptable. Clearly, on this reading, arguments, or at least their premises, may have to mediate between a state of affairs in the world and what the intended audience believes and requires. If our concern is that of a critic, who elsewhere he identifies as a "participant" (340), then the matter is more straightforward and on either of the imagined outcomes the argument would be judged fatally flawed. But the perspective of evaluation raises the key question of whether an argument is a good one if it exhibits the tension between the two criteria, which is effectively to ask which criterion should have priority.

To a certain degree, Johnson's solution to the integration problem is simple and noncontroversial: he proposes that informal logic should adopt the truth requirement, while rhetoric will adopt the acceptability requirement (2000a, 271). In fact, Johnson is proposing much more. In his mind, the truth requirement, and a perspective that adopts it, is to be preferred because it is more rational, and so any tension between the two criteria should be resolved in favor of the truth criterion (337).

There are several things to challenge in such a claim. In the first instance, appealing to a criterion of truth seems ill advised because the criterion itself is vague and generally problematic. In the second case, a truth criterion is unnecessary because the acceptability requirement is perfectly adequate and no less rational if we appreciate it from a rhetorical point of view. In developing the discussion of this chapter, I will support both these assertions.

❖ HAMBLIN'S ORANGUTANS

Johnson gives separate consideration to cases presenting the tension between the criteria. In the first case, where a premise is false but acceptable, he allows that it may be rational for someone to be persuaded by an argument that has a premise that subsequently turns out to be false, but he is concerned an arguer might knowingly advance a false premise because an audience will accept it. This is to present the issue in terms of the behavior and character of the arguer, avoiding the question of how the premise is known to be false (by the arguer, but not the audience).

Shifting from the perspective of the arguer to that of the evaluator, the same decision holds: "If he or she believes the premise is false, the evaluator has a compelling reason for not accepting the premise" (2000a, 338). Here, as later, the evaluator is judging the merits of the argument *in and of itself,* and not in relation to any audience or context. This helps clarify the two very separate operations at work in Johnson's theory of evaluation—one looking at the world and the argument's fit there, and the other looking to the audience. "A bad argument does not . . . cease to be a bad argument just because it is an argument that some people may be justified in accepting" (339).

The second case arises when a premise is true but unacceptable. Should an arguer advance a premise that the audience is not expected to accept even though it is true? If his theory was "rhetorically driven," Johnson would answer this in the negative. But on his model, this solution violates the requirement of manifest rationality, and the arguer is exhorted to find a way to make the premise acceptable. Nor would such an argument be good for an evaluator, who would also require support for the premise. Here the acceptability requirement has priority.

With these points made, Johnson addresses the position of Hamblin (1970), who rejects alethic criteria, that is, principally, the requirement that an argument's premises be true (234). Generally Hamblin argues that alethic criteria are neither sufficient nor necessary.

With respect to the first of these points, Hamblin questions the use of premises that are true if no one knows they are true. To illustrate the problem he provides several examples, including the following one about orangutans:

> [T]he argument that oranges are good for orang-utans because they contain dietary supplements might or might not carry some weight in the second half of the twentieth century but would rightly carry none at all as between two ancient Romans who had never heard of vitamins. (232)

A recipient of such an argument, suggests Hamblin, would not so much question the truth of the premise as question how the arguer *knows* the premise. That is, it is its epistemic status rather than its truth that is being questioned. Hence a requirement that an argument's premises be true is not sufficient; they must be *known* to be true. To whom should this be known? Johnson's tack, as we have seen, is to focus on what the arguer knows. But if, like Hamblin, we are talking about the *use* of the premises, we should be focusing on what the audience knows. In terms of the discussion of the previous chapter, this knowledge would be required within the cognitive environment.

The second part to Hamblin's charge, that alethic tests are not necessary, stems from the fact that not all people will be able to follow an inference from a true premise to a conclusion implied by it, so it is not enough for the conclusion to follow, it must be acknowledged to do so—another epistemic criterion. However, we might stop before this second move and suggest that if what is at stake is a requirement that a premise be known in the appropriate cognitive environment, then this also renders truth unnecessary because we are now talking clearly about the audience and what information is available. In terms of the dual directionality of Johnson's problem, the focus shifts away from the world to the context of the audience.

Johnson's concerns with Hamblin's rejection of alethic criteria revolve around the orangutan example. First, he finds the example too tersely presented. To be useful, we must imagine for it a dispute arising among ancient Romans over the nurturing of orangutans, a dispute that would involve alternatives and reasons for those alternatives. Second, the example itself is alleged to be misdiagnosed. The reason the Romans should reject the argument is not because they do not know the premise to be true, but because it would be unintelligible to them. To persuade rationally, an arguer should avoid premises the audience will not understand at all. "Thus, the problem for the Romans would not be knowing whether the premise is true but, rather, would be understanding its meaning" (Johnson 2000a, 185). Thus Hamblin's case against the truth requirement is judged unsuccessful, at least on this front.

There is always a potential for problems when employing hypothetical examples. If the example fails, this has serious, although not necessarily fatal, repercussions for the point it is intended to illustrate. Hamblin asks us to imagine a case where an audience cannot accept true premises because that truth has no meaning for them and cannot enter into their deliberations in any way. Rather than allow that this is one of the cases where acceptability would have priority, Johnson looks to unpack the example, to show that it is inadequate for the purpose intended. We should not overlook, though, that in cases where we fail to accept a premise, or appreciate its truth, we will in fact engage in a dialectical exchange of the kind envisaged by Hamblin and preferred by Johnson. Asking the arguer, "how do you know?" is a legitimate and common attempt to establish where the burden of proof lies.

Premises are acceptable, unacceptable, or questionable to a specific audience (and, in the terms set out in the previous chapter, to a universal audience). In Hamblin's orangutan case, the premise is, as Johnson rightly observes, unacceptable to this audience because the arguer cannot meet the burden of proof that he or she is obliged to meet. This is because what is required to support that premise and render it meaningful is not available at that time. Hamblin is undone by the hypothetical nature of his example. Bad choice. If the audience cannot understand such a premise, then, for the same reason, the arguer could not be expected to either. The orangutan example, however, is supposed to represent a *kind* of argument, and it is not the only one offered.

Consider Hamblin's first suggestion: "If I argue that the Martian canals are not man-made because there never has been organic life on Mars . . ." (1970, 236). Here the premise is not obviously unacceptable; rather, it is questionable, if we imagine a general audience of intelligent people. That is, while the premise that there has never been organic life on Mars is intelligible to us, we have grounds neither to accept nor yet reject it. It remains questionable to us (and in a weaker sense, cannot be accepted) until the arguer assumes the burden of proof to provide support and succeeds or fails in that effort. If he fails, we will not accept the premise. We reject it not because it is false (we remain skeptical on this point), but because it does not work as a reason for us to accept the conclusion that the Martian canals are not man-made. Yet, for those who insist on a correspondence between our proposition and the world, the premise "there has never been organic life on Mars" is either true or false. This is Hamblin's point.[2]

Again, Johnson's best response might be to add this to the category of cases in which acceptability is the primary criterion. But this should lead us to ask when this is *not* the case. That is, what cases have truth as the primary criterion, and are they enough to matter?

Another tack Hamblin takes in criticizing the truth criterion is to charge that truth and validity "are onlookers' concepts and presuppose a God's-eye-view of the arena" (1970, 242). With respect to the claim about validity, Johnson judges it both irrelevant, because validity is a logical rather than epistemic or alethic concept, and wrong, because we can assess whether a conclusion follows from a premise without any recourse to a nonhuman perspective.[3]

With respect to truth, though, Johnson allows that the criticism carries some weight. Or at least it carries weight with regard to some theories of truth, like "certain forms of the correspondence theory [that] presuppose omniscience" (2000a, 196). But other theories of truth, like the coherence, idealist, pragmatist, instrumentalist, or relativist, do not presuppose such a perspective, and so a theory of evaluation could avoid Hamblin's objection by framing its truth criterion in terms of one of these theories. He reiterates the point, noting that a correspondence theory of truth "would appear to be open to the sorts of criticism mentioned by Hamblin" (198). Instead, "a relativistic concept of truth would make for a theory that is largely indistinguishable from theories governed by dialectical criteria" (198).

Two things should be observed here: If by "dialectical criteria" we are to understand some notion of acceptability, then given the baggage that accompanies the idea of truth in argumentation (if we can pin it down to any particular theory), and granting that theories governed by truth criteria and dialectical criteria would be "largely indistinguishable," we would simply be better advised to adopt the notion of acceptability.

A second point is more problematic for Johnson and his theory of evaluation. The one theory of truth he allows to be susceptible to Hamblin's criticism and thus dismisses is the correspondence theory. Yet, as we saw earlier, this is the very theory his model ends up adopting: "The truth criterion concerns the relationship between the premise and the state of affairs in the world. The acceptability criterion concerns the relationship between the premise and the audience" (2000a, 336–337). In fairness to Johnson, what he is attempting in his work *Manifest Rationality* is not a developed account of the truth criterion, but an argument supporting its necessity and giving some sense of what such a criterion should involve (Johnson 2002, 323). But his own difficulty in clarifying a consistent notion of truth to underlie the truth criterion points to the problems that can be involved in pinning this down, and sharpens our question: What notion of "truth" is assumed by any truth criterion?

Beyond his eventual problematic adoption of a correspondence theory of truth, Johnson gives some other pointers about the nature of this truth and why it is required. He writes, for example, in ways that seem to relate it most clearly to the domain of science, explaining why he resists a wholesale adoption of a truth requirement:

> As one moves away from science and toward other spheres of reasoning—the practical sphere of human decision making: the areas of morals, ethics, politics and everyday human affairs—that doctrine begins to seem questionable. This is not because the criterion of truth is inapplicable to human affairs but rather because, as one reviews the nature and functions of argumentation in this arena, it seems clear that premises need not be true in order for the argument to be a good one. (196)

While this does not preclude the use of the truth requirement for arguments outside of the domain of science, it goes a long way toward encouraging such a restriction, perhaps because science is more amenable to views of truth along the lines of a correspondence theory.

Johnson's strongest argument for the truth requirement is an indirect argument that involves pointing out that theorists who thought they had abandoned the use of a truth criterion turn out to still be appealing to it in all kinds of ways. Thus, the argument appears to be, the truth requirement is necessary because people who do argument evaluation cannot avoid using it. It creeps in through the use of inconsistency, contradiction, assumption, and validity. And Johnson even believes it may be required to make "acceptability" intelligible. As an example of what he has in mind, he cites his own work with Blair (1993).[4] While they had not advanced a truth requirement for premise adequacy, they assumed it in judging premises inconsistent if they could not be true together, and in testing for relevance on the basis of whether the truth of a premise dictated the truth of a conclusion (2000a, 198). But while the underlying use of the term "truth" is undoubtedly there in the work of Johnson and Blair as well as many other argumentation theorists, this commits none of them to a full-fledged notion of a truth criterion that is *necessary*, nor does it explain how truth is being understood in such instances. If it is being used loosely in a way actually tantamount to "acceptability," then, again, there might be reasons for preferring the latter designation. We must delay a decision about this until we have a clearer idea of how both "truth" and "acceptability" are being used and whether there is a clear concept behind either of these terms.

❖ THE RHETORIC OF PHILOSOPHY:
   METAPHORS AS ARGUMENTS

The difficulty we encounter in determining the sense of truth to assign
to a truth criterion in the present context is that there are different
theories of truth, each of which offers its own account. Traditional candidates arise in the form of the correspondence, pragmatist, and coherence theories, but this does not exhaust the possibilities, others of
which were mentioned by Johnson.[5] Given the complexity of asking
about the nature of truth itself, the various theories instead offer explanations of how those who claim that a proposition is true use it, and
when they use it.

We see, for example, that Johnson is inclined to use it when
considering reasoning in the domain of science rather than in that of
morals, and employs it to capture an existing relationship between a
proposition and an external reality. In a similar fashion, when informal
logician Allen writes that "a proposition, p, is true if p" (1995, 218), we
can understand him to be asserting a relationship between the proposition and some external state, such that the proposition is true if the
external state actually exists. The most likely candidate for the truth
criterion being evoked by some argumentation theorists, then, is the
correspondence theory.

This theory boasts the credentials of longevity. While modern
versions can offer variants on the basic theme, the core has changed
little from when Aristotle wrote in the *Categories:*

> The fact of the being of a man carries with it the truth of the propo-
> sition that he is . . . for if a man is, the proposition wherein we
> allege that he is, is true . . . the fact of the man's being does seem
> somehow to be the cause of the truth of the proposition, for the
> truth or falsity of the proposition depend on the fact of the man's
> being or not being. (14b, 14–21)

This Aristotelian insight holds across the various versions, from
Wittgenstein's and Russell's isomorphism of proposition and fact, to
Austin's linguistic conception of a relationship between demonstrative
and descriptive conventions. Russell (1912), for example, talks of
propositions "mirroring" facts, thereby invoking (and perhaps distract-
ing us with) a particularly vivid metaphor to explain the relationship
expressed in the core term "correspondence." How *do* propositions, or

the sentences that express them, and facts correspond? How do we account for what it is we are striving to communicate when the reach of language ends and the world of things begins? This too is an age-old problem, evident in Plato's stylistic innovations to explain the relationship between the flux of experience and what he took to be the underlying, unchanging, reality. If language is a mirror of reality, how can we trust that the images are not distortions?

Strict correspondence would seem to require a one-to-one relation between the contents of propositions and the items of reality, this being the sense of saying that "p is true if and only if p." Stark without the dressing of metaphor, this reveals the problem that such devices hide, because it does not begin to explain what first fixes the relationship between what is said and what is, and then maintains that relationship.

Less demanding is to interpret correspondence as a relationship "with," rather than a relationship "to." Thus, but again metaphorically, "a key may correspond *with* its key-hole and one half of a stamp *with* the other half, while an entry in a ledger may correspond *to* a sale, and one rank in the army *to* another in the navy" (White 1970, 106–107). When we search for a fit between the constituents of propositions and facts in the world, we are confounded by the failure of propositions and the facts to which they correspond to "contain" the same number of constituents. This approach would also seem to assume a denotative theory of meaning. If my simple sentence "the bird is in the tree" is to fit the facts, then "bird" will denote the bird and "tree" the tree. But my proposition has a third element that captures the relation between the bird and the tree. How are we to understand this? Moreover, other simple sentences like "the hat is red" would seem to commit us to constituents of the fact that match both "the hat" and "red," and hence to holding that properties like "redness" exist independently of red things. Further difficulties emerge the more we dwell on such simple sentences and their propositional content, and this is without asking what correspondence pertains between "true" negative or conditional propositions and whatever accounts for their truth. Haack (1998) observes that none of the attempts to provide a theory that captures Aristotle's initial insight has been "unproblematically successful" (22), but she insists that this should not diminish the power of Aristotle's insight nor our concern for truth. It is difficult, however, to be so optimistic, or patient, when pressed by pragmatic concerns like those that occupy us here.

All this is to do little more than repeat some well-tried objections to correspondence theories of truth. The point is that argumentation theorists who wish to adopt such an approach as the candidate for the meaning of truth in any truth criterion have their work cut out for them. One promising place to begin is with the recent theory forwarded by Goldman (1999) that attempts to succeed in just the places the traditional accounts have failed.

Goldman advances what he calls a "descriptive-success" (DS) theory, where this means "faithfulness to reality" (1999, 60). On his account:

(DS): An item X (a proposition, a sentence, a belief, etc.) is true if and only if X is descriptively successful, that is, X purports to describe reality and its content fits reality. (59)

Goldman is also unable to get by without adopting a metaphor, and his choice is faithfulness or fidelity in human relations. He argues that a proposition corresponds to reality insofar as it is faithful to it and believes this captures the sense of "true" in phrases like "true to life" or "true to form." This leads him to a looser notion of "truth maker"—those correlates in the world that make propositions true. Recognizing the problems of identifying pieces of reality that correspond to negations, disjunctions, conditionals, and so on, and the general concerns with depicting facts in propositions, Goldman dispenses with the need for facts as the truth makers in his theory. Instead, propositions could be made true by concrete events or relations among abstract entities. "As long as anything that makes a proposition true is part of reality—construed as broadly as possible—this fits the correspondence theory as formulated by (DS)" (62). If a claim is true, then it is descriptively successful; if it is false, it is descriptively unsuccessful.

Goldman's correspondence theory of truth is part of, indeed the key part of, a truth-based (veritistic) social epistemology. Hence the model of argumentation he advances, with its rules for good practice, is one that sees truth as its proper aim (1999, Chapter 5). One further thing to mark about Goldman's theory is that it remains neutral on the question of what "reality" consists in (65). While he has his own take on the debate between metaphysical realists and antirealists, he believes his theory capable of accommodating a wide range of metaphysics.

So here we have a candidate for Johnson's truth criterion: A premise needs to be true in the sense of being faithful to reality and is tested by the success of its description. But should Johnson adopt such a theory, he would first seem obligated to subject it to the criticism against correspondence theories that he judged most compelling, that is the God's-eye-view.

Hamblin's objection needs careful consideration: when two people are arguing, he tells us, terms like "true" and "valid" have different currencies for the participants than they do for onlookers. The latter can judge the truth or falsity of statements according to what is observed. But within the dialogue, a participant's saying that something is true tells us only what he or she accepts. When someone says "S is true, the words 'is true' are empty and he might as well have said simply 'S'" (Hamblin 1970, 243). The emptiness or parenthetical character of these terms serves to divert us from the more important question of what the participants accept. In terms of what was said earlier, it diverts us outside the argument to a different perspective, that of an omniscient onlooker, whose grounds for saying "S is true," or "S is a faithful description of reality" are never questioned because of that assumed omniscience.

The quintessential onlookers in such cases are, Hamblin reminds us, logicians who, while allowed to express their views, should not mask their own judgments of acceptance as statements of logic. "The logician does not stand above and outside practical argumentation or, necessarily, pass judgment on it . . . he is, at best, a trained advocate" (244).[6]

Johnson allows that certain forms of the correspondence theory presuppose such omniscience (2000a, 196). By this, I take him to mean that they assume a perspective of knowing a correspondence of fit between propositions and reality without accounting for that within the argument. So to learn that the participant in an argument holds something to be true is to learn what that person accepts, rather than something about the truth of what is asserted. One of the ways around this problem, Johnson surmises, might be to adopt a relativistic theory of truth.

If we turn in this direction for an answer to our search, we again confront the problem of deciding from among a variety of relativist theories (perhaps, given this particular approach, a greater variety than for any other!). I do not want here to confuse a relativist theory of truth with relativism *per se* (however that might be conceived). While relativism has obvious consequences for how we think about truth, it tends to provoke passionate debates in which people rarely reveal their best face and often collapse into nonconstructive strategies like name-calling that would distract us too much from our search for a truth criterion.[7] Perelman's relativism I have discussed elsewhere

(Tindale 1999a, Chapter 4). While it is consistent with his approach to argumentation, it does not necessitate a relativist theory of truth along lines considered here.

The most extreme version of this theory would relativize truth to individuals. On such terms, a proposition may be true for one person but not another. Part of the problem is whether a proposition like "X is true relative to me" can fall within its own scope. It seems to invite an infinite regress: is the proposition that "X is true relative to me" itself true? Nor would this be a plausible theory for the argumentation theorist who wishes to adopt a truth criterion, because if we are to believe nothing else about such an adoption, it must be that a true premise is so both for the arguer and the audience. Less restrictive, but still impractical for the current purpose, would be a theory that relativized truth to communities, where "X is true" is interpreted as "X is true for community Y." This does not encourage discourse between communities and may again just reduce truth to acceptance.

Affiliated in some minds with the relativist theory of truth, and also mentioned by Johnson, are pragmatic theories of truth. Again, these are too complex to do full justice to here, but they start to point us in useful directions. They have received serious promotion, especially among American philosophers like Peirce, James, and Dewey. True beliefs, on this account, are those that have a certain instrumental value, that *work*. As Goldman interprets this: "A proposition is true if and only if it is useful to believe it, that is, useful to the prospective believer" (1999, 42). But this needs to be situated within a theory that does not understand such utility in an arbitrary way. There is a certain consensualist element to the way Peirce conceived pragmatic truth (Grayling 1990, 127), and James held that true beliefs were those that were confirmed by experience in the long run.

Again, the criticisms of such positions are standard fare. Critics who hold to an objectivist notion of truth and falsity will observe that on the pragmatic account false beliefs will often be useful to believe, which may be tantamount to the part of Johnson's integration problem that is concerned with false but acceptable premises. Also, if true beliefs are those verified by experience, then we face the prospect of odd outcomes such as finding a proposition like "Mrs. Smith died last week" true only after her body is discovered this week, but not before. Lurking in the background here is an insistence that "true" propositions must still relate to a state of affairs in the world, and hence truth and confirmation may become confused.

❖ ACCEPTABILITY

James's (1970) pragmatic view argued not only that true beliefs are verified over time, but that they are adjusted to deal with anomalies and preserve internal consistency. In this sense, there is an element of coherence suggested, and it is in coherence theories of truth that we may find our best candidate for a truth criterion.

Coherence theories deny, or express an open skepticism about, the existence of foundational beliefs with independent justification. Instead, if beliefs are to be justified (that is, deemed true), this must come through their coherence with other beliefs in a belief system, otherwise they are deemed false. Important work on this theory has been done by Rescher (1973). As with "correspondence," the central term here, "coherence," has a vagueness that needs to be clarified, and proponents of coherence theories tend to approach this in terms of the kind of system within which we see the coherence of beliefs arising. Rescher appreciates that there is an array of potential beliefs available to us and that guidance is needed in deciding which set we would be warranted in holding as true. Given that no external criteria can help us, Rescher suggests "plausibility-indexing" (on par with probabilistic likelihoods) to narrow down what is acceptable (116). But of course, in using this last term I show my hand here, for in terms of the coherence of beliefs in a system, as the final sections of the last chapter make clear, we are as well to adopt acceptability as to adopt truth. That is, given the difficulties we have seen associated with deciding what is meant by truth when it is to be applied as a criterion in argument evaluation, and given that the principal terms can be brought together in talk of coherence, then acceptability is to be preferred.

Johnson's strongest argument for the truth requirement, it will be recalled, is that theorists continue to rely on it in all kinds of ways (2000a, 197). Such reliance, given that it is expressed in no clear conceptual way, seems quite consistent with a coherence understanding of truth, particularly as it arises with respect to talk of consistency (one of Johnson's concerns).

As Govier (1987, 214) makes clear, "*Acceptability is not acceptance:* there is no need to reject the distinction between what is in fact taken as cogent by an audience and what that audience ought to take as cogent." Indeed, we would not wish to collapse acceptability into acceptance. While Perelman and Olbrechts-Tyteca proffer the adherence of an audience to a thesis or claim as a measure of success, it is too rigorous a requirement to propose generally and it runs afoul of the concern that an audience may accept problematic claims (Johnson 2000a, 193). Retrospectively, we can look at what an audience has accepted, or rejected, and evaluate whether they were justified in doing so. I set out the terms for such evaluations in the last chapter. Prospectively, and especially when constructing argumentation, the appropriate criterion is acceptability. Here premises are constructed such that the intended audience should be justified in finding them acceptable.

Johnson has no difficulty with an acceptability requirement *per se.* His problem is with the integration of this with a truth requirement in argument evaluation. When conflict arises between the two criteria, he resolves it in favor of the truth requirement because, simply, it is not reasonable to accept a false premise (2000a, 337). We must now consider this in light of the difficulties found in making sense of how "false premise" might be understood. The best candidate, I submit, is that a premise is "false" because it does not cohere with the others in the system. Put another way, the belief it expresses is inconsistent with other beliefs. For this reason, an arguer should not advance it and an audience would not be justified were they to accept it. But the acceptability requirement itself is quite sufficient to do this work. The premise is unacceptable because it expresses a belief that is inconsistent with other beliefs that are acceptable (where being acceptable does not assume acceptance). Johnson himself, when he returns to consider Hamblin's orangutan example, concludes that its failure is really at the level of "coherence" (2000a, 340). While by this he means that it is unintelligible, that is not the only sense we can attribute to coherence. Of course, unintelligible beliefs (if it makes sense to speak of such) will be inconsistent with, or fail to be relevant to, beliefs that are intelligible. We see this irrelevance in the orangutan example, to which I shall return.

As a representative case of "acceptability," Allen (1998) takes the account of Pinto, Blair, and Parr (1993), whereby propositions subsequently discovered to be false may be reasonable to believe, and thus acceptable. What strikes Allen about this account is that it is doubly relativistic: "A proposition, *p,* is not simply acceptable, but acceptable for a person, or persons, S, at a certain time, *t*" (1998, 3). This is indeed a good understanding of the acceptability requirement and one consistent with the stress I give to context in this book. Allen's strategy is not to dispute that acceptability needs to be judged from the point of view of an intended audience, but to argue that this does not preclude *also* judging it from a different point of view involving the requirement of true premises. It would then become a matter, presumably, of showing that more than one perspective was necessary or, at least, that the acceptability requirement was not sufficient alone. Neither Johnson nor Allen has so far shown this to be the case.

Allen also challenges the proponents of the acceptability requirement on another front—namely, that the acceptability of premises is decidable in the many cases in which their truth value is not. Allen has not seen a defense of this assumption and promptly questions it. Given the doubly relativistic nature of acceptability, deciding whether a premise is reasonable to believe at time "t" depends on the epistemic circumstances of the person doing the believing. He writes:

> To decide whether p is acceptable for S at time t, then, we must be able to tell what S's epistemic circumstances are at that time—or, more precisely, we must be able to tell whether S's epistemic circumstances at time t are such that it is then reasonable for S to accept p. And it will always, or usually, be easier to tell this than to tell whether p itself is true? I think we may fairly ask this question, and require an argument in support of an affirmative answer to it from those who prefer acceptability to truth as the criterion for premise adequacy on the ground, or partly on the ground, that we can't say what is true in most contexts. (1998, 3)

There is more than a hint of skepticism in Allen's question. The implication is clearly that it will not be easier to determine whether S's epistemic circumstances make it easier for S to accept p than it will be to determine whether p is true. (I do not see Allen making the stronger claim that it is *easier* to determine a premise's truth.) We are faced here with two tasks: determining a premise's truth, and deciding whether it is reasonable for a person, S, to accept a premise given S's circumstances. Neither is an "easy" task, but we have much more at our disposal for deciding the second of these than the first. We have the context in which the argument arises, with S as an essential component of that as detailed in Chapter 4. And we also have available the relevant cognitive environment, to the degree that this is apparent, that tells us the information to which S has access and the beliefs likely to be held and formed. Remember, the cognitive environment does not tell us *what* S believes, but what S could believe. Given the currency of an issue about which we may argue, this environment is always likely to be more specific than general. On the side of a premise's truth, as far as we have been able to determine, we have very little. One suspects, still, that the theory of truth that would suit the sensibilities of people like Allen is the correspondence theory. But we have seen considerable difficulties in understanding how this can be applied. I believe that the arguments of this and the previous chapter should answer Allen's skepticism and that, at the least, the burden of proof shifts back to the camp of those who would promote a truth requirement to give some account of the notion of truth that this involves.

It matters also why we need to think in terms of the two tasks that Allen identifies. Our interest is in whether an argument is good and how best to evaluate it. The double process suggested by Allen arises from the perspective that he shares with Johnson: the truth requirement is still attached to the idea of evaluating arguments in and of themselves, detached from the contexts in which they arise. It sees truth, that is, the value of the premise, as a property inherent in a premise, whereas the rhetorical view that espouses the acceptability requirement looks at a premise in *relation to an audience* and judges the acceptability of that premise in relation to the contextually given audience. *Perhaps* a statement has a value independent of its use in an argument, a value that we might choose to call its truth value. But for *argumentative purposes* this is irrelevant. Its value here arises in relation to an argument intended for a specific audience. On this ground, then, we do not require a truth criterion in order to evaluate arguments within the model of argumentation explored in this book.

For the purposes of argument evaluation, we should conform to the discussion of engaged and unengaged evaluations in the previous chapter. While that discussion was directed at questions about the universal audience, its pertinence to the acceptability of basic premises should be clear. Evaluation is a process that, while it may be conducted by a disengaged onlooker, must be viewed in terms of what is internal to the argumentative situation or event. This situation involves the participants and the relevant cognitive environment, it involves the dialogic context as this has been described. With these provisions made, we can state that a premise is acceptable if it coheres with the cognitive environment of an audience and the principle of reason within that audience. On these terms, a premise may be acceptable for an audience without that audience believing it (that is, an evaluator will judge they *should* accept it), because the audience does not successfully associate it with the relevant aspects of the cognitive environment, or differs in its interpretation. Establishing the grounds for that premise, should such a dispute arise, is part of the argumentative exchange and will involve a discussion about the burden of proof. Hence, to appreciate the acceptability of premises, one needs to know the audience. While, as noted above, there are difficulties associated with this task, it is a more accessible one than that which confronts the purveyor of a truth requirement. In particular cases acceptability may be grounded in different ways: in the words of reasonable authorities, for example, or, as we saw in the last chapter, in the logical consistency of the ideas involved. In all cases, though, it is the rhetorical situation that brings these things to light, since it provides the crucial components of arguers and audiences within the dynamic contexts that bind them.

❖ CONCLUSION

It must be noted in all of this that those most eager to enlist a truth requirement among their criteria of argument evaluation are those who see truth as the principal aim of argumentation. This is the case for Goldman and for Johnson, who sees it difficult for us to expect to arrive at the discovery of truth "if we do not require that the premises of our arguments satisfy that requirement" (Johnson 1999, 411).

Some of the disputes that we hope to manage (and perhaps resolve) through argumentation will be about "the way things are." This has held since the Sophists argued about the nature of experience and how people should interpret it in the public presentation of their positions. Importantly, though, these were debates about the nature of that experience, which largely left open the question of what lay behind it and whether we can know *that*. Gorgias suggested we could not; Protagoras felt that life was too short to ask questions about the gods, and the subject matter too obscure, and we can expect him to have made a similar response on the subject of an objective reality. These were not matters for argumentation, which has perhaps less ambitious goals, but no less important ones. Argumentation in its rhetorical form looks also to engender understanding, which may itself be a type of acceptability. Where disputes are not resolved but their nature and grounds understood, then we move forward, the past as open as the future, for it can still be decided in new ways, and will be. Argumentation is an invitation to self-persuasion given the essential reciprocity between participants. Fixation on "truth" creates the risk that we lose sight of this.

The data about the world and our experience do not, after all, speak for themselves (Potter 1996, Chapter 6). Seeing, like hearing, is an act of interpretation and we have to ask what it is that we are seeing. For the longest time scientists debating the issue of global warming were looking at the same sets of data and drawing very different arguments from them. Some saw conclusive evidence for global warming, while others argued that the opposite was the case. Though we may treat the proposition as a description, it is rather an interpretation and will be affected by other interests that affect us. This cannot be the realm of truth; this is the realm of what description or interpretation is acceptable. There we must consider the audiences involved. For we appreciate that different audiences in different locales understand given propositions in different ways. This is not to deny the reality of events that we experience; it is to stress our problems in describing them in acceptable ways. It is in light of our judgment of a proposition's acceptability for an audience that we decide whether further support or discussion is necessary. It is not a matter of truth here. In the realm of argumentation, if we are to progress toward our goals, we must concentrate on the question of acceptability.

The truth criterion, it has been suggested, has its place most clearly in the domain of science (Johnson 2000a, 196), and it has further been suggested that argumentation theorists' reticence to embrace this criterion is because they consider it a feature of formal deductive logic (Johnson 1999, 414). There seems a commendable reluctance to scavenge at what is taken to be the corpse of formal logic.

Perelman the rhetorical theorist, as we know, shared this perspective. He distinguished strictly between demonstration and argumentation. To talk of a proposition as "evident," for example, is to hold that "anybody who can grasp the meaning of its terms is certain of its truth" (1963, 110). Such certainty and truth cannot be achieved through argumentation, except when a dispute arises about self-evidence itself. Argumentation involves "not the contemplation of truth but of living a life the needs of which require rapid action" (117). Thus the best we have are opinions that have been tried and tested, survived objection and criticism, and in which we have a strong confidence, though no certainty. The rationality of such opinions is not guaranteed, and so we encounter "the ever-renewed effort to get them accepted by what in each field we regard as the universality of reasonable men" (133). These, then, we might regard as truths, but "these truths constitute no more than the surest and best tested of our opinions" (133).

We see this most vividly when we contemplate arguments about the past, something that many take to be finished and complete and so decidable in some definitive way. Yet the grounds for deciding this is another matter of dispute. Do we trust testimony (Coady 1992), or eschew it altogether for the inferential reconstructions of the historian's imagination (Collingwood 1970)? John Locke, fearing the first alternative, saw the thread of testimony diminishing over time as it becomes more distant from the events in question.[8] Perelman's response to this way of thinking leads him to adopt a particularly vivid metaphor. He questions the reliability of viewing beliefs about the past as founded only on a chain of reasoning, links of which may not be solid. Rather, he suggests, "When we have to reconstruct the past, the arguments which we use seem to me very much more like a piece of cloth, the total strength of which will always be vastly superior to that of any single thread which enters into its warp and woof" (1963, 122). The cloth metaphor bears resemblance to Haack's crossword puzzle metaphor mentioned earlier, but differs in several important respects. First, it does not present the matter to be engaged as a puzzle so much as a natural extension of our investigative natures, for which argumentative inquiry is so well suited. Second, the weave of the cloth knits together more finely than the interlocking solutions to a crossword and has a stronger internal structure of support. Metaphors only take us so far, of course. The point here is that Perelman and Olbrechts-Tyteca's argumentative project, which I have explored and developed, does not restrict us to the everyday affairs of human interaction. While this is the primary focus of its jurisprudential model of reasoning, it contains the tools and devices that allow us to talk more generally about our present experience and the past.

So we can say, for example, drawing on the many threads that give us a picture of the Romans and the cognitive environments available to them, that the truth about orangutans is ultimately not so much that the Romans would have found unintelligible talk of whether the vitamin content of oranges would be good for orangutans, but that for Romans of 450 AD (and the example refers to *ancient* Romans) talk of *orangutans*, creatures indigenous to the Southeast Asian islands of Borneo and Sumatra, would be unintelligible. The point is not to say that this further weakens Hamblin's example, which we have already decided to have been a bad choice. The point is that we may be prepared to say that it is "true" that ancient Romans could not have engaged in a dispute about vitamins and orangutans. What we are saying here is that, given our current understanding of the ancient world, and the evidence available to us, this is an acceptable belief, cohering with other beliefs we have about the period and the customs involved. To say that it is true is to say no more than that it is acceptable, and acceptable on quite strong grounds. But it could become questionable or unacceptable; the door never closes on our knowledge of the past. We revise and reject; we understand more completely (which is to say, we combine different insights into a deeper understanding). What we hold to be acceptable today may be revised as unacceptable tomorrow. That does not mean that we would then make a retrospective judgment that it was always unacceptable (that is the difference between judgments made under the acceptability requirement and those made under the truth requirement). It means that what once was acceptable (on reasonable evidence), at last date is no longer acceptable (on revised evidence). As we saw in the last chapter, what counts as reasonable evidence changes over time. That those who wish to adopt or re-adopt a truth requirement would not want to say that what was true is now false, is a reason for not adopting that requirement.

❖ NOTES

1. More, but not completely this, for we have also seen that they play an epistemic role and act as repositories for principles of evaluation.

2. Johnson (2003) observes that the problem with this argument is that we have reason to reject the conclusion because we no longer believe there to be canals on Mars. This does not itself, however, address the issue of the premise's acceptability, which is quite unlike that of the orangutan case.

3. I will not pursue this here, because my topic is the truth criterion. It may be the case, however, that Hamblin's God's-eye-view is another way (and undoubtedly a problematic one) of expressing the idea advanced at the end of the last chapter—that the universal audience both uses and legitimizes logical principles.

4. In 1999 Johnson develops a similar treatment but analyzes the work of more theorists with informal logic sympathies, including the work of the pragma-dialecticians mentioned in Chapter 1.

5. Good discussions of the merits and demerits of the primary candidates can be found in Grayling (1990) and White (1970). Also of interest is Bernard Williams's discussion (2002, Chapter 4).

6. While Goldman discusses Hamblin's dialogue logic (1999, 155), he does not specifically address this problem, but indicates that his own account of

argumentation contrasts with this because Hamblin has no commitment to truth as the proper aim of argumentation.

7. Hence Goldman takes on the "veriphobes" (1999, Chapter 1) and Haack (1998) ridicules the "New Cynics." However, insofar as Haack sees the basic strategy of the New Cynics to be a shift from attending to warrant (regarding the strength of evidence) to acceptance (regarding the standing of a claim in the eyes of a particular community), confusion is invited (92). Here (85–86) and elsewhere (Haack 1993) she adopts the metaphor of a crossword puzzle with its intersecting entries to suggest how a person's belief system about the world is developed and supported. For our own purposes, as will be stressed, it is important to separate acceptance from acceptability and thereby avoid confusion that might otherwise arise.

8. See the discussion of this in Coady (1992, 209–223), who also challenges the linear view of a thread of testimony through time, but on different grounds.

8

Rhetorical Conclusions

Argumentation, we have seen, situates us squarely in the social world and characterizes our behavior there. It finds us "in audience" just as we are "in language." In this way it contradicts the thrust of the Cartesian ego, which would find on the evidence of its thinking about itself a ground that cannot be doubted and on which other knowledge can be built. It contradicts this view because such "privileged" thinking enjoyed by the ego, in its very possibility, already assumes the interactions of the social world of language and audiences. The great rhetors and rhetoricians of our history, from Protagoras to Bakhtin, understood this social context as the arena of their activity and the source of material for them to configure. This is the ground of our experience—to address and to be addressed. We find ourselves and develop in the space between these two activities.

The "addressivity" that permeates and characterizes the argumentative situation is the most compelling "evidence" for why we should recognize rhetorical argumentation as preceding, grounding, and conditioning the logical and the dialectical. Ultimately, these last two emerge from and respond to the rhetorical situation, which is already argumentative. Let me reiterate that this is not to reduce either the logical or the dialectical to the rhetorical. We have seen strong, constructive features in both of these perspectives and, clearly, we *can* conceive argumentation from either of these alone and still have a fully consistent, useful way of constructing and analyzing arguments. The claim, though, is that taking the approach provided by either of these perspectives gives us an incomplete picture of how argumentation operates, and operates well. That fuller picture requires all three perspectives, with none reducible to another. In that full model, though, the one which is both fundamental and most indispensable is the rhetorical. Thus significant effort has been dispensed in fleshing out that perspective, indicating the kinds of things involved, along with their importance and value. Current argumentation theorists do not deny that the rhetorical has a role to play, but they do refuse it such a fundamental one. Thus, as we have seen, Johnson (2000a) subordinates the rhetorical to the logical, while van Eemeren and Houtlosser (1999c) subordinate it to the dialectical.

Johnson makes his case by insisting that attempts to explicate rhetorical notions come back to logical notions, like contradiction and consistency. Indeed, such ideas are important. But the most fundamental rhetorical notion that we have worked with in the book—although by no means the only one—is that of audience, and *this* is the idea that most makes the case at the same time that it cannot be understood as a logical notion. The principles of logic are abstract principles; they have no application, and therefore no concrete value to argumentation, outside of the contexts in which they are used. That they may seem to govern the reasoning of people who must uphold the principle of noncontradiction and so on, was explained in Chapter 6. There, our long inquiry into the *source* for our ideas of what is reasonable led us to audiences themselves, and in particular to the universal audience who serves as a moving standard of what should count. *Within* such audiences we found the logical principles being employed as tools. But the task was to explain the justification of those tools in terms of real audiences who use them, since every universal audience is anchored by a real audience. Thus we arrived at a place that Johnson occupied in defending the logical ground, but we arrived there from beneath that ground, from what underpins it.

Van Eemeren and Houtlosser (1999c) place rhetorical moves within a dialectical framework. As I explained this in Chapter 1, dialectic is deemed to deal with general and abstract questions. With its focus on the appropriate procedural rules for constructing good argumentation, the dialectical asks what should be done in general situations. Rhetoric, on the other hand, concerns itself with specific cases (van Eemeren and Houtlosser 2000a) and the features of context needed to convince specific people. Again, though, these dialectical principles have not dropped fully formed into the human arena as if through some divine dispensation. They are derived, tested, and modified from specific cases. The general is derived from, and justified by, our experiences of the specific, to which it can then be profitably applied.

More important, among the concerns raised by van Eemeren and Houtlosser is the norm assigned to rhetoric as opposed to that for dialectic. While dialectic embraces the idea of reasonableness, rhetoric aims at effectiveness. In this, then, van Eemeren and Houtlosser adopt the standard position of pragma-dialectics toward rhetoric. In spite of advocating criteria that mirror Perelman and Olbrechts-Tyteca's triad of choice, presence, and communion (1969, 172), van Eemeren and Houtlosser share the pragma-dialecticians' rejection of Perelman and Olbrechts-Tyteca's new rhetoric because it aims at effectiveness, understood with all the negative connotations traditionally associated with that term. While they are eager to enlist the aid of rhetorical features to further their dialectical project, they are equally concerned to guard against their influence: "effective persuasion must be disciplined by dialectical rationality" (van Eemeren and Houtlosser 2000b, 297). In this respect they echo Johnson's similar judgment that rhetoric lacks rationality (2000a, 270).

As powerful as this image of rhetoric remains, we have seen at several turns just how uneven it is. One of the limitations recognized in Perelman and Olbrechts-Tyteca's treatment of rhetorical figures (Chapter 3) was indeed the focus on effectiveness, at least if we understand this in traditional terms. Those terms see rhetorical argumentation as effective if it wins over an audience, persuades it. From there the leap is made to the judgment that since effective persuasion is the goal, any means can be employed to achieve it (Johnson 2000a, 163). Hence the opposition between effectiveness and reasonableness or rationality.[1] In the next two sections, then, by way of response, I will (i) clarify what has been said about rhetorical audiences, to show that they cannot be reduced to logical notions; and (ii) reiterate the goals of rhetorical argumentation, as they have been developed from Protagoras and other Sophists through to twentieth-century figures like Bakhtin and Perelman and Olbrechts-Tyteca, to show that no sacrifice of rationality or reasonableness is involved.

❖ THE RHETORICAL AUDIENCE

Several things deserve to be recalled here about rhetorical audiences, as these have been detailed in Chapters 3 through 7. While all important in their own way, perhaps what most warrants further emphasis is the engaged nature of these audiences, since this gives rhetorical argumentation much of its dynamic character. In contrast to the passive audience that often is assumed by logical argument, an audience that receives a finished product that it had no hand in producing, the rhetorical audience is actively involved in the genesis and development of arguments in several crucial ways. These are captured in the ideas of experience and collaboration.

It was in the study of Fahnestock's treatment of rhetorical figures that we recognized the importance of how arguments are *experienced.* Argumentation is engaged in by people with commitments, at a specific time related to previous and anticipated events. Moreover, argumentation has a movement to it: gathering points, building momentum, hesitating over what is to be stressed and underlined, retreating to clarify and reinforce, conceding and countering, rising to a pitch of insistence or challenge, and so forth. It may range in tone or volume; it may be figurative or plain.

To think in such terms is to take up the perspective of a participant—the audience—and ask, as we asked in Chapter 3, "how is this discourse/argument *experienced*?" How is it integrated with the lives and positions of those for whom it is intended and whose response it anticipates? The experiential aspect is most graphically acknowledged in the rhetorical notion of *presence,* whereby objects of discourse, phrases, or images are foregrounded so as to arrest the attention of an audience, to come alive for them. This animation of argumentation underlies the use of rhetorical figures as argumentation schemes, with their internal movement from evidence to conclusion that the audience is encouraged to experience.

The rhetorical audience, then, is engaged because it experiences argumentation in this dynamic way. Furthermore, a second related feature was explored in Chapters 3 and 4. Through the experiencing of argumentation the audience can become a *collaborator* in it. This invokes the nature of the rhetorical enthymeme, discussed in Chapter 2. Here, an invitation is extended to an audience to become active in the reasoning by way of completing it. Traditional understandings of the enthymeme readily assume this in the way that an argument as a product is left incomplete (usually through the "absence" of a premise) in a way that requires the audience to supply a component. A more dynamic appreciation of what can be at stake emerged from our discussions in Chapter 3 where it is the patterns of rhetorical figures, like the *antithesis*, that both draw an audience in and point ahead, allowing that audience to take the reasoning to the conclusion that the pattern dictates. More dynamic still was the deeper sense of collaboration that emerged from the sketching of a Bakhtinian model of dialogical argumentation in Chapter 4. Here the audience is a full collaborator in the sense of a coarguer, since the moves and choices of the primary arguer, the addresser, are constrained by the responses, actual and expected, of the addressee to such a degree that utterances are coauthored, bearing traces of all participants. Thus a second question posed earlier asked, "How does this discourse invite *collaboration*?" Again, this allows us to consider the argumentation as it is viewed by its audience, as something that invites response.

This has payoffs not just in the basic construction and evaluation of argumentation, both processes of which can now foreground the audience, but also in things like the recognition and treatment of fallacies. As I noted in Chapter 2, the traditional account of fallacy, derived from Aristotle, is deeply problematic and needs to be shorn of its Sophistic associations. Yet it conveys an essential insight, one that has puzzled generations of logicians but seems quite plausible to the rhetorical theorist. When Aristotle wrote in the *Sophistical Refutations* (164a20) that a fallacy is an argument that *appears* to be valid or genuine but is not, he invited an approach from the audience's perspective. For we must ask to whom it appears valid or genuine, and find for an answer that it is the audience. Similarly, we should ask to whom it is *not* valid or genuine, and we will find in answer another audience or some other part of the original audience. As I say, I would not want to endorse much more of the Aristotelian account of fallacy, but this aspect of it is compatible with the central idea of being addressed in discourse, of being "in audience," that I have emphasized.

The rhetorical audience, as we have understood it, is a real audience. If it is imagined, it is insofar as imagination is projected onto real communities of addressees. Hence the dualism suggested in the above reference to fallacies, where part of an audience "sees" validity but another part (of that same audience) recognizes that it is not there, points to my discussion of the most important audiences of the book—the universal audiences.

Universal audiences are repositories of reason, sources for what is reasonable. Like other aspects of audience, this is an important manner of engagement, of response to and involvement in argumentation. As we saw in Chapter 6, when we recognize the merits of another's point of view, we cannot be merely witnessing it from the perspective of our own subjective interests. We step out of that perspective and adopt the view of what we understand to be reasonable, and insofar as the other's points conform to this, we are convinced. This principle of reason within us—which is not always activated, but arises on the occasions when this recognition operates—is what we share over and above the particularities that distinguish us. Similarly, the arguments we put forward aim to activate this principle in others and must be designed to address them both in their particularity and on the level of the universal, since the latter is approached through the former. In argumentative situations, we function on both of these levels when we operate well, and on the particular level alone when we do not. Highlighted in Chapter 7 was the important criterion of acceptability, which focuses on the success of matching argumentation to both aspects of an audience.

Again, this is not a traditional picture of isolated Cartesian egos, confirmed in their own individuality. We are in audience from the first awakening of our cognitive lives, a point of view implicit in the theory and mythology of our rhetorical history. Plato's Protagoras in the dialogue named after him offers both myth and argument to explain the commonality of civic arts in the lives of all citizens (*Protagoras* 320c–323a). Civic wisdom is not restricted to an elite, as Plato may have preferred, but decreed by Zeus to be imparted to all. This identifies the common fund that Protagoras saw belonging to human communities, where "communal experiences and social knowledge" precede communicative encounters (Mendelson 2002, 36). Argumentation is the means by which we discover, form, and train this inchoate understanding, and audience, as our primary rhetorical way of being, underlies this. It can never be reduced to a logical tool.

❖   GOALS OF RHETORICAL ARGUMENTATION

I have stressed throughout this book that rhetorical argumentation aims at much more than persuasion, and the persuasion it does aspire to, in its constructive form, is invitational. Granted, the negative view of rhetoric, as exploitative discourse seeking only victory at any cost, so haunts the tradition that it seems at times unshakeable. Assuming, as we always will, that there must be fire when there is so much smoke, we cannot ignore this capability. As Gorgias says in the *Helen*, persuasion by speech is equivalent to abduction by force. But Gorgias's view of audience here is a passive one, and his value on this point is in alerting us to the power possessed by *logos* so that we might harness it. Bakhtin (1986) refers to the traditional view of rhetoric as its "lowest form" (152), for the abundant smoke accompanying this particular fire has done much to obscure the "higher" forms that this comment suggests also exist. Perelman and Olbrechts-Tyteca, when they advocate the goal of persuasion, are speaking, I believe, in just such positive terms, because there is a clear guiding ethic embedded in their project that would decry any exploitative tendencies.

An invitational rhetoric is already implied by the very nature of the audience I have been discussing. Deeply engaged in an argumentative situation as this has been elaborated in Chapter 4, identified as a particular audience by that situation, the audience cannot be passively persuaded by what it encounters. As coarguers complicit in the utterance, where this audience is persuaded, it will be so on its own terms. The practice of the Sophists made this clear, configuring experience to plausible ends; inviting the audience to consider things in light of its own experience and decide where the greater likelihood lay; proposing the weighing of opposing arguments in any case.

This last point also stresses how important the achievement of understanding can be as a goal of argumentation. If rhetorical argumentation can present two opposing arguments for consideration, then this shows that persuasion alone (of any kind) cannot be the goal. Arguers who feel an obligation to bring such balanced accounts forward are seeking something different. It is often in the contrast between positions, clearly and fairly presented, that we come to understand what is at stake in each. In a world of compelling social debates so resistant to resolution, where intelligent well-meaning people stand on both sides of an issue, then this kind of understanding is not just the best we might expect, it is a good in itself. Shared understandings of this nature move us forward in society, encouraging acceptance, promoting education, and allowing us to cooperate in spite of our deep disagreements.

Bakhtin's dialogism seemed particularly attuned to the desirability of such agreement, where this was not seen to involve an identity between positions. Agreement as understanding was a specific type of reply within argumentative situations, one toward which the arguer and respondent move through the utterance. While recognized as a difficult achievement (Todorov 1998), it is an important measure of success.

In a similar vein, Mercer (2000) observes how "[n]ew directions in human thinking often emerge when opposing viewpoints clash, and new courses of human joint action emerge when some ideas win out over others" (74). Understanding such "winning out" to involve a constructive self-persuasion that comes from insight and recognition, we can agree that argumentation is a valuable aspect of how we reason together through language.

There are several other "results," if not specific goals, of rhetorical argumentation that are worth observing here. One of these follows from what has been recalled of the argumentation drawn from Bakhtin's dialogism and involves the insights we gain into context, or the argumentative situation. "Context" is a rich idea, the understanding of which has developed considerably through recent literature (Crosswhite 1995; Tindale 1999a). The notions of involvement, anticipation, and response add to this richness. We can appreciate contexts to involve an interweaving of the participants' perspectives that adumbrates into their backgrounds, drawing features into a common fund of consideration. Moreover, that context is then structured as a site characterized by anticipation and response. The kinds of active projections into the other's perspective that this involves expands our sense of context considerably.

Finally, the above responses have attended to *what* is achieved by rhetorical argumentation. Again, while not an explicit goal, the *who* that can result is also worth keeping in mind. Leff's (2003) observations on rhetorical ethos, elaborated in Chapter 1, have, I hope, been reinforced by discussions of this book. While I have not always adopted his terminology of embodiment, enactment, and evocation, and while I have tended to give greater weight to the audience than to the arguer, still through discussions like those of rhetorical figures (Chapter 3) and Bakhtinian argumentation (Chapter 4), the ways in which the arguer personalizes her or his discourse so as to promote argumentative ends has been pointedly noted.

One characteristic of rhetorical argumentation, then, is the accentuation of the ethotic. Part of the task that an arguer faces when preparing to enter an argumentative situation is to appear credible and transfer that credibility to what is said. I used the discussion of

Socrates' speech in the *Apology* to develop something of this idea. Credibility is sought so as to give weight to an arguer and so shift the presumption in her or his favor. But this credibility has to be conferred by the audience, and hence in striving to appear a certain way the arguer must take up the perspective of the audience. This is another sense in which the arguer becomes the audience, seeing herself or himself mirrored there.

Lest this again seem exploitative and suggest an image of the arguer as chameleon or sycophant who is and says what others want, the model of argumentation I have been detailing here points to the development of an arguer very much at odds with such a suggestion. As Quintilian indicates in his deliberations on the goals of rhetoric (*Institutio*, 2.15.34), the emphasis should not be so much on just speaking effectively, but on speaking *well*, where the latter captures the importance of the ethical element involved. There is a model of argumentative competence suggested in what I have been developing that must affect the practitioners. Rhetorical argumentation demands sensitivity and responsiveness from its practitioners. One cannot engage in the deep understandings and exchanges involved without being altered in important ways. Our experience of being "in audience" is continually reinforced by the realization of how other audiences experience us. Insofar as what we become is a product of what we do and how we go about doing it, the arguers that emerge from these activities have a deeper sense of their social being and appreciation of others' views. We might also hope that with this comes a desire to contribute to the social goods that can be achieved, a desire ignited by the benefit of being a recipient of the same.

❖ CONCLUSIONS WITHOUT CONCLUSIVENESS

As the preceding sections indicate, I hope in this book to have made a serious contribution to our understanding of the participants in the argumentative situation—arguer and audience, appreciated rhetorically. It has been the exploration of the nature of rhetorical argumentation that has led to the disclosure and description of these participants. Turning this around, we can conclude that it is the nature of the audience and arguer, and what is at stake for us when we take up these roles (that is, move, for example, from our state of always being "in audience" potentially to actualizing it), that gives support to the privileging of the rhetorical in its relationship with the logical and the dialectical.

Another feature of our subject that provides similar support and has been similarly disclosed is the all-pervasive *context* of the argumentative situation. I noted above how the study of Bakhtin's dialogism opens up the notion of context, adding further layers of richness to our understanding. It does more: traditionally context has been approached as something fixed, which forms boundaries to the activity of argumentation. Thus we have been encouraged to focus on the product and see it as something complete and manageable within determinate confines. Rhetorical argumentation encourages us to escape the rigidity of this conception and see the context as something that is itself open to rhetorical influences.[2] Describing argumentation in Bakhtinian terms, and supplementing that description with ideas drawn from rhetorical scholars like Perelman and Olbrechts-Tyteca, reveals the essential fluidity of the argumentative situation.

Perelman and Olbrechts-Tyteca had emphasized this with respect to the audience, which is modified *in the process* of its engagement in argumentation (1969, 44; Perelman 1982, 149). Discussions in earlier chapters of this book have added similar descriptions of the "arguer" and "argument." These also undergo change through the reciprocal processes of the argumentative situation. This is why it was such a struggle to define "argument" rhetorically in the opening chapter. In its simplest form, it is the content of the exchanges between participants in an argumentative situation. Beyond that, the very nature of what we are trying to describe eludes precision.

So the argumentative situation is a site of ongoing renewal, of additions and retractions and, sometimes, considerable reconfigurations. If I can reach for a further metaphor here, I will enlist one that reaches back to the dawn of western thought. This is to conceive of the argumentative situation as exhibiting the flux and renewal of a river, which is never the same each time we "step" into it. Throughout this book I have stressed the animated forces at work in argumentation, from the movement within arguments to the changes to the idea of the reasonable in audiences. Now we see movement also as an essential characteristic of the argumentative situation. It is perhaps this movement of renewal and revision that best explains the preference for acceptability over truth as a criterion of argument assessment in Chapter 7.

The evaluation of arguments is made more difficult by this realization. The evaluation of argument products is as accessible as it is in part because those products are torn from the natural flow of argumentation and treated as fixed and complete. To be satisfied with this alone, though, we recognized to be a mistake, even an unfortunate one. We can evaluate argumentation for its acceptability, for its general appropriateness in relation to the relevant audiences, according to the criteria of Chapters 6 and 7. Yet there will always seem something provisional about such evaluations. Our argumentative goals of understanding, agreement, and self-persuasion, rather than truth or "correctness," make this less worrisome. We can still speak coherently of argumentation that is good, as well as that which is bad, and understand what accounts for the difference. Sometimes, where actions are called for, we must "finish" debates, allow that as much has been said as can be said for the present. But the movements of social life that are facilitated by argumentation will always ensure that these decisions can be revisited, reevaluated, and perhaps even "reargued"—although we can never step back into the original situation since each is always unique, given the changes of context.

Hence I must acknowledge the paradoxical nature of the title of this closing chapter. For in a very real sense there can be no rhetorical conclusions. The rhetorical resists conclusion. By its invitational nature, it is open-ended and deliberately inconclusive. It does not close debate; it does not "finish." Just as we live in audience, so we live in argumentative situations, whether dynamically alive, momentarily stalled, or deceptively dormant. Utterances arise out of dialogue as a continuation of it, and never enter from the sidelines (Bakhtin 1981, 276–277). Where one argumentative situation leaves off and another begins is always indistinct. At the same time, I have drawn many conclusions about the rhetorical, and so exploited an ambiguity alive in my title. These are conclusions in the sense of the last thing to be said, rather than the last thing that can be said. This is a discussion that is recoverable as far back as the Sophists, and which I join in midstream.

Sometimes, it seems, the argumentative situations in which we find ourselves have a novelty for which we are unprepared. We see this in clashes between cultures with quite different visions of the world, visions that appear incompatible. We see it in the intractable audiences who resist the most urgent overtures to cooperative argumentation. In situations such as this we may take a lesson from Alice and the White and Red queens, whose interactions we considered at the start of Chapter 1. Their encounter *as* encounter makes sense to us, which itself is significant. We can see what is lacking and what is needed for "real" engagement, or for the engagement that exists to start becoming productive. The participants have as much in common as they are different. Alice can enter into an understanding of the meaning of terms through the asking of questions. She can enter into an understanding of the structure and purpose of the world-views she confronts by asking questions. She can start to probe and understand the cognitive environment of the queens. As much as it may still seem that she has a long process ahead of her, an argumentative situation has been engaged and communication is possible.

❖ NOTES

1. In the criticisms being considered here these two are equated with each other in a way that they were not for Perelman and Olbrechts-Tyteca. In this particular discussion I will adopt the terminology of the critics.

2. I am grateful to Michael Leff for drawing my attention to the importance of this.

References

Allen, D. (1995). Assessing basic premises. In F. H. van Eemeren et al. (Eds.), *Proceedings of the third international conference of the International Society for the Study of Argumentation* (pp. 218–225). Amsterdam: Sic Sat.

Allen, D. (1998). Should we assess the basic premises of an argument for truth or acceptability? In H. V. Hansen et al. (Eds.), *Argumentation & rhetoric* [CD-ROM]. St. Catharines: Ontario Society for the Study of Argument.

Aristotle. (1984). *The complete works of Aristotle: The revised Oxford translation.* J. Barnes (Ed.). Princeton, NJ: Princeton University Press.

Bakhtin, M. (1981). *The dialogic imagination: Four essays* (C. Emerson & M. Holquist, Trans.). M. Holquist (Ed.). Austin: University of Austin Press.

Bakhtin, M. (1984). *Problems of Dostoevsky's poetics.* C. Emerson (Ed. & Trans.). Minneapolis: University of Minnesota Press.

Bakhtin, M. (1986). *Speech genres & other later essays* (C. Emerson & M. Holquist, Trans.). V. W. McGee (Ed.). Austin: University of Texas Press.

Barth, E. M. (2002). A framework for intersubjective accountability: Dialogue logic. In D. Gabbay et al. (Eds.), *Studies in logic and practical reasoning* (Vol. 1, pp. 225–293). Amsterdam: Elsevier Science B.V.

Berrill, D. P. (1996). Reframing argument from the metaphor of war. In D. P. Berrill (Ed.), *Perspectives on written argument* (pp. 171–187). Cresskill, NJ: Hampton Press.

Bialostosky, D. L. (1995). Antilogics, dialogics, and sophistic social psychology: Michael Billig's reinvention of Bakhtin from Protagorean rhetoric. In S. Mailloux (Ed.), *Rhetoric, sophistry, pragmatism* (pp. 82–93). Cambridge, UK: Cambridge University Press.

Billig, M. (1996). *Arguing and thinking: A rhetorical approach to social psychology* (2nd ed.). Cambridge, UK: Cambridge University Press.

Bitzer, L. (1968). The rhetorical situation. *Philosophy & Rhetoric, 1,* 1–14.

Blair, J. A. (1995). Premise adequacy. In F. H. van Eemeren et al. (Eds.), *Perspective and approaches* (pp. 191–202). Amsterdam: Sic Sat.

Blair, J. A. (1998). The limits of the dialogue model of argument. *Argumentation, 12,* 325–339.

Blair, J. A. (2000). Tindale's *Acts of arguing: A rhetorical model of argument. Informal Logic, 20*(2), 190–201.

Blair, J. A., & Johnson, R. H. (1987). Argumentation as dialectical. *Argumentation, 1,* 41–56.

Blakemore, D. (1992). *Understanding utterances: An introduction to pragmatics.* Oxford, UK: Blackwell.

Brickhouse, T. C., & Smith, N. D. (1989). *Socrates on trial.* Princeton, NJ: Princeton University Press.

Brinton, A. (1986). Ethotic argument. *History of Philosophy Quarterly, 3,* 245–258.

Burnet, J. (1924). *Plato's* Euthyphro, Apology of Socrates, *and* Crito. Oxford, UK: Oxford University Press.

Burnyeat, M. F. (1976). Protagoras and self-refutation in Plato's *Theaetetus. The Philosophical Review, 85*(2), 172–195.

Burnyeat, M. F. (1994). Enthymeme: Aristotle on the logic of persuasion. In D. J. Furley & A. Nehamas (Eds.), *Aristotle's rhetoric: Philosophical essays* (pp. 3–55). Princeton, NJ: Princeton University Press.

Carroll, L. (1977). *Symbolic logic: Part I, elementary, 1896, fifth edition, Part II, advanced.* W. W. Bartley III (Ed.). New York: C. N. Potter.

Carroll, L. (1993). *Alice in Wonderland and through the looking glass.* Ware, UK: Wordsworth Editions.

Christie, G. C. (2000). *The notion of an ideal audience in legal argument.* Dordrecht, Netherlands: Kluwer Academic.

Coady, C. A. J. (1992). *Testimony: A philosophical study.* Oxford, UK: Blackwell.

Cohen, D. H. (1995). Argument is war . . . and war is hell: Philosophy, education, and metaphors for argumentation. *Informal Logic, 17,* 177–188.

Cole, A. T. (1991). *The origins of rhetoric in ancient Greece.* Baltimore: Johns Hopkins University Press.

Collingwood, R. G. (1970). *The idea of history.* Oxford, UK: Oxford University Press.

Conradi, P. (2001). *Iris Murdoch: A life.* New York: W. W. Norton & Company.

Crosswhite, J. (1995). Is there an audience for this argument? Fallacies, theories, and relativisms. *Philosophy and Rhetoric, 28,* 134–145.

Crosswhite, J. (1996). *The rhetoric of reason.* Madison: University of Wisconsin Press.

Crosswhite, J. (2000). The nature of reason: Inertia and argumentation. In C. W. Tindale et al. (Eds.), *Argumentation at the century's turn* [CD-ROM]. Peterborough: Ontario Society for the Study of Argument.

Davis, S. (1999, April 10). Comment. *The Daily Telegraph,* p. 15.

Decleva Caizzi, F. (1999). Protagoras and Antiphon: Sophistic debates on justice. In A. A. Long (Ed.), *The Cambridge companion to early Greek philosophy* (pp. 311–331). Cambridge, UK: Cambridge University Press.

Devlin, L. P. (1965). Morals and the criminal law. In R. A. Wasserstrom (Ed.), *Morality and the law* (pp. 24–48). Belmont, CA: Wadsworth.

Ede, L. S. (1989). Rhetoric versus philosophy: The role of the universal audience in Chaim Perelman's *The new rhetoric.* In R. D. Dearin (Ed.), *The new rhetoric of Chaim Perelman: Statement & response* (pp. 141–151). New York: University Press of America.

Eemeren, F. H. van (Ed.). (2002). *Advances in pragma-dialectics*. Amsterdam: Sic Sat.

Eemeren, F. H. van, & Grootendorst, R. (1984). *Speech acts in argumentative discussions*. Dordrecht, Netherlands: Foris.

Eemeren, F. H. van, & Grootendorst, R. (1992). *Argumentation, communication, and fallacies*. Hillsdale, NJ: Lawrence Erlbaum.

Eemeren, F. H. van, & Grootendorst, R. (1995). Perelman and the fallacies. *Philosophy and Rhetoric, 28,* 122–133.

Eemeren, F. H. van, Grootendorst, R., & Snoeck-Henkemans, F. (1996). *Fundamentals of argumentation theory: A handbook of historical backgrounds and contemporary developments*. Mahwah, NJ: Lawrence Erlbaum.

Eemeren, F. H. van, & Houtlosser, P. (1999a). Delivering the goods in a critical discussion. In F. H. van Eemeren et al. (Eds.), *Proceedings of the fourth international conference of the International Society for the Study of Argumentation* (pp. 163–168). Amsterdam: Sic Sat.

Eemeren, F. H. van, & Houtlosser, P. (1999b). William the Silent's argumentative discourse. In F. H. van Eemeren et al. (Eds.), *Proceedings of the fourth international conference of the International Society for the Study of Argumentation* (pp. 168–172). Amsterdam: Sic Sat.

Eemeren, F. H. van, & Houtlosser, P. (1999c). Strategic manoeuvering in argumentative discourse. *Discourse Studies, 1*(4), 479–497.

Eemeren, F. H. van, & Houtlosser, P. (2000a). Rhetoric in pragma-dialectics. *Argumentation, Interpretation, Rhetoric, 1.* Retrieved June 4, 2001, from www.argumentation.spb.ru/2000_1/index.htm

Eemeren, F. H. van, & Houtlosser, P. (2000b). Rhetorical analysis within a pragma-dialectical framework: The case of R. J. Reynolds. *Argumentation, 14,* 293–305.

Eemeren, F. H. van, & Houtlosser, P. (2001). Clear thinking in troubled times: An integrated pragma-dialectical analysis. *Informal Logic, 21*(2), 17–30.

Eemeren, F. H. van, & Houtlosser, P. (2002). Strategic manoeuvering with the burden of proof. In F. H. van Eemeren (Ed.), *Advances in pragma-dialectics* (pp. 13–29). Amsterdam: Sic Sat.

Enos, R. (1993). *Greek rhetoric before Aristotle*. Long Grove, IL: Waveland Press.

Fahnestock, J. (1999). *Rhetorical figures in science*. New York: Oxford University Press.

Feyerabend, P. (1967). The theatre as an instrument of the criticism of ideologies: Notes on Ionesco. *Inquiry, 10*(3), 298–312.

Feyerabend, P. (1987). *A farewell to reason*. London: Verso.

Foss, S. K., & Griffin, C. L. (1995). Beyond persuasion: A proposal for an invitational rhetoric. *Communication Monographs, 62,* 2–18.

Fotheringham, A. (1998). What a visitor from Mars would discover. *Maclean's, 111,* 68.

Gagarin, M. (2002). *Antiphon the Athenian: Oratory, law, and justice in the age of the sophists.* Austin: University of Texas Press.

Gagarin, M., & MacDowell, D. M. (Trans.). (1998). *Antiphon & Andocides.* Austin: University of Texas Press.

Garssen, B. (2001). Argument schemes. In F. H. van Eemeren (Ed.), *Crucial concepts in argumentation theory* (pp. 81–99). Amsterdam: Amsterdam University Press.

Gaskins, R. (1992). *Burden of proof in modern discourse.* New Haven, CT: Yale University Press.

Goldman, A. (1999). *Knowledge in a social world.* Oxford, UK: Clarendon Press.

Govier, T. (1987). *Problems in argument analysis and evaluation.* Dordrecht, Netherlands: Foris.

Govier, T. (1998). Arguing forever? Or: Two tiers of argument appraisal. In H. V. Hansen et al. (Eds.), *Argumentation & rhetoric* [CD-ROM]. St. Catharines: Ontario Society for the Study of Argument.

Grayling, A. C. (1990). *An introduction to philosophical logic.* London: Duckworth.

Grice, P. (1975). Logic and conversation. In D. Davidson & G. Harman (Eds.), *The logic of grammar* (pp. 64–75). Encino, CA: Dicherson.

Grice, P. (1989). *Studies in the way of words.* Cambridge, MA: Harvard University Press.

Grice, P. (2001). *Aspects of reason.* Oxford, UK: Clarendon Press.

Grimaldi, W. M. A. (1996). How do we get from Corax-Tisias to Plato-Aristotle in Greek rhetorical theory? In C. L. Johnstone (Ed.), *Theory, text, context: Issues in Greek rhetoric and oratory* (pp. 19–43). Albany: State University of New York Press.

Groarke, L., & Tindale, C. W. (2004). *Good reasoning matters! A constructive approach to critical thinking* (3rd ed.). Toronto: Oxford University Press Canada.

Grootendorst, R. (1987). Some fallacies about fallacies. In F. H. van Eemeren et al. (Eds.), *Argumentation: Across the lines of discipline* (pp. 331–341). Dordrecht, Netherlands: Foris.

Gross, A., & Dearin, R. (2003). *Chaim Perelman.* Albany: State University of New York Press.

Guthrie, W. K. C. (1971). *The sophists.* Cambridge, UK: Cambridge University Press.

Haack, S. (1993). *Evidence and inquiry: Towards reconstruction in epistemology.* Oxford, UK: Blackwell.

Haack, S. (1998). *Manifesto of a passionate moderate: Unfashionable essays.* Chicago: University of Chicago Press.

Habermas, J. (1984). *The theory of communicative action: Reason and the rationalization of society* (Vol. 1) (T. McCarthy, Trans.). Boston: Beacon Press.

Hamblin, C. L. (1970). *Fallacies.* London: Methuen.

Hansen, H. V., & Pinto, R. C. (Eds.). (1995). *Fallacies: Classical and contemporary readings*. University Park: Pennsylvania State University Press.

Harris, R. (2001). Rhetorical figures in science. *Rhetorical Society Quarterly, 31*, 1–13.

Herrick, J. A. (2001). *The history and theory of rhetoric: An introduction* (2nd ed.). Boston: Allyn & Bacon.

Hirschkop, K. (1986). A response to the forum on Mikhail Bakhtin. In G. S. Morson (Ed.), *Bakhtin: Essays and dialogues on his work* (pp. 73–79). Chicago: University of Chicago Press.

Holquist, M. (1990). *Dialogism: Bakhtin and his world*. London: Routledge.

Hume, D. (1964). An enquiry concerning human understanding. In T. H. Green & T. H. Grouse (Eds.), *Philosophical works* (Vol. 2). Aalen, Germany: Scientia Verlag Aalen. (Original work published 1748)

Ignatieff, M. (1998). *Isaiah Berlin: A life*. New York: Viking.

James, W. (1970). *The meaning of truth: A sequel to* Pragmatism. Ann Arbor: University of Michigan Press.

Johnson, R. H. (1981). Toulmin's bold experiment: An appreciation and critique of Toulmin's *An Introduction to Reasoning. Informal Logic Newsletter, 3*(2), 16–27; *3*(3), 13–20.

Johnson, R. H. (1998). Response to Govier's *Arguing forever? Or: Two tiers of argument appraisal*. In H. V. Hansen et al. (Eds.), *Argumentation & rhetoric* [CD-ROM]. St. Catharines: Ontario Society for the Study of Argument.

Johnson, R. H. (1999). The problem of truth for theories of argument. In F. H. van Eemeren et al. (Eds.), *Proceedings of the fourth international conference of the International Society for the Study of Argumentation* (pp. 411–415). Amsterdam: Sic Sat.

Johnson, R. H. (2000a). *Manifest rationality: A pragmatic theory of argument*. Mahwah, NJ: Lawrence Erlbaum.

Johnson, R. H. (2000b, November). Unpublished paper presented at Trent University, Ontario, Canada.

Johnson, R. H. (2002). Manifest rationality reconsidered: Reply to my fellow symposiasts. *Argumentation, 16*(3), 311–331.

Johnson, R. H. (2003). The truth about the canals on Mars. In J. A. Blair et al. (Eds.), *Informal Logic at 25: Proceedings of the Windsor conference* [CD-ROM]. Windsor: Ontario Society for the Study of Argument.

Johnson, R. H., & Blair, J. A. (1993). *Logical self-defense* (3rd ed.). Toronto: McGraw-Hill Ryerson.

Johnstone, C. L. (Ed.). (1996). *Theory, text, context: Issues in Greek rhetoric and oratory*. Albany: State University of New York Press.

Johnstone, H. W., Jr. (1978). *Validity and rhetoric in philosophical argument: An outlook in transition*. University Park, PA: The Dialogue Press of Man & World.

Johnstone, H. W., Jr. (1996). On Schiappa versus Poulakos. *Rhetoric Review, 14*, 438–440.

Kennedy, G. (1963). *The art of persuasion in ancient Greece*. Princeton, NJ: Princeton University Press.

Kennedy, G. (1980). *Classical rhetoric and its Christian and secular tradition from ancient to modern times*. Chapel Hill: University of North Carolina Press.

Kennedy, G. (1991). *Aristotle on rhetoric: A theory of civic discourse*. Oxford, UK: Oxford University Press.

Kerferd, G. B. (1981). *The sophistic movement*. Cambridge, UK: Cambridge University Press.

Kuhn, D. (1991). *The skills of argument*. Cambridge, UK: Cambridge University Press.

Leff, M. C. (2003). Rhetoric and dialectic in Martin Luther King's *Letter from Birmingham Jail*. In F. H. van Eemeren et al. (Eds.), *Anyone who has a view: Theoretical contributions to the study of argumentation* (pp. 255–268). Dordrecht, Netherlands: Kluwer Academic.

Lodder, A. R. (1999). *DiaLaw: On legal justification and dialogical models of argumentation*. Dordrecht, Netherlands: Kluwer Academic.

Mailloux, S. (Ed.). (1995). *Rhetoric, sophistry, pragmatism*. Cambridge, UK: Cambridge University Press.

Makau, J. M., & Marty, D. L. (2001). *Cooperative argumentation: A model for deliberative community*. Prospect Heights, IL: Waveland Press.

May, T. (2002, April 24). Drowning children, Palestinians, and American responsibility. *Counterpunch*. Retrieved July 12, 2002, from www.counterpunch.org/may0424.html

Maybin, J. (2001). Language, struggle, and voice: The Bakhtin/Volosinov writings. In M. Wetherell et al. (Eds.), *Discourse theory and practice: A reader* (pp. 64–71). London: Sage.

McCabe, M. M. (1994). Arguments in context: Aristotle's defense of rhetoric. In D. J. Furley & A. Nehamas (Eds.), *Aristotle's rhetoric: Philosophical essays* (pp. 129–165). Princeton, NJ: Princeton University Press.

Mendelson, M. (2002). *Many sides: A Protagorean approach to the theory, practice, and pedagogy of argument*. Dordrecht, Netherlands: Kluwer Academic.

Mercer, N. (2000). *Words and minds: How we use language to think together*. London: Routledge.

Merleau-Ponty, M. (1962). *Phenomenology of perception* (C. Smith, Trans.). London: Routledge & Kegan Paul.

Morrison, B., & Motion, A. (1982). *The Penguin book of contemporary British poetry*. Harmondsworth, UK: Penguin Books.

Paley, W. (1963). *Natural theology: Selections*. F. Ferré (Ed.). Indianapolis, IN: Bobbs-Merrill.

Perelman, C. (1963). *The idea of justice and the problem of argument* (J. Petrie, Trans.). London: Routledge & Kegan Paul.

Perelman, C. (1968). Rhetoric and philosophy (H. W. Johnstone, Jr., Trans.). *Philosophy and Rhetoric, 1,* 15–24.

Perelman, C. (1979). The rational and the reasonable. In *The new rhetoric and the humanities: Essays on rhetoric and its applications* (pp. 117–23). Dordrecht, Netherlands: D. Reidel.

Perelman, C. (1982). *The realm of rhetoric* (W. Kluback, Trans.). Notre Dame, IN: The University of Notre Dame Press.

Perelman, C. (1989). The new rhetoric and the rhetoricians: Remembrances and comments. In R. D. Dearin (Ed.), *The new rhetoric of Chaim Perelman: Statement and response* (pp. 239–251). New York: University Press of America.

Perelman, C., & Olbrechts-Tyteca, L. (1969). *The new rhetoric: A treatise on argumentation* (J. Wilkinson & P. Weaver, Trans.). Notre Dame, IN: University of Notre Dame Press.

Perelman, C., & Olbrechts-Tyteca, L. (1989). Act and person in argument. In R. D. Dearin (Ed.), *The new rhetoric of Chaim Perelman: Statement and response* (pp. 43–68). New York: University Press of America.

Pinto, R. C., Blair, J. A., & Parr, K. (1993). *Reasoning: A practical guide for Canadian students.* Toronto: Prentice Hall Canada.

Plato. (1997). *Complete works.* J. M. Cooper (Ed.). Indianapolis, IN: Hackett.

Potter, J. (1996). *Representing reality: Discourse, rhetoric, and social construction.* London: Sage.

Poulakos, J. (1997). The logic of Greek sophistry. In D. Walton & A. Brinton (Eds.), *Historical foundations of informal logic* (pp. 12–24). Brookfield, VT: Ashgate.

Preston, J. (1999). Introduction. In *Paul Feyerabend: Knowledge, science and relativism. Philosophical Papers* (Vol. 3, pp. 1–15). Cambridge, UK: Cambridge University Press.

Quintilian. (1921). *Institutio Oratoria* (H. E. Butler, Trans.). Cambridge, MA: Harvard University Press.

Raine, C. (1979). *A Martian sends a postcard home.* Oxford, UK: Oxford University Press.

Ray, J. W. (1978). Perelman's universal audience. *Quarterly Journal of Speech, 64,* 361–375.

Reboul, O. (1989). The figure and the argument. In M. Meyer (Ed.), *From metaphysics to rhetoric* (pp. 169–181). Dordrecht, Netherlands: Kluwer Academic.

Reeve, C. D. C. (1989). *Socrates in the* Apology. Indianapolis, IN: Hackett.

Rescher, N. (1973). *The coherence theory of truth.* Oxford, UK: Clarendon Press.

Romilly, J. de. (1992). *The great sophists in Periclean Athens* (J. Lloyd, Trans.). Oxford, UK: Clarendon Press.

Rühl, M. (2002). *Arguing and communicative asymmetry: The analysis of the interactive process of arguing in non-ideal situations.* Frankfurt am Main: Peter Lang.

Rushdie, S. (2002). In defense of the novel, yet again. *Step across this line: Collected nonfiction 1992–2002* (pp. 49–57). Toronto: Alfred A. Knopf.

Russell, B. (1912). *The problems of philosophy.* London: Oxford University Press.

Schafer, A. (1998, February 28). There can be another me, but should there be another ewe? *The Globe and Mail*, p. A16.

Schiappa, E. (1991). *Protagoras and logos: A study in Greek philosophy and rhetoric.* Columbia: University of South Carolina Press.

Schiappa, E. (1995). Isocrates' philosophia and contemporary pragmatism. In S. Mailloux (Ed.), *Rhetoric, sophistry, pragmatism* (pp. 33–60). Cambridge, UK: Cambridge University Press.

Schiappa, E. (1999). *The beginnings of rhetorical theory in classical Greece.* New Haven, CT: Yale University Press.

Shotter, J. (1992). Bakhtin and Billig: Monological versus dialogical practices. *American Behavioral Scientist, 36,* 8–21.

Shotter, J. (1997). On a different ground: From contests between monologues to dialogical contest. *Argumentation, 11,* 95–112.

Sokal, A., & Bricmont, J. (1998). *Intellectual imposters: Postmodern philosophers' abuse of science.* London: Profile Books.

Somerville, M. (2000). *The ethical canary: Science, society and the human spirit.* New York: Penguin Putnam.

Sperber, D., & Wilson, D. (1986). *Relevance: Communication and cognition.* Cambridge, MA: Harvard University Press.

Sprague, R. K. (1962). *Plato's use of fallacy: A study of the Euthydemus and some other dialogues.* London: Routledge & Kegan Paul.

Sprague, R. K. (Ed.). (1972). *The older sophists.* Columbia: University of South Carolina Press.

Taylor, A. E. (1956). *Plato: The man and his work.* New York: Meridian Books.

Tindale, C. W. (1999a). *Acts of arguing: A rhetorical model of argument.* Albany: State University of New York Press.

Tindale, C. W. (1999b). The authority of testimony. *ProtoSociology: An International Journal of Interdisciplinary Research, 13,* 96–116.

Tindale, C. W. (2004). Hearing is believing: A perspective-dependent account of the fallacies. In F. van Eemeren & P. Houtlosser (Eds.), *The practice of argumentation.* Amsterdam: John Benjamins.

Tindale, C. W., & Gough, J. (1987). The use of irony in argumentation. *Philosophy and Rhetoric, 20,* 1–17.

Tindale, C. W., & Welzel, A. (in press). From argumentation to bargaining: The role of ethotic moves. In M. Raith et al. (Eds.), *Procedural approaches to conflict resolution.* Berlin: Springer Verlag.

Todorov, T. (1984). *Mikhail Bakhtin: The dialogical principle.* Minneapolis: University of Minnesota Press.

Todorov, T. (1998, March 13). I, thou, Russia. *The Times Literary Supplement,* No. 4954, 7–8.

Toulmin, S. (2003). *The uses of argument.* Cambridge, UK: Cambridge University Press. (Original work published 1958)

Vlastos, G. (1991). *Socrates: Ironist and moral philosopher.* Cambridge, UK: Cambridge University Press.

Walton, D. (1992). *Plausible argument in everyday conversation.* Albany: State University of New York Press.

Walton, D. (1995). *A pragmatic theory of fallacy.* Tuscaloosa: The University of Alabama Press.

Walton, D. (1996a). *Argumentation schemes for presumptive reasoning.* Mahwah, NJ: Lawrence Erlbaum.

Walton, D. (1996b). *Argument structure: A pragmatic theory.* Toronto: University of Toronto Press.

Walton, D. (1997). *Appeal to pity: Argumentum ad misericordiam.* Albany: State University of New York Press.

Walton, D. (1998a). *The new dialectic: Conversational contexts of argument.* Toronto: University of Toronto Press.

Walton, D. (1998b). *Ad hominem arguments.* Tuscaloosa: The University of Alabama Press.

Warnick, B. (1997). Lucie Olbrechts-Tyteca's contribution to *The new rhetoric.* In M. M. Wertheimer (Ed.), *Listening to their voices: The rhetorical activities of historical women* (pp. 69–85). Columbia: University of South Carolina Press.

Wenzel, J. (1979). Jürgen Habermas and the dialectical perspective on argumentation. *Journal of the American Forensic Association, 16,* 83–94.

White, A. R. (1970). *Truth.* New York: Doubleday.

Willard, C. A. (2002). Review of *Acts of arguing. Argumentation, 16,* 505–506.

Williams, B. (2002). *Truth & truthfulness: An essay in genealogy.* Princeton, NJ: Princeton University Press.

Woods, J. (1988). Pragma-dialectics: A radical departure in fallacy theory. *ISSA Newsletter, 4,* 5–15.

Woods, J. (1994). Is the theoretical unity of the fallacies possible? *Informal Logic, 16,* 77–85.

Woods, J., & Walton, D. (1989). *Fallacies: Selected papers 1972–1982.* Dordrecht, Netherlands: Foris.

Index